Ken,
to the fond memories of
"the champ" a unique
and very special
JOE American Hero,
LOUIS my dad -

Very Best
Joe Louis Barrow
10/25/88

JOE LOUIS

50 YEARS
AN AMERICAN HERO

by
Joe Louis Barrow, Jr.
& Barbara Munder

McGRAW-HILL BOOK COMPANY

New York   St. Louis   San Francisco
Hamburg   Mexico   Toronto

3 4 5 6 7 8 9 DOC DOC 8 9 2 1 0 9 8

ISBN 0-07-003955-0
ISBN 0-07-003956-9 {COM. EDITION}

Library of Congress Cataloging-in-Publication Data
Barrow, Joe Louis.
    Joe Louis : 50 years an American hero / by Joe Louis Barrow, Jr., and
    Barbara Munder.
        p.   cm.
    Bibliography: p.
    ISBN 0-07-003955-0
    ISBN 0-07-003956-9 (Commemorative Edition)
    1. Louis, Joe, 1914–   . 2. Boxers (Sports)—United States—
Biography. I. Munder, Barbara. II. Title.
GV1132.L6B37   1988
796.8'3'0924—dc19
[B]

Book design by Eve Kirch

To the memory of my father
and
the many individuals he influenced

NATIONAL URBAN LEAGUE, INC.
JOE LOUIS YOUTH FUND

The Joe Louis Youth Fund is a youth development program of the National Urban League. Cofounded by Joe Louis Barrow, Jr., and Shell Oil Company, the program is intended to support the League's youth programs through sales proceeds from *Joe Louis: 50 Years an American Hero* and other direct contributions to the Fund.

Established in 1910, the National Urban League is a not-for-profit, community-based agency headquartered in New York City, with 112 affiliates in 34 states and the District of Columbia. Its principal objective is to secure equal opportunity for black Americans and other minorities.

The National Urban League works to improve educational accomplishments, to develop employment skills, and to instill self-motivation and self-reliance in young people. While many of the league's efforts must be directed toward solving immediate problems such as teen parenthood, school dropout, and crime prevention, it also develops long-range programs that assist in acquainting youth with the world of work, developing specialized skills, and preparing youth for jobs in an increasingly competitive technological age.

In founding the Joe Louis Youth Fund, the National Urban League, Joe Louis Barrow, Jr., and Shell Oil Company, have asserted that youth can be champions, can overcome adversity, and can make a difference in their lives and the lives of others.

For additional information:

> National Urban League, Inc.
> 500 East 62nd Street
> New York, NY 10021
> (212) 310-9000

Contributions to the National Urban League, Joe Louis Youth Fund, are tax-deductible.

CONTENTS

ACKNOWLEDGMENTS

In the fall of 1985, when I began thinking about this project, a special word of encouragement came from many people, particularly my friend Steve Haber. As the endless efforts to receive sponsorship assistance continued, a golfing acquaintance, Bob Bremson, emerged as a dear friend who tirelessly provided reassurance that the project would succeed.

To the many folks at Shell Oil Company, and particularly to Merrill Seggerman: thank you. Without your deep belief that this was a project worth sponsoring and my father an individual worth remembering, this book would not have happened.

My heartfelt gratitude, of course, goes to Barbara Munder, a *coauthor*, not a *with*. Barbara kept the faith, and because of that, we have a book today. Barbara's commitment never wavered throughout the sometimes long and arduous process of book writing, particularly during my "last-second edits." A friend for sixteen years she has been; a friend for life she will remain . . . merci!

Dozens of interviews with individuals who influenced or were influenced by Joe Louis made this book possible—relatives, friends, and acquaintances, employees and employers, those who lived for every Joe Louis fight; and most important of all, a very special lady, my mother Marva. Without the willingness of all to share their remembrances and experiences, this book could never have been written.

Likewise, I am most grateful to two of the institutions that house the Julian Black Scrapbooks of Joe Louis: the Smithsonian Institution's National Museum of American History in Washington, D.C., and the New York Public Library's Schomburg Center for Research in Black Culture. While it would be impossible to cite each newspaper clipping contained in the 109 volumes assembled by Joe Louis's manager, Julian Black, suffice it to say that they were all instrumental in preparing this biography. Particular thanks, however, go to several newspapers that were especially generous in sharing their Joe Louis archives with the authors: *The New York Times* and *The Detroit Free Press* in the United States and *The Times*, *The Daily Express*, *The Daily Mirror*, and *Boxing News* in London.

We wish to make special mention of Jimmy Jacobs, preserver of boxing memories, who kindly loaned us his collection of key fight scenes; sadly, Jimmy died of pneumonia this anniversary year. Our thanks go too, to three people who helped us understand the fight business and through their actions make the game more human: Josephine Abercrombie, Stan Hoffman of the Houston Boxing Association, and Jack Kendrick, poet, screenplay writer, and amateur boxer.

Once the research was complete, several people made this book eminently more readable. To them we are most grateful. First and foremost among these is our friend, mentor, and editor, Peter Landau, who helped shape and focus the manuscript and later, with a deft pencil, refined and tightened the writing.

Our gratitude also goes to our friends at McGraw-Hill: to Senior Editor Tom Quinn and General Books Vice President John Martin who had the vision to believe in the project and to realize that Joe Louis was more than just a boxer and this more than just a boxing book; and to Marketing Vice President Kermit Boston, translator Renata Karlin, and administrative assistant Blanche Patterson, whose special skills and commitment made a difference. From Barbara, a special word of thanks must also go to Jack Patten, publisher of *Business Week*, for his patience, encouragement, and marketing prowess.

A warm expression of appreciation goes to Linda Jones, my assistant, whose hours of diligent research, repeated retyping of manuscript and interviews, and cogent comments made calm prevail in both Denver and New York and the process easier.

To Arthur Ashe, the black athlete whose tennis skills won him a Wimbledon championship, and whose sense of black history provided him with the dedication to research *A Hard Road to Glory*, we wish to express our thanks for writing a foreword that sets the stage for this book, and offers a unique perspective on my father's accomplishments.

But the last word of acknowledgment must go to those closest to us, for without their precious love, support, and understanding, we couldn't have devoted the time and energy to complete this undertaking: our respective spouses, Deb and John, and Barbara's daughter, Alexis.

To all the above our grateful appreciation . . . thanks for helping us preserve the memory of Joe Louis.

FOREWORD

During his athletic prime, Joseph Louis Barrow was the best known and most admired black man on earth. There had been black men in America before the Great Depression of the 1930s who made incalculable contributions—Crispus Attucks, Nat Turner, Frederick Douglass, W. E. B. DuBois, Booker T. Washington, among others. But their contributions notwithstanding, in the main they were known only by name and deeds, and herein lies the power of sports in black life.

Nearly every black person and most whites in America knew who Joe Louis was. They knew his face, his voice, his record in the ring, his family, and his life history that so closely mirrored the background of other striving blacks. He was the first black role model to appear regularly in movie newsreels.

Louis literally represented "his race" at a crucial time in black American history. Boxing and track and field were the only sports in which blacks were able to go as far as their talents would take them. Sports were the only endeavors—

outside entertainment—where blacks could even hope to rise above an artificial ceiling placed on advancement. The "Brown Bomber," as he was affectionately called, surpassed all expectations.

This world champion came by his public persona because of a strong-willed mother and the legacy of Jack Johnson, the first black world heavyweight champion back in 1908. That his mother reared him in a loving and religious home is not unusual, but Jack Johnson had cast a burdensome shadow over all future black heavyweights. At the beginning of his professional career in 1934, nearly every decision taken by Louis's managers was made to counteract the controversy left by Johnson. Essentially, Louis had to prove his respectability before being allowed to prove his ringmanship.

Louis's ringmanship became that by which others were judged. His straightforward, slightly plodding moves were in contrast to those of Sugar Ray Robinson, the flamboyant black welterweight who turned boxing into ballet. Louis's fists, however, completely vindicated an opinion by one of his schoolteachers, who said he had a future in "working with his hands."

Those hands kept all of black America huddled around radio sets when he fought from the mid-1930s through the 1940s. His loss to Max Schmeling in 1936 was cause for days of mourning. The writer Langston Hughes saw grandmotherly black women sitting on curbsides weeping after this twelfth-round knockout. But phoenixlike, Louis won the world heavyweight title a year later, and exacted revenge from Schmeling in the first round in a 1938 rematch.

Louis was forever a man who remained a part of his people. He was accessible to a fault and generous beyond measure. At heart a gentle soul, he was only transformed by the ring into a master of the sweet science of boxing. He freely performed nearly 100 exhibitions during his army tour of duty and unwisely donated two championship purses to relief funds for the navy and army. Retrospectively, none of this denigrated him in the eyes of black America.

Perhaps Louis's primary contribution was in positively representing what could be done if blacks were allowed to compete fairly with whites under the same sets of rules. Black America simply had no "number one" in anything except boxing and track and field. There were no black mayors, senators, cabinet members, major corporate heads, or tycoons; those positions were proscribed and off-limits. Where else to show our talents but in sports and entertainment, and who better than the world heavyweight champion?

That he lived his final days in the employ of a Las Vegas casino hotel is also not unusual. The temptations had been just too inviting in the preceding years, and his resources were drained. Black America had had no powerful corporations of its own to offer succor to their grand champion, but an attempt should have been made nevertheless.

The Reverend Jesse Jackson spoke eloquently of Joe Louis Barrow at his funeral. In referring to the tremendous social breakthrough effected by Jackie Robinson in integrating team sports, Jackson said, "Before there was a Jackie, there was a Joe." And Joe had stood alone in that solitary ring so many times and represented us well in the dreary Depression-filled decade before World War II. It is fitting then that his son now provide more insights about his extraordinary father.

Arthur R. Ashe, Jr.

INTRODUCTION

It was almost as if America would shut down tight, cloaking itself in a pervasive, eerie silence. On frigid winter nights, on milder evenings in the spring and fall, and most often on blistering evenings in the summer, all visible activity in the country's cities and towns and villages and hamlets would grind to a halt. The streets would be empty; the quiet would be almost palpable.

This was the unfailing preamble to the dozens of occasions in the 1930s and 1940s when my father, Joe Louis, fought one of his opponents. Americans, black *and* white, would huddle around any available radio. As time for the opening bell approached, children would be roused to listen and even Europeans would rub sleep from their eyes as they awakened to alarm clocks set for the middle of the night. In the minutes that followed, millions of people around the world would hang on every word of the ringside broadcasters. Even those who had never before taken notice of boxing became engrossed, picturing the blow-by-blow descriptions in a magical way that television with all its realism could never duplicate.

The significance of all this was perhaps most apparent in the South, where radios were still scarce. Often, the only radio was in the village store or the local gas station, where blacks and whites would gather together to hear the fight. Usually, the white folks would sit in chairs; the black folks would stand along the walls or outside an open window. Typically, the blacks would listen with total concentration; just like the black boxer in the ring hundreds or even thousands of miles away, they revealed no emotion. The white folks, especially in my father's early boxing years, would be saying things like "Hit him. . . . Hit him. . . . Kill the nigger bastard."

Inevitably, my father would win. Once he did, the blacks would leave the store or the station very quietly, without a sound. Such was the intimidation of blacks by whites, particularly in the South, that they would walk in silence to their own part of town. When they reached their shanties, however, they whooped and hollered with joy. In larger cities, blacks would join hands in the streets and parade up and down, tooting or banging anything capable of emitting a loud and jubilant sound. Never before or since, to my knowledge, has an individual in sports repeatedly created such a spontaneous outpouring of emotion, stretching across many nations.

It took many months of conversations with the famous people who knew my father and with ordinary people in many parts of the world to put this curious and unique cultural phenomenon of the 1930s and 1940s into perspective. The revelation first occurred in Detroit, where my father grew to maturity and where my cousin, Tom Barrow, in 1985 launched a challenge to Mayor Coleman Young. As I traveled from shopping center to factory, from senior center to neighborhood church, speaking on behalf of Tom, I repeatedly heard about the Brown Bomber's—my father's—exploits. All, it seemed, wanted to share with me their own very special memories: where they were on the night of a particular fight, how they celebrated, how my father influenced their lives.

The time had come. For the past 37 years, I had unconsciously buried, denied, and at times consciously ignored my heritage. Maybe I didn't fully realize the special place in social history my father held. Maybe I, selfishly, was too involved in my own life. Or maybe my father's divorce from my mother and his subsequent separation from my sister and me—a situation that seemed to suit him satisfactorily—was just too painful to face. Whatever the reason, in 1985, I realized that I had to do something to document the impact he had on so many people and discover who my father really was. So I embarked upon a revealing, sometimes painfully tormenting, journey into my father's past.

Joe Louis was my father, but he was a great deal more to those of his own generation. He was a hero. I came to realize that they knew him better than I did. I had not seen my father on average more than four times a year from 1949, when my parents divorced, to 1981, when he died. That statement in itself is a rather sad and revealing commentary. I was fortunate; although my parents divorced when I was young, my mother soon remarried, and my stepfather, Albert Spaulding, a medical doctor, was there to provide me and my sister Jackie with the support we needed. Nevertheless, I would look forward to seeing my father on his infrequent visits to our home in Chicago. I remember going out to dinner with him to restaurants on the south side, only to share him with autograph seekers and well-wishers who simply wanted to say hello. I guess, as a youngster, I just didn't understand why I had to share my father with the world.

My father was never much of a conversationalist. I noticed that when he was with his buddies, they had loose, easy-flowing discussions. But when he was with me or other family members, we had to take the lead. I always found myself asking him questions in an effort to learn his thoughts and to fill the pregnant pauses. He never really initiated a conversation, although I do remember one time he did, because it was so surprising to me. I was working for the United Bank of Denver, and he asked me about my chosen career. What was I doing? Did I like it? What did it entail? He seemed pleased and proud that I was in banking, a profession that required mental rather than muscular power.

He wasn't a naturally affectionate person. One particular display of emotion, therefore, has stayed with me. It was in 1976, when I went to Las Vegas to play in the Frontier Airlines Pro-Am Invitational Golf Tournament. I was signing the register at Caesar's Palace when a friend said, "I think there's somebody over there who wants to say hello to you." I turned and saw my father. He said, "How you doing, ole dude?" I said, "Great, ole dude." He gave me a big hug.

Frankly, this just knocked me off my feet. Most of the time, I felt he seemed to care a great deal more for those who were one or two steps removed from him than those who really loved him. Emotionally, he seemed more attached to other people than to the family. In hindsight, I believe that was because Joe Louis was so accessible to other people. Everyone who met him felt he was a friend, not just a new acquaintance. My father didn't have the entourage of bodyguards around him that others in his position have had. He wasn't aloof. And he wasn't frightened by the public.

His lasting impact on history was made evident to me in Detroit. One day, while I was speaking on behalf of my cousin in a Detroit shopping center, an elderly woman accompanied by her grandchildren approached me. Obviously in awe, she asked, "Are you really the Brown Bomber's son?" When I responded in the affirmative, she said with a gleam in her eye, "You just don't know what it was like when your dad was around.'' Enthusiastically, she began telling stories of my father's heroics to her offspring's children as she walked away. I couldn't help but notice their blank stares. I realized they had never heard of Joe Louis.

Until then, everyone I met had known who the Brown Bomber was. But here was the generation gap in action. A legend was dying with those who had listened in rapt attention to their radios in the 1930s and 1940s. In addition, those who knew him best were either gone or very elderly, with fading memories. The beloved Chappy, my father's trainer and mentor, had passed on in 1942; Julian Black and John Roxborough, his managers, had died in 1967 and 1975, respectively; his third wife, Martha, was in and out of comas due to uncontrollable diabetes; and his seven brothers and sisters had dwindled to five.

Throughout that election year, the pieces of the puzzle, so long buried in my subconscious, began to come together. By the end of the campaign, I also felt a sense of urgency. If I wanted to learn the story of who my father was and what he stood for, and if I wanted to preserve his legacy, I had to act *immediately*. Now that I have had hundreds of interviews and conversations and have read and reread the Joe Louis scrapbooks donated by his manager to the Smithsonian Institution's National Museum of American History, his character and his exploits have unfolded before me: his strengths and his fortitude, his sins and his foibles, his idiosyncrasies and his humor.

The journey that produced this book took me from his birthplace in a four-room house in the cotton fields of Chambers County, Alabama, to the Hollywood mansions of the stars who admired him when he reached celebrity status. I spoke with the surviving boxers he faced in the ring: the German heavyweight champion who gave my father his first professional beating, Max Schmeling, surrounded by boxing memorabilia and photos autographed by various U.S. Presidents in his Hamburg office; Billy Conn, the gravelly voiced Irishman who was de-

feated twice by my father, in his home in the Squirrel Hill
section of Pittsburgh, which he jokingly says, referring to the
purses he received from the Louis-Conn fights, "Joe bought
me"; and Jersey Joe Walcott, whose challenges my father successfully fended off twice late in his career, once in our joint
radio interview with Radio KOA Denver and again at a wreath-
laying ceremony at my father's grave site at Arlington National
Cemetery.

I spoke at length with his three wives: my mother, Marva
Louis Spaulding, who married my father in 1935, divorced him
in 1945, remarried him in 1946, and divorced him again in 1949;
Rose Morgan, his second wife, who had a 2-year marriage that
was annulled in 1958; and his third wife, Martha, who remained
with him until his death. I visited those who served my father
—his manager, his lawyer, and his personal secretaries—as
well as a leader of our nation, former President Gerald R. Ford.

Finally, I spoke with common folk, too numerous to single
out by name, and influential individuals, including Maynard
Jackson, Andrew Young, and Georgetown's John Thompson,
who would describe for me the impact my father had on them
and other Americans of the era.

The juxtaposition of all these individuals must have been as
jarring and startling to my father as it was to me. His life was
like a roller coaster ride. He saw the top and he saw the bottom.
He started in poverty on an Alabama farm, reached stardom
and riches beyond most people's comprehension during the
post-Depression thirties, and ended his life humbly—with limited means and physical disabilities. Throughout, however, he
retained his dignity and remained special and visible to the
country and its people in a unique way at a time in American
history when they needed him most.

Pride: that's what I feel today at the end of that 3-year
journey. But it wasn't always that simple. The result is this
story about my father.

CHAPTER ONE

Sweet Revenge

"Sport is sport. It has nothing to do with hate."
—Max Schmeling

An anguished cry that seemed to come from the very soul of the challenger pierced the huge stadium. Blow after punishing blow put him onto the ropes. One, two, three times in rapid succession, he was knocked to the canvas. The last time, little more than two minutes into the first round, the bruised and battered man did not rise.

More than 70,000 boxing fans had gathered in New York's Yankee Stadium on the night of June 22, 1938, to see what was, after the legendary Dempsey-Tunney bout, the second largest boxing event in the history of the sport. The gate reached close to $1 million. It seemed as if all the Hollywood greats were there—Clark Gable, Gary Cooper, Douglas Fairbanks. Senior government officials, including the postmaster general, governors of many states, and the German ambassador to the United States had front-row seats. And all of New York society was in attendance. Sitting ringside, they heard the bloodcurdling scream that came from Max Schmeling, the result of a powerful right from Joe Louis, signaling to Louis as clearly as a knockdown that the end of the fight was at hand.

Although Louis, the world heavyweight champion since 1937, had entered the ring that night a two-to-one favorite—having a 5½-pound edge over his opponent—many sportswriters actually favored Schmeling. By their count, the formidable German who was hoping to become the first heavyweight champion to regain his title had two weapons on his side. One was his deadly right-hand punch, that had finished Louis in the 12th round of their 1936 nontitle match. The other was a psychological advantage; Schmeling was the only boxer who had ever knocked out the champion. Max Schmeling, who stood 6 feet 1 inch and tipped the scales at 193 pounds, had almost twice as many fights to his credit as did Louis. Experience and three years (1930–1932) as heavyweight champion were on his side. He had thirty-six knockouts, won thirteen by decision, won three fights on fouls, lost three verdicts, and had four draws. The German was considered an intelligent, methodical fighter.

Most experts agreed, however, that Louis was the better boxer. As for what his best punch was, however, there was general disagreement because he was such a complete fighter. Both his fists were devastating. He was acknowledged to have the best 6-inch left jab in the history of the sport. His left hook was considered a deadly wallop and a sure knockout when it connected. But his right could be powerful, too. As Louis told *The Ring* before the fight: "You fellers keep saying I have a great left hook. Why do you forget my right hand? Don't you know that I have scored almost as many knockouts with the right as I have with the left?" In addition, he was fast. Joe could land three punches for every two of his opponent's.

Louis was perfectly proportioned for his chosen profession. Over his 6-foot 1½-inch frame, he carried an evenly distributed 198½ pounds, his ideal fighting weight. His chest, 42 inches normally, was a magnificent 45 inches when expanded. His 76-

inch reach was impressive and his lethal fist was a mighty 11¾ inches in circumference. Louis was nine years younger than his opponent, and he had a psychological edge of his own: he wanted revenge. He wanted to beat the only man who had knocked him out in his professional career. Not only that, he wanted to retain his heavyweight crown without the cloud of the previous knockout.

MARVA LOUIS SPAULDING
Mrs. Joe Louis (1935–1945, 1946–1949)

Everywhere we'd go before the fight, all we heard was, "We want you to get Schmeling." It seemed his whole life hinged on that one fight.

Millions of words were written during the buildup to this fight for the heavyweight championship of the world. Many of them centered on the pre-World War II political environment—Max Schmeling, German, representing Nazi supremacy; Joe Louis, American black, representing freedom and equality. By 1938 horrifying stories of German concentration camps were beginning to filter into the American press. Jewish organizations were threatening to boycott the fight as they had the 1936 contest between the two boxers. Promoter Mike Jacobs, in an effort to head off a box office disaster, convinced these organizations that an American-German contest would further their cause, rather than damage it. Nevertheless, visitors to Louis's Pompton Lakes, New Jersey, training camp included American supporters of the Nazis.

Prior to the fight, Louis was invited by President Franklin Roosevelt to visit the White House. The President grasped the boxer's biceps and said, "Joe, we need muscles like yours to beat Germany." About the same time, Hitler, as if in response, cabled Schmeling: "To the coming World's Champion, Max Schmeling. Wishing you every success." This praise stood in stark contrast to the repudiation Schmeling received from the Third Reich prior to the 1936 fight. The German boxer was overwrought by the political signals.

Before entering the ring Schmeling also felt isolated. Joe Jacobs, the German's manager in the United States, was refused entry into the boxer's dressing room prior to the fight and his corner during the fight by the New York Boxing Commission. Jacobs's publicity antics for Tony Galento, another fighter he managed, had enraged them. Doc Casey, often a second for the German, was so fearful of the political environment that he excused himself from Schmeling's corner.

MAX SCHMELING
Former Heavyweight Champion

I sailed into New York harbor on the SS Bremen about six weeks before the fight with your father. I was surprised to see the picketing. Demonstrators on shore carried signs saying "Schmeling Go Home." I was told, "You are just fighting for the money. You will bring the money to Hitler to build military weapons." I received threatening letters that were often signed with "Heil Hitler" or "Hit Hitler." This was the reverse of the reception I had received in my 1936 confrontation with Joe.

It gave me a bad feeling because I always thought I was liked in America. I found out later that the propaganda wasn't against Max Schmeling, the fighter, but against Max Schmeling, the German. Every German, even if it wasn't true, was at this time thought to be a Nazi by Americans.

We quickly left New York for my training camp upstate. But even in training camp, from the time I got up to run until I retired for the evening, there was picketing. Initially, I laughed about it. But day in and day out, week after week . . . eventually you don't laugh any more. You just think about it.

On the day of the fight, I was escorted, along with Max Machon, my trainer, to Yankee Stadium by police. The area around the Stadium, I noticed, was roped off by hundreds of policemen. On my way to the ring, I was surrounded by more than twenty policemen. As I walked down the long path to the ring, I put a towel over my head to protect myself from the cigarette boxes, banana peels, and paper cups that were thrown at me.

In addition to the volatile international political environment, the fight also brought into focus an undercurrent of black versus white supremacy in the United States. It was ironic that a black boxer who had hitherto been called by American sportswriters "the mocha mauler," "Mike Jacobs's pet pickaninny," "the coffee-colored kayo king," among other derogatory nicknames, had suddenly become an American symbol. Even fifty years after this fight, Max Schmeling emits an intensity when speaking of the reception he received in New York. As I sat in his Hamburg office surrounded by boxing memorabilia and a bronze bust of the fighter, I thought maybe through that experience Max Schmeling was able to understand what blacks were living each and every day during the first half of the century.

In the black community, Schmeling, the man who had previously beaten Louis, was perceived as the personification of evil. Black Americans were down, way down, and felt that Joe Louis had to avenge himself—for them. It was almost as if that segment of America had somehow disappointed the country when their hero lost in 1936. If Louis beat Schmeling in the rematch, it would be not only a national victory—with political implications—but also a vindication of black America's ability to carry the flag.

MAYNARD H. JACKSON
Former Mayor of Atlanta

In 1938, Louis was viewed as the patriot, the clean-living family man, the upstanding hero who would not embarrass black people. Black folks have always been afraid of our heroes embarrassing us with the white people. There's something deep in our heritage. I think it is coming out of slavery.

When I was growing up, you heard families say, "Come here, let me put some Vaseline on your knees. What would white folks think if they saw you with those ashy legs? Come here, boy, let me brush your hair. What would white folks think if they saw you with your hair like that?"

There was a tendency, especially during your father's era, for blacks to approve of someone black only after he had been approved by the white community. Joe Louis, because he was accepted by whites, was the first legitimate national black hero. He was not just a hero to blacks but the first legitimate national hero who happened to be black.

With these diverse pressures on him, Louis's training for the Schmeling bout was the most intense of his career. In late April he went to Stevensville, Michigan, for two weeks of preliminary workouts. In the middle of May, the boxer moved to Lafayetteville, New York, for some light roadwork. Louis remained there, with a brief break to go to New York to sign the June fight contract with Schmeling, until he left on May 28 for training camp at Pompton Lakes. At the New Jersey training camp he was joined by his sparring partners George Nicholson, who had given him his best workouts for an earlier bout against Nathan Mann, and Dave Clark, a boxer from Detroit.

Early on, Louis and his advisers decided on his fight strategy. They would counteract Schmeling's strength, his powerful right, and exploit his weakness, an inability to respond quickly to a two-fisted attack at close range. "So that's where I'll be on fight night," said the confident champion, "as close to Maxie as his undervest, giving my own impression of Henry Armstrong [the fisty welterweight champion] ripping in those short-arm hooks and swings." Louis was convinced that his speed and power in close would keep Schmeling too busy blocking to land a forceful right.

A few days before the fight, Louis withdrew from those around him, speaking only with a few intimate friends. He was mentally as well as physically preparing for this encounter. He was like a wound-up spring. The day before the bout, Jack Blackburn, Louis's trainer, affectionately called Chappy, bit him on the shoulder, tasting the perspiration. He turned to Julian Black and John Roxborough, the boxer's managers, and said, "There he is. I did mine. He's as good as hands can make him. Now it's up to the rest of you."

Some say that Louis entered the ring that night hating Max Schmeling. Not at all. Joe simply wasn't that kind of man. He once said to British Broadcasting Company's commentator Harry Carpenter: "I don't remember hating anybody in boxing, not even Max Schmeling. Sure, I was mad after he knocked me out in the first fight, but not because I got knocked out. I was mad because he said something about me being a foul fighter. I was never that. When I went into the ring against him the second time . . . I wanted to knock him out as a man who was in there trying to knock me out. But to hate him, that's another thing. You don't hate that easy. Hating is something that comes deep. I never learned to do that. That's something only bad people learn."

Louis arrived at the stadium several hours before the fight. In his dressing room were managers Black and Roxborough, trainer Chappy, and friend and advance man Freddie Guinyard. The room was stark but functional, a padded table and a medicine chest the sole furnishings. The warm-up session was a routine that developed between Louis and his handlers. Partially because of its continued success—but mostly because of the boxer's superstitious nature—it rarely varied. He threw a medicine ball with Guinyard. Chappy taped his hands, first his left, then his right. He shadowboxed for half an hour, which was 20 minutes longer than usual. Then during a brief visit from Mike Jacobs, his promoter, Louis promised a quick knockout: in three rounds.

Although Louis was calm, his seconds were unusually nervous. When one of them dropped some tape, he said, "You're not fighting. What are you so nervous about?" He put on his black and red trunks and familiar blue silk robe with red trim over a flannel robe and walked out of the dressing room at ten o'clock. The roar of 70,000 fans at Yankee Stadium responding to the entrance of the champ was deafening. Schmeling, dressed in gray, was already in the ring.

Many of the usual introductions and preambles that attend heavyweight championship fights were shortened because of fears of what might happen in the politically charged atmosphere. Usually, time is taken to introduce the important people and former boxing champions who are in attendance. This time, only former champions Jack Sharkey, James Braddock, and Max Baer were acknowledged. Uncharacteristically, Louis danced on his toes in his corner, trying to keep his muscles limber and his body warm. Otherwise, as usual, he appeared stone-faced and unemotional. Schmeling stood still with a sullen expression on his unshaven face. His arms dangled by his sides, and his eyes appeared to Louis to be mere slits below his protruding eyebrows.

Seconds after the bell rang, Louis delivered two left jabs and a left hook which repeatedly jolted Schmeling's head back. The spring uncoiled. Seeing his temporarily stunned and exposed opponent, the champion quickly followed those first blows with an onslaught of awesome punches—a left hook, a right uppercut, a straight left, and a right cross interspersed among others—forcing Schmeling against the ropes within thirty seconds. It was only then that the German was able to throw a weak right over Louis's left to his jaw. His first punch of the fight missed its mark.

MAX SCHMELING

I always wanted to be a fighter who went into the ring with several moves planned—like a chess player. I was a slow starter. I wanted to take the first few rounds of the 1938 fight to find out what Joe's strategy would be. But he was quicker than I. He started like a winner. He knew right away that I was hurt and took advantage of my weakness.

On June 22, 1938, Joe Louis was unbeatable. Your father had everything in him to win. He was prepared. I was prepared. But on that day, there was nobody who could have beaten him—not even Jack Dempsey in his prime. There is no excuse for my performance. It is simply a fact.

Schmeling continued to fight defensively, leaning against the ropes while Louis threw an overhand right. The boxers clinched with the champion working on the challenger's body. They backed away, but the Champ reentered the fray with jabs and a right to the German's head. After a brief pause, Louis continued pummeling his opponent—jabs, a left hook, an overhand right. Some ringsiders felt that death was imminent in the ring, so savage was the attack.

Fear clearly covered Schmeling's face as Louis once again put him onto the ropes. A blocked right uppercut, a weak left, another left, and an overhand right that may have been the punch that won the fight followed. That final, terrific right to the jaw threw the German against the ropes partially turned.

"With each blow," Joe Williams of the *New York World Telegram* would write, "you imagined Louis saying, 'So I fouled you, eh?' . . . Boom! . . . 'So you gave me a beating I'll never forget, eh?' . . . Boom!"

Schmeling was dazed, holding on to the top rope with his right hand. Two more lefts led to a blow to his back that would briefly be called a foul by the German's seconds. It was so forceful a body punch that it broke the third lumbar vertebra of his spine. A combination of lefts and rights followed, causing Schmeling's knees to give way and his chin to drop to the ropes, thereby supporting his body. Referee Arthur Donovan started to give him a standing count, but the challenger, too battered to think, reentered the fight after only a two count.

MAX SCHMELING

Most of the fight was a complete haze for me. Joe quickly took control. I was just a target for him. I remember the fight only from the films I saw later. I do, however, recall I turned around when Joe tried to hit my heart. He hit my kidneys instead. That wasn't your father's fault; it was just the circumstances. I turned my back to him at the wrong time. I had, by that time, lost all sense of direction and coordination. Afterward I went to a hospital in New York for ten days and to one in Germany for an additional six weeks.

Twice thereafter, Schmeling hit the canvas: the first time face forward after a vicious left-right combination, the second on all fours after a lethal left hook to the head and a final devastating right to the face. In both instances, the German was so groggy that he failed to take the full count, repeating the mistake Louis made in their 1936 confrontation.

The end for the now helpless boxer came quickly. Louis threw a left jab, a right to Schmeling's injured left side, a left hook, and a right to the jaw. The challenger fell forward unconscious. Pandemonium broke out. Fans were on their chairs shouting and throwing anything within arm's reach into the air. By the count of three Max Machon, the German's trainer, threw in a white towel as a sign of surrender, a signal not accepted in 1938 by the New York Boxing Association. Donovan picked it up and flung it toward the ropes and continued his count. Dazed, the boxer still on the canvas was as listless as the towel dangling on the ropes. Machon rushed into the ring in an effort to help Schmeling. Realizing the futility of it, Donovan stopped the count at eight. At 2 minutes and 4 seconds into the first round, by a technical knockout, Joe Louis was declared "the winner and still champion."

Few could later recall the details of the fight, so rapid and powerful was the onslaught by the Brown Bomber.

BOB HOPE
Entertainer and Boxing Fan

I was a real fight fan in the 1930s. [Years earlier Hope fought out of Cleveland under the name Packy East. He had twenty-one amateur fights and lost them all.] I used to go to the Hollywood Legion Hall every Friday night to see the fights. So, of course, I wouldn't miss the Louis-Schmeling fight. I took three or four people with me, and we sat in the press area near ringside. Just as the fight began, a guy behind me yelled, "Hey, Bob." I turned around to talk to him. A roar went up from those around us. When I turned back to see what had happened, I saw Schmeling on the floor. Some fight fan, I had missed half the fight! It was that quick.

As much newsprint and radio airtime were filled after the fight as before, recording what one journalist called "the most professional one-round destruction of one man by another" since Jack Dempsey met Jess Willard. Some 50 years after the fight, sportscaster Howard Cosell recalls verbatim Bob Considine's graphic ringside reporting: "Listen to this, buddy, for it comes from a guy whose palms are still wet, whose throat is still dry and whose jaw is still agape from the utter shock of watching Joe Louis knock out Max Schmeling. It was, indeed, a shocking thing, that knockout—short, swift, merciless, complete."

Louis, in a syndicated article, said that he was particularly proud of the fourteen clean right-hand blows which he threw during the fight—"they were Schmeling's own specialty but I managed to put him to sleep with his own draught." And put him to sleep he did.

MAX SCHMELING

You know, it's a funny thing; I never had a bad feeling about being beaten in that fight by your father. Sport is sport. It has nothing to do with hate.

Oh yes, there is just one more thing that I remember. I wasn't invited by Hitler to visit him after the second fight, as I was after our 1936 fight. I was dropped by the German high command like a hot potato.

CHAPTER TWO

Origins

"As a baby, Joe could holler loud as a wildcat."
—Turner Shealey

"There's something different about Chambers County," some locals say. "It's the way the red soil smells." Chambers County is a part of eastern Alabama formerly occupied by the Creek nation. In 1832 it was ceded by the Creeks to the United States, via a treaty giving the head of each family 320 acres and the chiefs 640 acres. Many of these acres, however, were immediately sold to land speculators.

Most of the early settlers of LaFayette, the county seat of Chambers County, were "members of some church, favored morality, and did what they could to encourage education and to build up good schools and churches," according to historical records. When cotton was king, LaFayette was a busy and thriving market for the surrounding county. It is outside LaFayette, at the base of the Buckalew Mountains, that my father, Joseph Louis Barrow, was born on May 13, 1914.

I was excited but apprehensive when I visited Chambers County for the first time seventy-three years after my father's birth. Growing up in Chicago and living my entire life in the North, I knew of the South only from books and television. I felt all the concerns a northern black might feel. Would I encounter the racism that was being expressed in Forsyth County, Georgia? Would relatives I had infrequently seen or never met accept me? I shouldn't have been worried. I was delighted with the reception I was given by my aunt and other family members and the "celebrity" status I received when I visited local white historians. Their account of my heritage unfolded before me.

To get to my father's birthplace, you follow Route 50 to Bells Chapel Road, a dirt road. Some people suggest you avoid the Buckalew Mountain area if you fear encountering rattle-snakes, water moccasins, or, worse yet, a still. But if you persevere, you behold some extraordinary natural beauty: red clay contrasting starkly with the green of 60-foot pine trees. I doubt my ancestors, however, stopped to savor it.

TURNER SHEALEY
Joe Louis's Second Cousin

As a baby, Joe could holler loud as a wildcat. A lot of babies holler; a lot be quiet. Joe was one that hollered loud. He'd get mad and you could hear him all every which way. I loved to possum hunt: get a dog and go in the woods at night and catch possum. I'd get my dog and go in the woods to keep from hearing him holler.

See, times were hard. All the older family members had to go to the field. He wasn't looked after like he should've been. And that'll get a baby upside down.

There were two ways for blacks to farm in the South in the early 1900s: as sharecroppers or as renters. Sharecroppers on a one-horse farm of several hundred acres were furnished with

land to cultivate, a house, and a mule or horse by the landowner. At harvest, the sharecropper would give the farmer
one-half the crop as payment. During the year, the cropper was
advanced the equipment and supplies he needed to cultivate
the land and the clothes and food he and his family required.
He paid for these items out of his percentage of crop. Little,
if anything, remained after he repaid his debts.

A renter, on the other hand, paid the landowner a 500-pound
bale of cotton at harvest for a one-horse farm. He had to supply
his own stock, equipment, and fertilizer. Since a renter had
more independence and privileges, renting was preferred to
cropping by southern blacks. Regardless, as there generally
was no written contract, deed of trust, or definite oral understanding between owner and renter, there were frequent dis-
agreements. Even when a black tenant did receive a contract,
there were endless misunderstandings. The system quite simply
bred dishonesty and waste, and blacks felt their plight was
helpless and even hopeless. As a result, there was a constant
movement of blacks from one farm or plantation to another.

During the twelve years of my father's life in Alabama, the
Barrows were both renters and sharecroppers. They moved to
a different farm after almost every crop. In 1914, the year he
was born, his parents, Lillie Reese Barrow and Munroe Barrow, were renting a parcel of land in Chambers County from
Peter Shealey, Lillie's uncle. They were cultivating about 25
to 30 acres, half cotton and half corn. Their house was wood-
framed, with a long hallway separating four rooms. Six other
Barrow children were living in this house at the time of Joe
Louis's birth. Five months later, Turner Shealey, a second
cousin who was orphaned, moved in with the Barrows. And
the following year, the last Barrow child, a daughter named
Vunies, was born. The older children worked in the fields with
their parents; the middle ones did odd jobs, such as gathering
wood; and the youngest stayed home. The older brothers and

sisters typically served as surrogate mothers and fathers to the younger ones.

EULALIA BARROW TAYLOR
Joe Louis's Sister

Joe and I were quite young when we lived in Alabama, so we'd stay around the house mostly during the day or be in school. In the evening we'd play fire ball. You make a ball out of rags, tie it tight with a string, soak it in kerosene, light it and throw it to each other. You had to be quick to get rid of it before it'd burn you.

On Sundays we'd go to church. You couldn't play hooky because everybody got in the wagon to go to church. Kids were obedient to their family then. We didn't know what it was to disobey Momma. Momma used to always teach us to tell the truth. If she ever whipped us, I can remember her saying, "I'm not whipping you for what you did. I'm whipping you for lying about it."

Louis's father, Munroe, was hospitalized for mental illness off and on between 1906 and 1916. He'd come home, stay perhaps six months, then go back to the Searcy Hospital for the Negro Insane in Mt. Vernon, Alabama. He fathered eight children— Susie, Emmarell, Alvanious (Bane), Ponce deLeon (Leon), Lonnie, Eulalia, Joe, and Vunies—several of whom inherited his size. He stood 6 feet 3 inches and weighed almost 200 pounds. In 1916, after the birth of Vunies, he was institutionalized until his death. Most of the children were too young to be influenced by or even to remember their father.

Thereafter, most of the house and field work was done by Lillie assisted by her uncle, Peter. My grandmother was a strong, independent woman. At 5 feet 6 inches and 170 pounds, she was large for her generation. As a devout Baptist, she raised her children to respect their elders, be law-abiding, and help their neighbors. "It comes honestly to Joe to be good to his mother," says a cousin. "His great-grandfather, Anthony Barrow, who worked and gained his freedom during the days of slavery, was not satisfied until he had bought his mother's freedom."

The family stayed for the harvest of one crop on the Shealey farm, then moved eleven miles west of LaFayette to Red Grove. They made one crop there and moved on to Waverly, Alabama. Two crops later, they moved to another farm in the same community. After sharecropping there for one year, they moved to Canaan, where Lillie Barrow married Pat Brooks, a widower with nine children of his own.

TURNER SHEALEY

It was pretty bad with the poor man in the South. All of us had to obligate ourselves to the merchants to get a livelihood. We had to be subservient to get sufficient funds to operate a crop. If you made enough cotton—that was the only cash crop that the farmers had back then—you could stay on the farm. If you didn't, and if you looked like a pretty good fella, he might allow you another chance for a second year.

If you wasn't, and you didn't do what you shoulda did, why they would close you out. They'd take everthing you had—all the crop; the foodstuffs you had grown in the garden; your animals such as hogs, mules or cows; the farmer's tools—and you had to move away from his plantation and go obligate yourself with somebody else. Maybe he'd take the chance at you if he would need some hands, having vacant farms with nobody to fill them, and be glad to give you a try. Sometimes, it was a couple of miles away and sometimes it was much farther. The Barrows didn't often make enough to pay off, and they had to move a lot.

After Lillie and Pat Brooks married, the family moved to Camp Hill, where the combined clan lived until they moved north.

Camp Hill was a small town with only one main street. Brooks worked for a wealthy white construction engineer who built bridges throughout Alabama. According to Joe's sister Vunies, "He was this white man's right hand." Life for the Barrows improved. They had a car and an organ and were able to afford rugs for the floor.

Brooks, a light-skinned, lanky man, was strict but generous toward his large family. "Anyone who would marry a lady with so many kids had to be a nice man," comments one relative. But Lillie was the dominating influence on the children. She showed no favoritism. Children and stepchildren soon blended together. One, Pat Brooks, Jr., who was the same age as Dad, became his closest friend and confidant when they were growing up. Uncle Pat, as I remember, was soft-spoken like my father and had a unique sense of humor. When I was young and we were all together, he and Dad used to tell jokes and laugh a great deal—they seemed inseparable. Dad was deeply saddened when Uncle Pat died suddenly and untimely of a stroke in the 1960s. It was a great loss to him.

All the Barrow and Brooks children attended the local school. Some, particularly the younger girls, were good students; others, including Dad, were not so inclined. There was, however, little incentive to attend school or to become interested in schoolwork. Southern black schools were predominantly one-room wooden structures in the local churches, with woefully inadequate facilities. Instruction for all levels was the responsibility of a single teacher. Graduation from an Alabama school came after eight years, which totaled only forty-six months of study.

TURNER SHEALEY

We didn't have but one teacher until the higher grades. I reckon I was probably in my teens before they would have two teachers to a school. We'd go every day when the weather was good. We little fellas, first-year beginners, when the weather gets too bad or too cold, we couldn't make it. It be something like two and one-half miles from here over there to school. Way we went was by a pathway. We wouldn't go all the way around the road; we'd cut through the fields.

Church was pretty good back then, I reckon. The preachers, they wasn't too highly educated, but they had a lot of spirit. Seemed like the people were spiritual then. I guess it took our minds off our problems.

The Barrow heritage, like that of all southern blacks, is mixed, but primarily stems from Africa. My father's maternal grandparents were sold into slavery in Winston-Salem, North Carolina. George Shealey, a white plantation owner, bought my great-grandmother and her two children. There is also Blackfoot blood on our maternal side. Munroe Barrow was the son of Lon Barrow, son of Anthony Barrow. Anthony Barrow was the son of James Barrow, a prominent white planter in the Buckalew Mountains. My great-grandmother on the paternal side, Victoria Harp Barrow, was half Cherokee (a descendant of a chief) and half white.

It is suspected that my black ancestors entered the United States through South Carolina's busy slave port of Charleston. More than 65,000 slaves were imported into South Carolina from Africa during those years. Considered "connoisseurs" of Africans, the South Carolina slave owners chose slaves from the African Gold Coast first, then the Windward Coast, and finally the upper Niger Valley, the region peopled by the Mandingos, who were used primarily as house servants.

When the slaves were freed, Solem Bell, a neighboring white landowner, sold my maternal great-grandfather 120 acres for $5 an acre to be paid for in crop over time. My great-grandfather was one of the first men to buy property in Alabama after slavery was abolished. Barrow ancestors recall stories of Bell's visiting his former slave Peter in his new home (where Dad would later be born). He would join the family around the kitchen table for dinner, a highly unusual act for a white land-owner in the 1800s.

Although some of the family's encounters with white south-erners may have been better than those of their fellows, life for the Barrows and Brookses in the 1920s remained barely above the subsistence level. In spite of this, it took a major incident to encourage them to look for better prospects.

VUNIES BARROW HIGH
Joe Louis's Sister

I heard my mother describe the night that changed our lives. After visiting a sick friend she and my stepfather drove home about twelve or one in the morning. The Ku Klux Klan stopped them and was going to pull them from the car. Someone in the crowd recognized my stepfather. He said, "That's Pat Brooks. He's a good nigger." They didn't bother my parents. My stepfather, however, made up his mind that night he was leaving Alabama.

Seventy years later, when you visit Chambers County, it's clear that the local people are still proud of their most famous son. Many individuals in the county today, for instance, claim to be distantly related to Joe Louis Barrow.

CHAPTER THREE

Moving North

"I could never understand how he became such a great fighter. As a child, he never fought."
—Vunies Barrow High

In 1926 the Barrows and Brookses traveled by train to Detroit and became part of the great migration north. The industrialization and urbanization of the region following World War I had set the stage for a vast population shift: Poor people in the South, especially blacks, were finding that they couldn't afford to live on the farms any more; unemployment was high and social conditions were dreadful. So with wages rising in the North and blacks, as a result of the decline in European immigration, able to get some of the new jobs, they deserted the farms in droves. They were enticed by recruiters who traveled throughout the South, advertisements in southern black newspapers, and letters from relatives already settled in the North. All promised economic rewards and greater tolerance in northern urban centers.

Detroit was a particularly popular destination because of its economic growth. Indeed, during the 1920s it would show the largest gain in black population of any U.S. city. And it was there that Pat Brooks, urged by two brothers who were already established in Detroit, went to look for employment. He was hired by the city as a street sweeper. Several months later, his stepson, deLeon Barrow, joined him.

DELEON BARROW
Joe Louis's Brother

In Alabama, when I got around about 15, I was working in a little old mill where they make lumber. I made $12 a week. I used to give my mother $6, and I'd keep $6. I'd put $5 in the Bible and live on the $1 a week. That's all it'd take me.

We moved to Detroit when I was 17. I know one thing about Detroit in 1926: if you lose a job, you can go right out and get another one. I was lucky; I never get out of a job.

My stepfather was working for the city. They didn't pay but 50 cents an hour. That's $4.50 per day. At first I was doing some construction work. In 1928, I left my job and went to work for the Ford Motor Company. I always worked the steel mill—45 years, 2 months, and 21 days. All the Barrow boys, including Joe, worked at Ford's. Joe was at Ford's River Rouge plant three or four months in 1934.

Ford paid well. You only had to work eight hours a day for $5 a day. Nobody was paying that kind of money. Then we got raised to 80 cents an hour. After sixty days, you got a raise to $1. I worked up to $8 a day. When the Depression came, they knocked me all the way back to $4 a day. It was "take it or leave it."

Finally, in the early summer of 1926, Brooks sent for the remainder of the family. Lillie brought nine children—four Barrows and five Brookses—and they settled in an old eight-room house on Detroit's Macomb Street, the most spacious house any of them had ever been in. Behind it, in the attic of a barn, the boys built a boxing ring. Although Lillie wasn't aware of it, many of the neighborhood children used to box there. "That's where Joe really started out," recalls deLeon Barrow authoritatively. "Thurston McKinney, a buddy of Joe's, and a bunch of them boxed their way from that barn to the Brewster Recreation Center."

When he arrived in Detroit, Louis began attending the Duffield School. But since his academic credentials were somewhat suspect, a teacher recommended a transfer to Bronson, a vocational training school. Louis attended Bronson until he was about 17, quickly gaining proficiency in carpentry. Much of his handiwork soon showed up in the family's house. Meanwhile, his closest friends through much of his life came from Black Bottom, a section of the east side of Detroit. Many of them had gathered in the Duffield School grounds after school or at the Calvary Baptist Church. These included Thurston McKinney, who really introduced Louis to boxing, and Freddie Guinyard, who became his advance man and personal secretary during his early boxing career.

Since times were tough—and money scarce—before school Louis worked in the Eastern Market; there, for 50 cents a day, he would unwrap the tissue paper around the fruits and vegetables and help the merchants display their goods. Then after school, he and Freddie Guinyard worked for Pickman and Dean, a Detroit ice company. They delivered ice by horse and wagon in the summer and coal in the winter. The youngsters were paid by their size, and since Louis was large for his age, he received $1 a day; Guinyard, who was barely 100 pounds, got 50 cents. When they wanted someone to carry more than 25 pounds of ice, Guinyard pointed to Joe.

FREDDIE GUINYARD

Joe Louis's Friend and Personal Secretary

Joe and I met at the Calvary Baptist Church in Detroit when we were 12. He was three months older than I, but if you let Joe tell it, I'm ten years older! I'd see him on Sundays at church, at the Eastern Market, and on the ice wagon.

One morning, the man we used to work for on the ice wagon was sick. We decided to go to the place where he'd rent the wagon and horse and tell them to hitch it up—we was taking it to the man. Instead, we ran the wagon ourselves. This was my thought. Joe wasn't ever taking it on himself to do something like this. I was the instigator. Most fights he got into was for his stepbrother Pat Brooks or myself—protecting us.

As close as I was to Joe, I didn't know he was taking boxing lessons until one time I saw his picture in the newspaper. By then, he was doing good in the Golden Gloves. Knowing him like I did and the way he thought, I knew he didn't think anybody could beat him.

Louis's older sister, Emmarell, unwittingly helped foster her brother's fledging career, as well as his first romance, with her stepdaughter, Mathilda Davis. She gave him 35 cents a week to do household chores and some of her marketing. Joe, encouraged by Thurston McKinney, used the money to train at the Brewster Recreation Center under Atler Ellis. Louis, who lived nearby, showed up frequently at Emmarell's house—as much a result of Mathilda's presence as the weekly allowance his sister paid him.

EMMARELL BARROW DAVIS

Joe Louis's Sister

Your daddy minded everybody. You could trust him. You could tell him to do something, and he would do it—except make black-eyed peas!

Momma worked and would leave him home to cook. One day she told him to prepare some black-eyed peas. After she left, he told our sister, Susie, to cook them. That night, Papa tasted them and said they had rocks in them. Joe had forgotten to wash them before telling Susie to cook them. Did he get whipped!

Lillie Barrow wanted to expose her children to cultural opportunities, even if it meant scrimping. Vunies took piano lessons, for instance, and Joe studied the violin—or so his mother thought. She paid 50 cents a week for a violin and gave her son 50 cents a week for the lessons. Louis, however, used the money to pay for a locker at the Brewster Recreation Center, a ruse that wasn't discovered until the violin instructor visited Mrs. Barrow's house to ask where his student had been. At first Lillie was annoyed. But once she saw how determined her son was, she uncharacteristically relented, saying, "Very well, if you're going to be a fighter, be the best you can." At least that was in line with her philosophy that a job worth doing is worth doing well.

In any event, with Lillie Barrow's blessing, Joe Louis Barrow was on his way. Almost immediately, his name was shortened. The reason was simple and quite accidental. While he was filling out the application for one of his first amateur fights, Joe wrote so large he could fit only *Joe Louis* on the card. Not realizing the implications of the name change, he was told, "Don't worry about the 'Barrow.' 'Joe Louis' will be enough." Then, when he entered the Golden Gloves, his sister made a jacket for him with *Joe Louis* embroidered on the back. The abbreviation of his name was permanent.

Louis was a quiet and docile child. He grew up in a strict Baptist household—which allowed no card playing, no drinking, and no dating by the girls until they were 16½ years old. "Until I was 17, I had to be in the house before dark," recalls

Joe's sister Vunies. "You could sit on the porch when it got dark, but you couldn't be out." The Barrow youngsters went to church three times on Sunday: to Sunday School in the morning, the service at 11 a.m., and the Baptist Youth Program at night. Even though the fledgling boxer was large, he avoided the Catherine Street Gang, the group of local toughs, preferring, in his limited free time, to sneak into the movies or to play ball. So his choice of a career puzzled his family.

VUNIES BARROW HIGH
Joe Louis's Sister

I never could understand how he became such a great fighter. As a child, he never fought. I was the fighter.

I had real red hair. It was very long, and my mother put it in two braids. The kids used to call me names because of it. One day when I was in the sixth grade, I lost the first fight of my life. A girl almost killed me. Joe came by while she had me on the ground. He walked right by, went into the house and told Momma, "Your young lady's out there fighting again." He really didn't approve of fighting—especially between girls.

We didn't have a lot of money, but we had a rich life. We had love, plenty to eat, a roof over our heads, and shoes on our feet. Some of it stayed with Joe. He really loved his fellow man. Lillie Barrow Brooks was responsible for him not being another Jack Johnson [the high-living black heavyweight champion of the early days of the century].

Louis's quiet nature was partially the result of a disability, a speech impediment that he was never able to overcome. He mumbled, sounding as if he had a mouthful of marbles. Difficult to understand, he consequently didn't say much. But when he did, it made sense. By the time he was in his 20s Louis's character was set—he never went to bed without reading the newspaper carefully, thought about things long and hard before making a decision, and had an excellent memory which he never let you forget. People thought he was slow-witted. Quite the contrary: the young man was quick, with a dry sense of humor.

VUNIES BARROW HIGH

Joe could jive my mother. We had an organ in the house, but my mother, who was not musically inclined, didn't know anything about the violin. When my mother thought he was taking violin lessons, she would say, "Why don't you play something for us, Joe?" He would stand up and draw the bow across the strings rapidly in grand style. We all thought it was wonderful.

He also could get the best of my stepbrother Pat who had a weak stomach. Joe loved sweets in those days. When my mother made a fancy dessert, like a lemon meringue pie, Joe would say something like "I was out in the alley, and I saw a rat." Pat would jump up and run into the bathroom, and Joe would eat his pie. That was his droll sense of humor!

Early on, Louis's skills blossomed at the Brewster Gym under Atler Ellis's experienced eye. To assist him in the young boxer's training, Ellis enlisted the aid of Holman Williams, a young black middleweight amateur who would later turn professional, as a sparring partner and teacher. Ellis first matched his protégé against Johnny Miler, a light-heavyweight who was a member of the 1932 U.S. Olympic team. Miler, like most of Louis's opponents during his career, was white. He was also extremely competent, knocking Louis down seven times in two rounds. "Joe's face was all skinned up. He took a bad whipping,"

Walter Smith, a fellow amateur boxer of Louis's and now a cornerman for champion Thomas Hearns, told the *Detroit Free Press*. "Miler was the U.S. (amateur) champion at that time. And Joe . . . that was his first fight. There were no restrictions on age or experience in those days."

Rather than demoralizing him, the loss intensified Louis's concentration on boxing. He left his job at Ford and entered the fight game wholeheartedly. Louis was subsequently credited with fourteen knockouts in a row, few lasting more than a round or two. For each of these, he received merchandise checks, which he turned over to this mother, who now agreed "there might be something to this boxing."

The young boxer was diligent in his training regimen. It was one of his most fundamental traits, and the few occasions in his life when he deviated from the habit proved disastrous. Smith, several weight classes below Louis's then light-heavyweight status, worked out with him on many occasions. "Joe had fast hands, and I think he got them by working with smaller guys," he reflected years later. "He'd train with middleweights, welterweights, guys with real fast hands, and that helped him when he became a heavyweight. He had to move fast to hit small, quick people."

"You couldn't help but like the guy," Smith recalled. "Every night, we'd tease him . . . he laughed more at the jokes we'd tell on him than we did. But when he got in the ring, he had that deadpan look and that followed him through his whole career."

And so powerful were Louis's punches that fifty years later, Smith could still remember their effect. "He had a good left hook and left hand. He had a punch we called the DOA—a left hook to the stomach and a right cross to the head. If you couldn't get out of the way of both of them at the same time, you'd be dead on your ass. That's what it really stood for."

Louis made two significant decisions in 1933. He entered

the Golden Gloves, a step toward turning professional, and on the recommendation of Holman was taken on by a more experienced trainer, George Slayton, manager of the Detroit Athletic Club. Traveling the country and winning most of his fights, the young boxer began to gain respect in amateur circles.

He had a dazzling record as an amateur until he met Clinton Bridges, a Golden Gloves Intercity light-heavyweight titleholder. Bridges proved too experienced for Louis and outpointed him in 3 rounds. Louis tasted defeat again in 1933 at the hands of Stanley Evans at a fight in a Highland Park theater in Detroit. "I had watched him train and I knew if he hit you, you were down," Evans told a *Detroit Free Press* reporter years after the bout. "I had to outsmart him. I had to have more ring generalship. I'd block his punch and counter, or beat him to the punch." Evans was awarded the 3-round decision.

Evans met Louis again that year in a light-heavyweight fight at the Detroit Golden Gloves Championship. In this second match, Louis won the decision, establishing a recurring pattern in his career: when he met someone a second time, he improved on his first performance. For his part, Evans solved the Louis threat by moving up in weight class. "When I stepped on the scales in St. Louis, I put weights in my pockets so I weighed in at about 178 instead of 174," he explained. "Everybody said I could lose a couple of pounds and go as a light-heavyweight, but I said no. I pointed at Joe and said, 'That fella's a light-heavyweight, and he's going to win, too.' "

A string of knockouts sent the young Detroit boxer to the 1933 Golden Gloves National Championship in Boston. There, Louis was defeated for the fourth and final time in his amateur career. That time, it was against Max Marek, a Notre Dame football star. The following April, Louis's amateur career reached its peak when he won the National AAU light-heavyweight championship in St. Louis. Overall, in fifty-four amateur bouts, he won forty-three by knockout and seven by decision and lost four, all by decision.

Meanwhile, the Detroit Athletic Club's Slayton asked John Roxborough, one of Detroit's wealthy, well-known blacks, to visit Brewster Gym to watch Louis. Some twenty years before, Roxborough had been one of the best basketball players in the Midwest. He had made his money in the numbers and by 1934 was an influential figure in black gambling in Wayne County, Michigan.

Roxborough came from a respectable family. His brother was a state senator, his nephew was with the State Department, and several family members had an insurance firm in Detroit. Roxborough quickly saw Louis's potential and agreed to manage him. After he did so, his approach was not unlike that of a preacher whose sermon was, "Do as I say, not as I do."

Under Roxborough's wing, Louis's talents flourished. But by 1934, Roxborough's personal finances were strained by an impending divorce. He turned to Julian Black, a numbers man and nightclub owner in Chicago, for financial assistance—in return for a percentage of Louis. Black was a fine-looking man, with straight black hair and a smooth, brown complexion. Like Roxborough, Julian Black was street-smart. But where Roxborough was diplomatic, Black was abrupt and straight to the point. Where Roxborough was warm and outgoing, Black was all business.

The Roxborough-Black regime was a successful comanagership, which lasted until World War II. Although it was said that Louis was ill-managed, nothing could be further from the truth. Realizing the boxer's success was to their own financial advantage, Roxborough and Black were always kind but strict toward their ward. As close as they were to Joe, however, they were incapable of controlling his frequent frivolous spending sprees. He was simply too generous—his generosity was a positive character trait when held in check, but when untempered would prove his undoing.

ALVANIOUS BARROW
Joe Louis's Brother

Joe was always free-hearted. When he would come to Detroit, he'd always have a stack of $10 bills, and he would just pass them out to everybody. One time he was here, and he passed out the $10 bills to everybody in the house. Some more kids came up. They had heard that he was up here. He passed them out to them. I think he must have given out sixty $10 bills that day.

Louis was particularly benevolent to those in his hometown. In turn, Detroit and the people of Detroit were unflagging in their devotion to Joe Louis. People would tag behind him when he walked in the Detroit streets. On one occasion his sister Eulalia recalls she saw such a crowd following her brother, and she started running, too. Flabbergasted by her actions, she stopped and reflected, "What in the world am I running behind him for?" The simple answer is that Joe Louis was just that magnetic.

Instances of Louis's charity are almost too numerous to recount, but several in his early years stand out. One Christmas shortly after he had turned professional, Joe visited Detroit's Duffield Elementary School. He had bought hundreds of dollars' worth of gifts for all the students and walked up and down the halls distributing them as well as words of encouragement to the children, who left their classes to greet him. On another occasion early in his career, he repaid the city of Detroit $250 —the amount Louis's family received in welfare checks after his stepfather was injured in an automobile accident.

Louis loved Detroit, and Detroit, to this day, continues to

honor him. The city has named its major sports and concert facility the Joe Louis Arena, placed the *Sports Illustrated* Monument to Joe Louis at the corner of Jefferson and Woodward Streets, and commissioned a sculpture of the boxer that stands prominently in the Center Atrium of Cobo Hall, Detroit's main convention center.

CHAPTER FOUR

Born to Fight

"Joe could knock your head off with a six-inch punch. All he wanted was an opening and he could find one in a split second. If a fighter made a mistake, he was gone."

—Marshall Miles

In 1934 John Roxborough and Julian Black moved Louis's headquarters from the Brewster Recreation Center in Detroit to Chicago's Trafton Gym, where his training could be intensified and his skills polished. For the young boxer's development they turned to a new handler, Jack Blackburn, a former lightweight champion. Blackburn had previously worked with two exceptional fighters, Bud Taylor and Sammy Mandell, and was known for the way he honed their natural talents. By his own account, Blackburn fought two or three times a week between 1903 and 1909 and lost only once. Five feet nine inches and 135 pounds when he was in fighting trim, he was noted for his dangerous left and for his cunning. Blackburn was often in the unenviable position of finding few lightweights willing to fight him—and not many heavyweights willing to risk being humiliated by losing to someone who was so much smaller. In spite of his color and size, he still faced the best of his era, including Joe Gans, the Old Master; Sam Langford, the famed Boston Tar Baby; and light-heavyweight champion Philadelphia Jack O'Brien.

The story goes that initially Blackburn didn't want to train Louis. "What is this Louis?" he suspiciously asked Black and Roxborough when they approached him. "A white boy?"

"No, he's a colored boy who can bat 1.000 in any league," retorted Roxborough.

"No sireee," said Blackburn. "Not for me. You can't make no good money with a colored boy. He won't have no chance. You can count me right out."

Putting his persuasive abilities—and Blackburn's need for money—to the test, Roxborough convinced the trainer to see the young boxer. It took just one look. Observing Louis's finely proportioned body, lightning reflexes, and punching power, Blackburn relented—but on the basis of a guaranteed salary, not a percentage. (When Louis started winning, this arrangement was changed.)

Although Blackburn and Louis developed a great affection for one another—they called each other "Chappy"—there was no doubt that Blackburn had a darker side. He had grown up during an earlier generation of boxing. Much of what occurred in the ring was illegal and unfair. During his boxing days, although he wore a size eight shoe, Blackburn would wear a size twelve so he could put his money into it. He was paid in $20 gold pieces; and if he didn't hide his money in his shoes, the promoter and the manager would be gone by the time he finished boxing. His handlers on occasion would put plaster of paris on his hands when they were wrapping them; he would dip his hands into the bucket of water that was in the ring. Now, you know what that will do in the next ten minutes!

Blackburn had a hard life and bore razor scars across his

cheek to prove it. In 1909, his boxing career ended when he was sent to prison. The newspaper reports vary, but it is known that a man was shot and killed one night in Philadelphia. Blackburn was convicted of the crime. Still, Chappy began as Louis's trainer and eventually turned out to be his adviser, mentor, and father figure. He wasn't afraid of Louis, but the boxer was wary of him. Blackburn had more power over Louis than any other living man.

FREDDIE GUINYARD
Joe Louis's Friend and Personal Secretary

Chappy was special. He would talk to Joe in a different way than most people. He'd talk to me in that way, too. When I first started working for Joe, I wasn't on a salary. I could spend anything I wanted. All I had to say was, "Joe, I need this." One day Chappy told me, "Freddie, you ask Mr. Roxborough to put you on a salary. Then, you have more than just being here. Just being here, he can tell you to get out any time. But if you got a salary, you've got something more." That was the best advice I ever had.

Fighters in the thirties lived different from the fighters today. Joe come right up under the old fighters, and Jack Blackburn tried to instill some of his ideas into him. I know some fighters today that have sex with their girlfriends and wives before a fight. That was a no-no in the thirties and forties. That's one reason why Joe and Marva had it out. They didn't want her to come in the training camp. She wasn't one to seek the glamour of being there. She just wanted her husband.

Chappy was one of the best trainers in the business. He began by teaching Louis to defend himself. Next came a lesson in how to align his body perfectly and how to move so that he could throw a punch. Blackburn perceptively told Louis, "You can beat anyone you can hit, but I have to teach you how to get in the proper position to do so." The shuffle, a term often used to denigrate Louis's ability to move quickly, actually allowed him always to have a perfect launching pad from which to release a punch. Finally, the lessons progressed to punching. Chappy taught Louis every weapon in his arsenal, but the most powerful was the Blackburn jab that turned into a lethal hook. Louis once described his left jab as different from that of former champ Gene Tunney: "He snaked his out on the retreat; I uncork mine while I'm shuffling in, shoving the left foot out and dragging the right after it. That gives the punch 100 percent more steam."

Roxborough and Black had a lesson of their own to teach Louis: Avoid being like Jack Johnson, the black champion who dominated the heavyweight ranks for seven years. Johnson's tenure began with his defeat of the 5-feet-7-inch Canadian Tommy Burns, on Boxing Day 1908, and it ended in 1915 in the controversial "fixed fight" against Jess Willard in Havana, Cuba. In the eyes of white America, Johnson never wore the crown well.

Many blacks, on the other hand, felt Johnson was never allowed to reign with dignity. He was plagued by the Ku Klux Klan. Before his defense of the title against Jim Flynn in 1912, for instance, he received a note from the Klan that said, "Lie down tomorrow or we string you up." He was falsely accused of being a "loafer" and playing "cat-and-mouse" with his opponents in the ring. Johnson himself described his style in terms of defensive tactics. In Spain—after he tried bullfighting—he said: "If I were a bullfighter I'd make the public think I was within inches of death, but I'd keep my margin of safety always. I did in the ring. My God, against the men I beat when I was at my best, I was padding backwards round the ring for three rounds out of four. Defense always wins fights in the end, if it's good enough."

Johnson's personal style, however, deeply offended the segregated society of his day. After a victory in the ring, the black boxer's face would break into a broad grin, a natural reaction that whites mistook for a sign of black supremacy. He married two white women and had an affair with a third, and under threat of imprisonment he fled the country in a self-imposed exile that lasted from 1913 until 1920. He was often photographed, always smoking a cigar, with women and flashy cars —an image white America and some blacks of the day couldn't accept of the world's heavyweight champion.

The standards Roxborough instilled in Louis were clearly a response to Johnson's excesses:

- Never have your picture taken alone with a white woman.
- Never go into a nightclub alone.
- Have no soft fights.
- Have no fixed fights.
- Never gloat over a fallen opponent.
- Keep a solemn expression in front of the cameras.
- Live and fight clean.

Some believe it was a burden for Louis to adhere to this advice. But actually, his upbringing and personality made these principles easy to follow. Whether they were black or white, Louis didn't want to make a mockery of any of his opponents—it wasn't in his nature. In truth, he was attuned to the era in which he was to play such a large role. He knew he would potentially have only one opportunity at the heavyweight championship title. To Louis, boxing was a business; the objective, to win.

Regardless, Roxborough and Black weren't taking any chances. They were cautious about those with whom they'd let the young boxer associate. In particular, they were apprehensive of Louis's boyhood chums from the Black Bottom section of Detroit.

FREDDIE GUINYARD

I caught up with Joe in Chicago. I got a job with the songsters The Mills Brothers. I was just a little bit higher than a shoe-shine boy. I found out Joe was training for his first pro fight at a gym called the Bacon Casino. It was 50 cents to get in. I told them I was a friend of Joe's. They said, "Friend or foe, put the 50 cents in the box." Eventually, I got them to get Joe. He stopped training to let me in.

Now when Joe and I started running around together after he won his first fight in 1934, people would write Mr. Roxborough and tell him, "If you let Freddie Guinyard run around with Joe Louis, you won't have a fighter." I didn't stick up nobody or hit them in the head with a blackjack, but most crap games when they were raided . . . I was there.

At first, Mr. Roxborough and Mr. Black wouldn't let me see Joe. But I'd go around the back of his house near the cemetery, come up the backyard, and go upstairs and we'd talk. After Joe bought his first car, we used to go around the theaters, pick up the young ladies and take them for a ride. One girl's mother told her if she caught her in that car with Freddie Guinyard and Joe Louis again, she'd break both of her legs. Not one, but two!

I have to admit that I wasn't the best environment for Joe Louis. But from childhood, Joe had given me part of his money. He used to shovel snow in Detroit; I was too little. They'd give Joe $3, and he'd give me $1 of that. So, if you've got any decency in you at all, you wouldn't do anything to throw him off from going straight.

After seeing the sullen demeanor of their boxer without his friends, Roxborough and Black relented. Guinyard, and later other boyhood pals, became part of the entourage—arranging for transportation and sparring partners, collecting tickets at training camp ($1 was charged for admission to watch Joe train), and performing other miscellaneous chores. Roxborough had a pocket watch; when he took it out and looked at it, it was time for one of his subordinates to tell spectators to leave.

Roxborough and Black first matched Louis against Chicago's top heavyweight, Jack Kracken, who was best known for going the distance against Primo Carnera, the Italian giant. Many questioned the wisdom of the match. "Kracken will kill that boy," one local fight manager predicted. Louis, however, proved them wrong. He celebrated his debut as a professional on July 4, 1934, by knocking out Kracken in the Bacon Casino on Chicago's south side in less than 2 minutes of the first round. The 20-year-old received $59 for his evening's efforts—more than he earned in a week working at Ford.

A week later, Louis faced a friend, Willie Davis, at Bacon's. This time, the knockout took four rounds, earning Louis $62. Two months and several fights later, he was matched against Alex Borchuk in Detroit. But this time, even though the young fighter finished off his opponent in four rounds, he was not left unscarred. Louis returned to Chicago missing one tooth. Joe ended 1934 with twelve fights—all wins, ten by knockout—under his belt. His ring earnings, as well as his reputation, steadily increased. He had received $3000 for a three-round knockout of Lee Ramage; by his first fight in 1935, a ten-round decision over Patsy Perroni in Detroit's Olympia Stadium in January, the purse was $4000.

With Louis's early boxing success came an opportunity that proved to be the pivotal one in his drive for the heavyweight championship of the world. His managers were approached by Mike Jacobs, a New York boxing promoter. Jacobs was an Eastern European Jew who came from a background almost as impoverished as Louis's. He grew up in an Irish neighborhood on the West Side of New York to which his parents had immigrated from Eastern Europe via Dublin, Ireland. As a boy, Jacobs also worked hard to get out of the environment into which he had been born. He moved quickly from being a "digger," a boy who bought opera or theater tickets for scalpers, to being a scalper.

During World War I Jacobs became involved in scalping boxing tickets, and it was through a relationship he developed with Tex Rickard, promoter for Madison Square Garden, that boxing became his career. In 1916 he began advancing Rickard money for title fights in return for blocks of prime tickets to scalp. By 1921 he had become an invaluable behind-the-scenes power broker at Madison Square Garden. Jacobs's relationship with the Garden came to an abrupt halt, however, when Rickard died and Jimmy Johnson, rather than Jacobs, became the Garden promoter.

Jacobs, however, was secretly asked by three influential sports journalists from the Hearst newspaper chain to start another boxing club. Damon Runyon, columnist; Edward J. Frayne, *New York American*'s sports editor; and Bill Farnsworth, *New York Journal*'s sports editor, had previously been promoting boxing in the Garden in support of Mrs. William Randolph Hearst's Free Milk Fund for Babies, a New York charity that received a percentage of the proceeds from the fights held in the Garden.

When the Garden reduced the Milk Fund's cut, the journalists surreptitiously decided to branch out on their own. They offered Jacobs the same arrangement they had with the Garden —money for the Milk Fund in exchange for publicity for the fights—plus a percentage for themselves. The Twentieth Century Sporting Club was born. Jacobs began to promote boxing cards at the former New York Hippodrome at Sixth Avenue and Forty-fourth Street.

Jacobs first saw Louis fight in Los Angeles in 1935. In a

rematch against Lee Ramage, Joe scored a two-round knock-out. Jacobs realized that Louis was an extraordinary boxing talent. He approached Roxborough and Black to take Louis to New York in June for a major bout, saying, "John, you and Joe are colored. I'm a Jew. It's going to be hard for us to do anything. But if you stick with me, I think I can do it."

He proceeded to show Louis's managers what he could do. Since he already had Runyon, Frayne, and Farnsworth on his side, he set out to line up the remainder of the sports press. Jacobs hired a private train, stocked it with liquor and food, and invited thirty journalists to travel from New York to Detroit to see Louis fight Natie Brown.

In the first round, Joe knocked down Brown, the first knock-down in Brown's professional career. He followed up with a series of pulverizing lefts, but failed to knock him out. For the remainder of the ten-round bout, Brown crouched almost dou-bled over, in an attempt to avoid Louis's devastating punches. Although tentative for the bulk of the fight, Louis was im-pressive. Still, the press found his otherwise flawless perfor-mance "mechanical." And as he emerged from the bout unmarked, the reporters also questioned whether the youthful fighter could take a punch as well as he could deliver one.

After the fight, Joe Louis signed a contract with Mike Jacobs on the understanding that he would attempt to win every fight in the earliest round possible. As Roxborough's principles in-dicated, there would be no fixed fights in Joe Louis's career. The Natie Brown fight marked the young boxer's seventeenth victory since he had turned professional eight months earlier. A fan remarked, "He was sure enough born to fight." Louis's natural athletic ability, coordination, and powerful build were assets, but of equal importance were his love of the sport and his dedication to rigorous training. Roxborough and Black matched him against five opponents over the next two months to help prepare him for his June 25 bout in Yankee Stadium against former heavyweight champion Primo Carnera. It would be New York sports fans' introduction to Joe Louis.

Boxing experts considered Carnera Louis's toughest opponent to date. Weighing 260½ pounds (64½ pounds more than the young boxer), the Italian heavyweight was known for his roughhouse tactics in the ring: he used his weight to push his opponent around and stepped on his toes while punishing him with his punches. Although he was a stand-up fighter, which Louis preferred, he was 6 feet 5¾ inches and had a long reach. In preparation, the Detroit boxer trained with a trio of giants —Leonard Dixon, Ace Clark, and Ceil Harris—all taller than Carnera. Louis entered the fight an eight-to-five favorite.

The political elements later to be seen in Louis's fights with Max Schmeling were also apparent prior to the Carnera fight, days before Italy began preparations to invade Ethiopia. Some thought the fight might be construed by the 60,000 in attendance as a young American hero versus a towering Italian giant of Mussolini's army. As the fighters entered the ring, announcer Harry Balough appealed to the audience in the name of sportsmanship. The fans actually provided no cause for alarm, but Joe Louis's six-round destruction of the former heavyweight champion did. His face, when he entered the ring and throughout the bout, did not reveal his intentions—to demolish his Italian opponent unequivocally. In the first round he concentrated on Carnera's head with a series of left and right punches that caused the former champion's teeth, unprotected by a mouthpiece his handlers had forgotten to give him, to pierce his upper lip and spurt blood. Similar blows to Carnera's head marked the second round.

Louis shifted his punches to Carnera's body during the third round and back to his head in the fourth. The Italian boxer was never able to crowd his opponent; Joe held him at bay with powerful punches. In the fifth round, Carnera captured his opponent in a clinch. With incredible strength Louis pushed the Italian into the ropes and followed up with a series of rights.

The blood from his earlier cuts spilled from his lip down onto his chest.

Surviving the round, the former champion entered the sixth round clearly exhausted. In the corner, Carnera told his seconds, "I don't want any more of that." Louis, however, didn't oblige. A series of rights knocked the Italian boxer to the canvas. After a second attempt, he finally rose at the count of four—only to be dropped again by a right to his jaw. Carnera was up again at four, but Louis pursued his opponent with a combination of punches, sending Carnera down a third time. He rose, murmuring something to referee Arthur Donovan; one ringsider recalled Carnera's pleading, "Geev it to heem; geev it to heem!" Donovan immediately stepped between the fighters. At 2:32 of the sixth round Louis won the fight on a technical knockout, for which he received more than $44,500, his largest purse to date.

Joe shared his earnings, as well as the New York victory celebration, with his family. His mother and most of his brothers and sisters were ringside to see him fight for the first time. "Carnera fought from bell to bell," deLeon Barrow, Louis's brother, said years later, recalling the evening, "and he didn't get no credit for it." After the fight the Barrows—deLeon, Lonnie, Emmarell, Eulalia, Vunies, and a whole lot of cousins—went to a nightclub on Seventh Avenue. Joe joined them, a rare action for the boxer, who usually headed home after a bout, ending the evening with waffles and chicken. Like the Barrows, most fans, black and white, recall exactly where they were on that evening.

GERALD R. FORD
Thirty-eighth President of the United States

I remember listening on the radio to the Carnera fight when I was at the University of Michigan. I recall because I was always an avid reader of the sports page. Here was the

emerging Joe Louis, a young, very promising boxer in the
Detroit area, against this behemoth who was 260 pounds.
Joe just whipped him badly.

There was little time for the boxer to rest or celebrate. Less
than two months later Louis faced King Levinsky in Chicago's
Comiskey Park. Levinsky, known for his powerful punches,
was to be a warm-up for an upcoming bout with Max Baer,
another former heavyweight champion. Louis barely worked
up a sweat, flooring his shattered opponent in the first round.

Before the fight, Chappy told Louis that he couldn't go into
the ring with him; excessive drinking had finally taken its toll.
Joe told Blackburn that he would knock out Levinsky in one
round so his trainer would only have to walk up the ringside
steps once—a promise to his beloved mentor he would repeatedly make before bouts. In return for the one-round knockout, Joe asked Chappy to stop drinking for six months. His
trainer agreed; Louis, never one to welch on his end of a bar-
gain, held Chappy to the agreement.

Levinsky, like many of Louis's opponents, was petrified of
the young boxer's growing reputation as a devastating puncher.
Before the bout, Mike Jacobs was warned by one of his cohorts
in Levinsky's camp that the boxer was so nervous that he might
be incapable of entering the ring. Jacobs, after going into Levinsky's dressing room to confirm the report, started the fight
one hour ahead of schedule.

When Louis returned to Detroit after the bout, he found his
boyhood chums, like most blacks during the Depression, out
of work and on welfare. With the assistance of Thurston
McKinney, he formed the Brown Bomber Softball Team, pro-
viding the twenty-two-member team with their gray and red
uniforms and their touring bus. Louis planned to play with the
team between bouts.

DELEON BARROW
Joe Louis's Brother

Your father was a good softball player. He used to play first base with the Brown Bombers whenever he could. Joe had a devil of a team. They played everywhere . . . down south, Texas, California. In the wintertime, I used to keep the team bus in my barn. One winter Thurston McKinney came out and told my wife he was going to put the bus up on cement blocks for the winter. He took the wheels and sold every one of them. Next spring they come looking for the bus and I said Thurston come and took the wheels. Well, Joe had to buy a set of new wheels for the bus.

Louis reveled in these brief and infrequent reunions with family and friends, finding they were the only times he could truly relax. Meanwhile, Mike Jacobs was busily negotiating the boxer's bouts for the rest of the year. Jacobs matched him against Max Baer, another fighter he promoted, for what he assumed would be a heavyweight title fight. Baer, at Jacobs's urging, fought Jimmy Braddock earlier in the year. Unfortunately for all those associated with the Twentieth Century Sporting Club, Baer lost to Braddock, resulting in Madison Square Garden's retaining promotional rights over the heavyweight crown.

The battle between the two boxing organizations for control of the heavyweight championship title fight thus heated up. Louis was clearly the best box-office draw for a title fight, but Braddock, the new champion, was represented by Madison Square Garden, which refused to split the fight proceeds with Jacobs. So Jacobs proceeded with the scheduled September Louis-Baer bout. In preparation, Joe and his trainer had a private slow-motion viewing of the motion picture of Baer's fight against Carnera and subsequently scheduled an indoor training session from which they barred the public. Chappy analyzed

Baer's style, focusing on his dangerous right and perfecting Louis's defense against it. He taught his boxer to feint when shuffling in. (Before the fight, both fighters had married: Joe's wedding with Marva Trotter took place just hours before the match. Baer, considered the glamour boy of boxing, married Mary Ellen Sullivan 88 days before the bout.)

Louis's training regimen paid off. In front of 95,000 fans in New York's Yankee Stadium, the Brown Bomber gave Baer a brutal beating in less than four rounds. By one reporter's calculation, Louis missed just 2 out of more than 250 punches in the 11-minute, 50-second bout.

The first round was the only one in which the former champion appeared to have a chance. At the end of the first three minutes, he and Louis exchanged a flurry of punches and counterpunches, in which both boxers hit the mark. Joe came through unmarked, putting to rest the theory that he could throw punches but not take them. Some ringsiders felt Baer quit after the first round; others believed he was simply so stunned by the Detroit slugger's powerful blows that he couldn't respond thereafter. Regardless, by the second round, the former heavyweight champion was bleeding profusely. Confused, he hit his opponent twice after the bell. The third round sealed Baer's fate: twice Louis knocked him to the canvas, the first knockdowns of the German-American's career. The second time, he would have been counted out had the bell not saved him at the count of four.

The fourth and final round was a convincing one for Louis. Near the end of it, the Brown Bomber hit Baer with a series of lefts followed by a right to the jaw. Baer grabbed his opponent. Once separated, Louis swung a final right and left to his jaw, sending him once again to the canvas. He rose to his knee, but by that time the referee had reached the count of ten. Baer wrote his own stinging epitaph when, after the fight, he ruefully told reporters, "I would have struggled up once more, but when I get executed, people are going to have to pay more than $25 a seat to watch it.''

The four-round annihilation of Baer, a highly respected former heavyweight champion, sent Joe's reputation soaring. Quiet moments with family and friends, and unobserved train station entrances and exits, were incidents of a bygone era. Louis had become a national celebrity, and nowhere was this more apparent than in his hometown of Detroit.

DELEON BARROW

One Sunday morning right after the Max Baer fight we drove to Elizabeth Park. Some people were playing softball, so Joe got on the team. Now, they don't even know who Joe is. After about two innings they found out who he was. Good God, we had to get all the police out there in Trenton to get us out of there. People started hollering Joe Louis was there. They come from all over. Even the boats come in off of Lake Erie. There seemed to be thousands of people surrounding us.

Louis finished 1935 with an equally devastating knockout of Paolino Uzcudun, a Spanish heavyweight past his prime. In the fourth round, when the Basque fighter momentarily separated his arms to see his opponent, he received a right-hand punch that many boxing experts of the day considered one of the most powerful punches they had ever witnessed. It lifted him off his feet and tossed him to the other side of the ring. Uzcudun rose at the count of eight with a face so battered that referee Arthur Donovan stopped the fight. He was so demolished by Louis's punches that twenty minutes later in his dressing room he collapsed again.

Joe's earnings were steadily mounting. To put them in perspective: During the first one and a half years of his professional boxing career, Louis's purses totaled $371,645. Of this, $346,688 was received for his last four fights—Carnera, Levinsky, Baer, and Uzcudun—comprising 43 minutes and 15 seconds of fighting activity. Although the purses had to be split with managers and expenses and taxes had to be deducted, and although there were others who had earned more (the Dempsey-Tunney purse in 1927 was $990,445), in 1935 it was still a fortune for a 21-year-old boxer. Consider the following: In the same year, you could buy a fully equipped DC-3 aircraft for $100,000; rent a room in New York's Waldorf Astoria Tower (where Cole Porter and John Paul Getty had apartments) for $35 a night; or buy a National Football League team for $10,000. The average annual salary in the United States at the time was $1250.

Although boxing fans may argue about who was the best heavyweight champion, all agree that Joe Louis must be ranked near, if not at, the top. Even as early as 1935, his second year as a professional, experts knew he was a boxer to watch. Always superbly conditioned, Joe Louis fought with a magical composure. Some say that he introduced modern boxing—a much more graceful, scientific sport than that of the John L. Sullivan era. Ringsiders were always surprised when opponents fell because they didn't see Louis hit them. His punches seldom traveled more than six inches.

MARSHALL MILES
Joe Louis's Manager, 1944–1959

Joe was a good fighter. He could protect himself very well. He had the hardest short punch I ever heard of. Joe could knock your head off with a six-inch punch. Most fighters need space—Joe didn't. In addition, he had the instinct to know when to finish off an opponent. All he wanted was an opening and he could find one in a split second. If a fighter made a mistake, he was gone.

Joe could move pretty good. A lot of people say he shuffled, but he could move pretty good. To land your best punches you have to be flat-footed. The strength comes from your side and your legs. Joe was always in the best position to land a powerful punch.

And his punches came automatically. That's the reason I've seen him hit fighters in exhibitions. He didn't want to do it, but they'd just make one mistake. He would see the opening and instinctively go in there. We'd take fighters on the road with us, and they would get mad because Joe sometimes would hit them.

Louis's technique, strategy, and fine physique were due to his rigorous training schedule. Roadwork would begin at 5 a.m. in the summer, 7 a.m. in the winter. In the winter, he put on shorts, a woolen shirt, a sweater, a track suit, a knitted skull cap, woolen gloves, and heavy boots for his workout. He'd start at two miles and work up to eight or nine miles a day, changing from walking to running as he thought appropriate. As he jogged along, he would occasionally bend down to pick up stones to strengthen his back muscles. After a rubdown, Louis rested until breakfast at 9:30 or 10:00 a.m. A brisk mile-and-a-half walk with his sparring partners would follow the first of his two daily meals.

FREDDIE GUINYARD

I used to do roadwork with Joe. Jack Blackburn and Carl Nelson, Joe's bodyguard, would be driving alongside to give instructions and to run the dogs off. Joe and I and two or three sparring partners were running. One morning I asked Jack when we got up, "I'm not fighting a soul, why am I out running?" He laughed, saying, "I wondered how long you were going to take that."

One morning it was cold as the devil when Joe got up.

He said to Jack, "Chappy, I can't run I'm so tired. I didn't sleep at all last night. I had a dream that I was running and somebody was dropping coal on me all the way. I ran all night." Chappy looked at him and told him to go on back to bed. Later, accusingly, he asked me, "Did you tell Joe to tell me that damn lie?"

A two-hour sparring session beginning at 2 p.m. would be alternated daily with a general training session. With boxers' faces greased with oil or Vaseline, the sessions would begin with five minutes of shadow boxing to warm up. As in a regulation bout, Louis sparred four to six three-minute rounds with a minute interval. Next came three minutes each on the small bag, the heavy bag, the jump rope, and then calisthenics. Fighters having three or four different styles—each paid $25 per round plus expenses—would be hired to prepare him for his ring opponent.

Bill Bottoms, the chef who was with Louis from his amateur days until the war, prepared all his meals. Joe's two daily meals were fairly spartan, considering his size and his rigorous regimen. Breakfast during training consisted of a large glass of apple juice, two poached eggs, and three or four lamb chops or a thick beef patty. Fifteen minutes after his meal, he would drink a couple of glasses of water. Two weeks before a fight, all fats were taken out of his diet, including the bacon Louis loved. Dinner was heavily protein. He had one or two glasses of water followed by a salad, soup, a one-pound steak grilled medium rare, corn or string beans followed by tea. A quarter of an hour later he would have several glasses of water.

FREDDIE GUINYARD

Bill Bottoms, the cook, was a crabby old bastard. All cooks are. I can cook and I used to cook different things at night.

Bottoms didn't want nobody in his kitchen. Roxy, who liked the little things I'd cook up, said, "Let him cook."

Joe would eat anything. Now his family, like my family, were rice eaters. They would fix peas, rice and things like that when he went home. But when he walked into a restaurant, to hell with the damn peas. We had had our fill of that!

We went to Buffalo when he was still a young fighter. There was a restaurant there, Dan Montgomery's, that had the best Black Angus steaks outside of New York [City]. Kidding, they gave Joe a steak almost half the size of the table. He ate it all! The man that gave it to him said, "I'd never believe it."

Dinner was followed by recreation of choice. Louis liked to play cards or table tennis, watch a movie, or hear Bill "Bojangles" Robinson tell stories. His cronies, including Cab Calloway and Duke Ellington, might join him in such end-of-the-day relaxation, often staying overnight in the main house. Others who did so were "running buddies," friends he would also cavort with primarily in the black neighborhoods during his free time. They (Sunnie Wilson, Leonard Reed, and Billy Rowe among them) were generally unpretentious, down-to-earth people, from the same humble background as Louis.

Joe met Sunnie Wilson through his childhood friend Thurston McKinney. Wilson, like McKinney, was interested in amateur boxing. He managed a few amateur boxers in the basement of a Detroit church. His vocation was show business. He managed the Chocolate Bar, a "black and tan" (interracial) club in downtown Detroit. Leonard Reed managed another club, the Plantation.

Billy Rowe, too, met Louis early in his boxing career. He was the theater editor for the *Pittsburgh Courier*, the largest black newspaper. In an effort to meet the up-and-coming boxer, Rowe talked a friend who was a milliner into giving him a hat

for Joe. Overhearing his attempt to get the interview, Louis
opened the door and said, "Come in. You're the only person
in New York who wants to give me something for nothing."
After Louis and Rowe became friends, the *Courier* assigned
their theater critic to cover Louis's fights. The camaraderie
was to last more than forty-five years. Louis's, Wilson's, Rowe's,
and Reed's common preoccupation with nightclubs, the theater, and showgirls was to be irrevocably binding.

Making Louis tougher was a constant and creative challenge
for his managers. When in Chicago Chappy would take him to
the stockyards to drink fresh blood from the slaughterhouse
every four or five days, beginning two weeks before a fight.
One morning as he tilted a glass of blood to drink he said to
Chappy, "This is the last drop I will ever drink." It was. Manny
Seamon's (Louis's trainer after Chappy died in 1942) recipe for
toughness was the regular application of fish or beef brine to
Louis's hands and face. "If you want to be a champion boxer
you can't be a glamour boy as well," advised Seamon. "It's
been tried and it doesn't work. First, the bright lights and
proper training don't mix. Second, there are times when a boxer
is called upon to do things which don't exactly make him welcome in company."

As much as Louis respected and relied on Chappy's advice,
he actively participated in his own training. Joe Louis wasn't
formally educated, but he could make a quick study of opponents' foibles and had excellent ring sense. During training, he
would stand in the ring and show his trainer how he could
throw a punch better or more effectively defend against a blow.

MARVA LOUIS SPAULDING
Mrs. Joe Louis (1935–1945, 1946–1949)

Joe was really disciplined in his training routine. I would
stay in Chicago and go to the city in which he was to fight
a week to ten days before. No girls were allowed in the

training camp. I would visit the camp, have dinner, and return to New York. I never saw or spoke to your father the day before a fight. His handlers would call me and say, "He's fine." If I had a problem, it would have to wait until after the fight.

Practical jokes were also part of the training regimen, and Louis himself was often the recipient. On the way to one camp, he and his cohorts stopped at a service station. When Louis went into the rest room, one of them put a rake, which was lying on the ground, across the door. When Louis opened the door, the rake slid down and hit him on the head. He shadowboxed with the rake for about five minutes. It was jokingly referred to in that training camp as one of his best fights. But Louis was just as frequently the instigator. His pals enjoyed his wry sense of humor, even when they were the brunt of the joke.

MARSHALL MILES

I had a beautiful girl come up to the camp to visit me one Sunday night. Afterwards, I took her back to New York. I didn't come back to the camp until Tuesday, as Monday was my day off. As I'm coming back, I see a familiar car up in front on the highway. I get close to it and I see my girl in the backseat. Fuming, I went on into camp. Joe's sitting on the front porch with a sneaky grin. He had sent my girl two dozen roses and had asked her to come up to see him.

After dinner, he was walking down beside the lake. I followed. I said, "So you got my girl, huh?" He just laughed. I said, "I don't like that. You're going to jump in the lake." He didn't believe I meant it because he couldn't swim. I pulled this .45 on him and shot right by his foot. He jumped in! When his bodyguard came running, I said, "Put him in a hot tub and rub him down. He'll be all right."

Louis was superstitious. For many years he felt that he had to get down to 198 pounds for a fight. To reach his target, he would take off 2 or 3 pounds in the dressing room—walking fast or shadowboxing. His dressing sequence was another idiosyncrasy. He always put on his left shoe and his left glove before the right. Chappy was the only one he permitted to wrap his hands.

There was no idiosyncrasy, however, when it came to the boxer's routine in the ring. There Louis was all business. Blackburn, Black, and assistant trainer Manny Seamon were always in Joe's corner. One handler would sit midway along the ropes on one side and another would sit behind the opponent's corner. Anything of importance said by the opponent or his handlers would be passed by sign language to Louis. A loud hollow clap by Chappy meant "You're lagging. Get a move on." A downward thumb meant "Watch for a low blow." Another signal was "Keep your left hand up." A cornerman would also watch for foul play. He would look, for example, for the use of cocoa butter on the opponent's skin. A blow on oiled skin can cause a leather boxing glove to slip off, blunting a punch's effectiveness. A second was assigned to feel the tension of the ropes surrounding the ring. It was important that they not be too loose because boxers —when they leaned on them—could, for strategic advantage, enlarge the size of the ring, or, worse yet, fall onto the ring's apron. The handlers also checked the padding of the ring surface. Too much padding doesn't allow adequate movement, tiring a boxer's legs; too little padding can mean injury, in the case of a fall.

Between bouts in his early career Louis spent time with his running buddies and his family. His growing purses were readily distributed among his family and friends. Louis shared his newfound wealth with those he loved, many of whom were not reluctant to receive or take advantage of his generosity.

DELEON BARROW

When he was fighting, every time he would come to Detroit I would get a handful of tickets and give them out. He would give me four or five tickets for his former boss and the same number for me and my boss. He would always remember Ford.

Joe gave money and fight tickets to everybody. Lonnie (our brother) and Albert (our cousin) run together. Everywhere Joe went, them two were there also. I remember one time when Joe was fighting an exhibition in St. Louis. They went—driving their car to somewhere in between St. Louis and Chicago and catching the bus the rest of the way. When they got there, Joe gave them $500 apiece and a ticket to see the fight. They sold the ticket and got back on that bus and come on back to Detroit.

CHAPTER FIVE

Louis's Stunning Upset

"The American press made a God out of him. Joe himself believed that he was unbeatable."
—Max Schmeling

In the first two years of his professional career, Joe Louis's record was unblemished—twenty-seven victories, twenty-three by knockout. The young boxer was as invincible as was democracy in the political world, or so it appeared early in 1936.

At the same time, German Max Schmeling, the former heavyweight champion of the world, was on the comeback trail, chalking up a string of victories on the European boxing circuit. And as Schmeling's wins mounted, his prospects for another title fight improved. Moreover, Joe Jacobs, the German's U.S. manager (no relation to Mike Jacobs), assumed champion James Braddock would prefer to fight Schmeling rather than Louis and that Madison Square Garden, Braddock's promoter, would prefer to deal with him, rather than Mike Jacobs.

But it didn't work out that way. The New York Boxing Commission determined that Louis deserved the first shot at Braddock's title. Irreconcilable differences resulted in a stalemate: the Garden's Jimmy Johnson insisted the Twentieth Century Sporting Club give up its independence in exchange for a title fight. So Jacobs, sensing an opportunity for a lucrative gate, instead negotiated a Louis-Schmeling fight for Yankee Stadium in June 1936. The winner would be the undisputed contender for the heavyweight title; if Louis won, Johnson would be forced to stage a title fight.

When the boxers entered the ring on that night, Louis was a ten-to-one favorite. Writer Jimmy Cannon, who chose to travel with the Yankees baseball team rather than remain in New York for the Louis-Schmeling bout, told his boss, "It won't be much of a fight." Most experts predicted that the Brown Bomber would knock out the German in three rounds or less. Just one look at the boxers' previous ring records was evidence enough to lead one to that conclusion. Schmeling had barely taken Paolino Uzcudun in 1935 in their twelve-round bout; Louis had annihilated the South American boxer in four rounds. Schmeling was knocked out by an injured Max Baer; Louis, in four rounds, destroyed Baer. In addition, the German was slow, had only a powerful right in his arsenal, and was 31 years of age, 9 years older than Louis.

There were some boxing experts, however, who believed that Schmeling's experience was being overlooked. The German had first visited the United States in 1928 at the invitation of Madison Square Garden's Tex Rickard. By that time, he had defeated all the middleweights in Germany for that country's title, gained Germany's light-heavyweight title in 1927, and won the European light-heavyweight crown the next year. In the United States, Jacobs matched him against Johnny Risko, who had, in an upset, destroyed Jack Sharkey; Schmeling finished Risko in nine rounds; he subsequently stopped Paolino Uzcudun in fifteen.

In 1930, under Jacobs's tutelage, Schmeling was guided through a series of elimination bouts culminating in a fight against Jack Sharkey for the heavyweight title vacated by Gene Tunney. Schmeling won the crown by something of a fluke. A left by Sharkey in the fourth round appeared to hit the German below the belt. Schmeling went to the canvas and Jacobs urged him to remain there. The referee awarded the fight to Schmeling, the first and only heavyweight to win the title on a foul. Sharkey got his revenge and the title two years later in a rematch in a hotly contested fifteen-round decision. Although Schmeling's career subsequently went into a slump, by mid-1934 he was on the comeback trail. He knocked out Walter Neusel in August, kayoed Steve Hamas in a rematch in 1935, and four months later won the twelve-round decision against Uzcudun.

Schmeling, the authorities argued, was game. It was predicted that no matter how many times Louis hit him, as long as he was on his feet he would continue to punch. Most importantly in the eyes of the sporting press, he was not afraid of the younger boxer, whose reputation had terrified many of his previous opponents. Their fears were understandable—the press portrayed Joe Louis as a ''stalking panther,'' a ''jungle killer.'' Louis appeared to many to be more machine than human, his unemotional expression in the ring contributing to this reputation.

Max Schmeling was not a typical Louis opponent. He truly believed he could win. He had traveled to the United States in December 1935 to see Louis for the first time in his impressive victory over Paolino Uzcudun. More than fifty years later, Schmeling still remembered the stoic expression Louis wore on his face, making him appear almost nonchalant; the confident way his handlers silently moved around him between rounds; and the fact that he predominantly used his left. ''It was the hardest left I've ever seen,'' recalled Schmeling. While watching it ringside, he also observed a flaw in his future opponent's style.

Night after night when Schmeling returned to Germany, he reviewed films of Louis's previous bouts in slow-motion frames until he was convinced that he was right. He and his trainers methodically analyzed the American boxer's fighting style: where he stood, how he held his hands and positioned his feet, and what distance he stood from his opponent when he threw a punch. Schmeling's training routine revolved around attacking the perceived Louis weakness and countering his opponent's strengths. He planned to move with Louis's powerful right to reduce its impact and to undercut his opponent's left hook by moving in close. What remained was the Brown Bomber's left jab, which was dangerous, but not as destructive as his other weapons. Schmeling's regimen also focused on getting into the best physical condition possible. He estimated he would have to take Louis's strong left ten to fifteen times in the first round and counted on his legs, especially the left, to make the difference in a decisive moment. To ensure adequate time for mental and physical preparation, Schmeling arrived in the United States by ship several months prior to the bout. Nothing in Schmeling's camp was left to chance.

MAX SCHMELING
Former Heavyweight Champion

I received a cable from Mike Jacobs to fight your father. But I was very careful before I accepted. I didn't want to be just another man who got licked by Joe Louis. I went over to the United States to see Joe when he fought Paolino in December 1935. I was sitting in the front row. In the fourth round, Joe knocked him into my lap. It was the first time Paolino ever got licked, ever got beaten by KO. Joe was impressive in that bout, but I thought not unbeatable. All the newspapers came to me and said, "Max, you want to fight this Joe Louis? What do you think about him?" I told them I saw a mistake Joe made in this fight. "What was it?" they asked. I told them, "I won't tell you." Actually, I secretly hoped this mysterious sounding phrase would be a psychological weapon against Joe.

Joe was a good puncher. He was technically a very good boxer. He had a very good left hand. I think, however, he was young. I was 31, and he was 22. I had more experience, and I was a good counterpuncher.

Meanwhile, reports from the Louis training camp indicated that the American boxer was out of shape after a four-month layoff. His previous fight had been a one-round knockout of Charley Retzlaff on January 17, 1936, in Chicago, just two and a half weeks after the Paolino fight. (Retzlaff, Joe said afterward, gave him the most severe beating he had suffered to date.) Other reports indicated that Louis was overweight and sluggish during training.

Few believed the publicity; it was thought to be hype aimed at building up the gate. (One exception was actress Marlene Dietrich, who predicted Schmeling's knockout victory. Another surprise vote of confidence came from Mike Jacobs. After silently observing the German's workout ten days before the bout, he offered him a contract should he win.) Yet, for a variety of reasons, the prefight hype didn't draw the expected crowd. The ringside seat price of $40, the highest yet for a boxing match, was one factor. Another was the American Jewish reaction to the early signs of anti-Semitism in Germany. By late 1935, Heinrich Himmler had begun a state breeding program to produce perfect Aryans, and Hitler's Nuremberg Laws had deprived German Jews of their legal rights. By 1936, Hitler repudiated the Locarno Treaty and German troops reentered the Rhineland. American Jewish organizations saw the Louis-Schmeling fight as a forum for voicing their outrage. Although a proposed boycott was called off, it had an effect on the crowd turnout. Finally, rain, always a nightmare for promoters of outdoor events, delayed the bout by one day. Although all this didn't appear to affect the boxers—both arrived at the weigh-in ceremonies unperturbed—the crowd was 45,000, a little more than half the expected turnout.

After ten minutes of introductions of the luminaries present —the period seemed excruciatingly long—the fighters squared off.

GERALD R. FORD
Thirty-eighth President of the United States

I was a ranger at Yellowstone Park that summer—I was what they called a 90-day wonder. We listened to that fight on the radio. It was shocking and it was sad because by that time, I had gotten enthusiastic about this young man who was doing so well. It was beyond my comprehension that Max Schmeling could defeat him.

Following a few tentative movements, Schmeling felt the first sting, a left jab to the face. The German responded with a right cross. In his corner after the first round, he ruefully told manager Joe Jacobs and trainer Max Machon, "He's a deadly puncher, this fellow." Encouraging their fighter, they responded, "You can punch too." The next two rounds were replays—Louis scoring with his left, and Schmeling countering with his right. Although by the third round Schmeling's left eye was already bloodied, he was gaining confidence. Louis, who was ahead by a slight margin after the first three rounds according to the judges' scorecards, later quizzically told a reporter that he found Schmeling's style difficult to figure out: "He had his long left sticking out, with his left jaw protected in a cup on his left shoulder. His right hand was cocked and ready. I couldn't score a clean hit.''

The turning point for Schmeling came in the fourth. Louis began with a left hook; the German countered with a solid right to the American's jaw. Louis jabbed; Schmeling responded with another right, anticipating the next jab. It hit squarely, jolting his head back, but he was still able to release a strong right cross which landed squarely in the Brown Bomber's face. Louis in defense protected his head, but the German, now on the offensive, in quick succession threw a right uppercut, a left cross, and a long right that landed squarely on the chin. Louis was knocked to the canvas—the first knockdown of his professional career. Dazed, he rose from the canvas after a count of only three, not taking advantage of the allotted time to recover. The fourth and all succeeding rounds, with the exception of the seventh, were Schmeling's. Louis never fully recovered from the blow in the fourth.

FREDDIE GUINYARD
Joe Louis's Friend and Personal Secretary

Joe later told me, "From the fourth round until I was knocked out, I didn't know where I was. I was fighting on instinct."

I was used by his trainers to find out his mental attitude. See, few people knew how to talk to Joe. You had to use the circuitous route. Initially, after the Schmeling fight, he didn't say anything to me about the fight. We'd talk small talk. One morning, ten days or two weeks later, while we were doing roadwork, Joe told me how he felt after the fourth round. I went to a pay phone and called Mr. Roxborough.

They wanted to know what he said about a particular fight. His mental attitude was as important as his physical training.

At the start of the fifth round, Schmeling landed another right bomb, and with the German continuing to be the aggressor, the two boxers traded punches until the bell. At the end of the round, Louis dropped his arms, preparing to return to his corner. Schmeling then hit him with another solid right, causing Louis's legs to buckle. Joe was dragged to his corner by his handlers, who protested the punch. Schmeling claimed the deafening roar of the crowd had made it difficult to hear; the referee concurred.

Through the sixth round, the fight went steadily against Louis. Schmeling repeatedly bombarded his opponent's jaw with rights. Consequently, the seventh round was an exhilarating surprise to the Brown Bomber fans in the crowd. Throwing a fusillade of body punches, the young boxer landed a powerful left hook in Schmeling's stomach. The German fighter bit his lip in agony, causing sportswriter Joe Williams, commenting on the round later, to say, "When you get around to gamesters, you can write the German's name in flaming letters, too."

Regardless, the seventh proved to be Louis's last gasp. Two low blows cost him the eighth round. No longer had he sting in his punches, and a light jab by Schmeling almost knocked him down in the ninth. Consequently, the German in the following round did what no other fighter had previously dared to do—openly mock the young boxer. But then the previously undefeated fighter had never before repeatedly missed with his devastating right-hand punches. In the eleventh round both boxers slowed the pace. Schmeling prepared to finish a stunned and tired Louis; Louis attempted to regain his composure and his strength.

After another low punch from Louis in the twelfth round, Schmeling, fearing Joe might win on a low-blow knockout, went for a knockout himself. He landed one right after another until he finally dropped the young boxer to the canvas with a right and a two-fisted barrage to his head and neck. The Brown

Bomber wound up on his knees against the ropes, falling to the canvas on his side. Gamely, he tried to get up, dropped on his back, and rolled over on his stomach with his right glove resting over his head. He lay there motionless while he was counted out, for the first time in his career, by Art Donovan. "When the referee counted, it came to me faint, like someone whispering," he later recalled. Schmeling, euphoric from the win no one anticipated, including the Nazi regime, leaped into the air exuberantly, arms straight over his head. The improbable had happened. The superman of boxing had been knocked out.

MAX SCHMELING

In the second round, I hit him. It was too high, but he was staggered. In the fourth round, Joe used his left. I had to take that left from him so I could go in with my right. He closed my eye with that punch, but that's where he made his mistake, the flaw I wouldn't tell the press before. His mistake in this fight was to drop his left for a split second after he used it. He was open for a right. When he did, I went in. He went down. Joe got up after two to three counts, instead of staying down for the full count.

He came back strong and was very dangerous in the fifth, sixth, seventh, and eighth rounds. His mind in the ninth round seemed to wander. I think he was thinking too much about the fourth round. In the twelfth round, I had him again. He was again staggered. Still I had to give him everything I had to knock him out.

I think it's good to get beaten in the beginning of one's career. Until this time, the American press made a god out of him. Joe himself believed that he was unbeatable.

Schmeling, bearing the scars of battle, including a closed left eye, was escorted by fifteen policemen to his dressing room.

Along the way they pushed back well-wishers and those who wanted to see the man who had defeated the heralded Brown Bomber.

But more important, the unexpected victory changed Schmeling's life, especially in terms of his standing in his own country. Virtually ignored officially by the Nazi regime prior to the fight (although Hitler in a private interview urged the boxer not to proceed with what appeared to be a foolhardy and embarrassing quest), Schmeling was welcomed home a national hero. He was flown back to Germany via a special berth on the famous German zeppelin, the *Hindenburg*. He received congratulations from Propaganda Minister Joseph Goebbels; his wife, actress Annie Ordra, was sent flowers by the Reich; thousands of people were on hand in Frankfurt when the *Hindenburg* landed; and he was escorted to Berlin—along with his wife and mother—to have lunch with Adolf Hitler. Films of the fight were converted by the German government into an enthusiastically received movie, *Max Schmeling's Victory, A German Victory*.

Yet more than fifty years later, so strong are the remnants of anti-Nazism that Schmeling remains defensive about these actions by the Third Reich.

MAX SCHMELING

I was invited to meet with Hitler. Everybody in America was writing about this meeting. But it was just natural, you know. Joe was invited by Roosevelt. This is usual. A good sportsman, if he has a success, will be invited by his government leader to meet with him.

For his part Louis, as a vanquished warrior, was scarcely noticed as he was carried from the ring, preceded by one of his sisters, who was painfully sobbing. His left jaw was swollen to the size of a melon and both of his hands were badly bruised. The thumb on his left hand and a knuckle on his right were damaged. His face hidden under a straw hat, Joe was quietly rushed out of Yankee Stadium by his advisers. Taken to a downtown hotel, the young boxer was emotionally incapable of dealing with the turn of events. It was inconceivable to him that he had been knocked out. He was stunned that his face had been so badly battered and bruised by another boxer. Twenty-four hours later, he was finally taken to Harlem's Theresa Hotel, where Marva had fled after the fight—the first fight that Marva had seen since the Max Baer bout the night they were married. It was to be the last.

MARVA LOUIS SPAULDING
Mrs. Joe Louis (1935–1945, 1946–1949)

I thought boxing was brutal. That was why your father never allowed me to go to fights. He said, "You get too nervous. You don't understand fighting." I did learn about the sport, however, and that helped. He told me, "I watch their eyes. The eyes tell you everything." Fighters' bodies, I learned, were covered in Vaseline so the punches would slide. Sometimes when they appear to be taking a pounding, the punches are actually going under their arms.

Joe, however, rarely got bruised. For years, he didn't even get a mouse on his cheek. The Schmeling fight, however, was different. After he was brought back to the Theresa Hotel, he wouldn't let anybody, not even his friends or the reporters that loved him, see him. I put cold and hot compresses on his face every thirty minutes. All our meals were brought in. Your father was crushed, mentally and physically, after the defeat. He got into bed fully dressed and lay there like a mummy refusing to speak. Initially, he couldn't accept the responsibility for the loss.

After three or four days, we slipped out of New York by train and went to Chicago. The street outside our apartment was jammed. Several weeks later, he began to go out, but only after dark. The chauffeur would take us to some isolated place, and we would just walk. You know they called Muhammad Ali egocentric. Joe was just as bad. He was always concerned about his appearance.

Louis may have been stunned, but so were his fans. How could the man about whom Jack Dempsey said, "I'm just as glad I don't have to fight him" be defeated? So incredible was the loss that Jack Blackburn, after the fight, told reporter Alfred Dayton, "Something was wrong. Nobody is hitting Chappy with all those rights when he is right. I have an idea it was in the second that the left went wrong. I can't say positively for he didn't talk between rounds or let us know that he had hurt his hands. I was sure, though, that something was wrong, for Joe certainly was not himself." Others agreed with Blackburn's assessment.

DELEON BARROW
Joe Louis's Brother

Joe's jaw was swelled up so big, he couldn't even talk and he was vomiting. Instead of going to the Theresa Hotel, the first night he went to a downtown hotel. They taken him clean out of the neighborhood, thought there was something wrong with him, they done doped him or something. I believe he was doped for that fight. Cause he ain't never act right in that fight. Joe didn't ever hit Schmeling with his right hand over two times, and Joe's right hand was swelled up. And what's it swelled for, I don't know, he ain't done nothing with it.

Even schoolchildren had their theories. At New York Public School 35, which was attended by journalist Art Buchwald, the children expressed sentiments like "Schmeling fouled Louis" or "Hitler had someone poison Joe's food." Clearly, it couldn't have been a fair fight: if it had been, Joe Louis, their hero, would have won. With equal certainty, Buchwald recalled on Louis's death, they knew, "the next time around Joe would kill Schmeling and save the honor of America." There were only three things the kids in Buchwald's crowd in Hollis, New York, in the 1930s were sure about: "Franklin Roosevelt was going to save the economy, Joe DiMaggio was going to beat Babe Ruth's record, and Joe Louis was going to save them from the Germans."

Reporters, too, were baffled. *The New York Sun*'s Grantland Rice said, "The Louis defense against Schmeling's right was not even up to the average amateur standard. The near superman of many fights suddenly turned into a duffer with nothing to offer but fighting instinct and a stout heart. The fact remains that the fighter who was knocked out by Baer—who dropped a decision to Jack Sharkey—who ran just about even, with a shade against Paolino in their last two fights—who was badly cut up and beaten by Steven Hamas in Philadelphia—made Joe Louis look like an amateur. Schmeling had the head and the heart to win." Other boxing experts had their theories: at 22 and with only two years of professional boxing, Louis was inexperienced; or he was overconfident after a string of earlier successes.

And those who never thought Louis was truly a worthy heavyweight contender felt vindicated in their opinion. "Schmeling's victory is the finest thing to happen to boxing in a long time," Jack Dempsey said ungraciously. "Who did Louis fight anyway? Baer, who was scared to death; Uzcudun; and Carnera. The big bubble broke Friday night. Joe Louis will be licked by every bum in the country."

Although there may be some merit to many of the explanations, numerous interviews with those close to Louis at the time indicate that the most plausible explanation is the simplest: Max Schmeling was physically and mentally better prepared on that night in 1936. For the two previous years Louis had fought twenty-seven times. During that period of constant fighting and training, the young boxer had become a hero to black Americans. He had gone from earning $5 a day to $240,000 an evening. An overnight sensation, he was sought after by actors and actresses, sports club owners, and politicians. Fame inevitably went to the 22-year-old's head. After the Retzlaff bout in January 1936, Louis craved the rewards of his labor. During the four months off before entering training camp for the Schmeling bout, he enjoyed himself.

Unfortunately, at his training camp at Lakewood, New Jersey, he didn't really get down to business. The atmosphere was that of a carnival. At the entrance, a big sign read, "Joe Louis Boxes Today." Arrows pointed the way to ringside. Between sparring sessions, under the hot sun, Louis played golf, a newly acquired avocation. Women, hitherto strictly prohibited, were in attendance. In an effort to persuade Louis to focus his attention on boxing rather than on golf or starlets, Roxborough asked Marva, never permitted at previous camps, to visit every day. Although warned by his trainers and friends of the possible repercussions of his actions, the young boxer refused to listen. For the first time in his career, he took control of his own destiny. And he struck out.

FREDDIE GUINYARD

Joe was different before the first Schmeling fight. I see it in Tommy Hearns; I see it in other fighters. Nobody knows from Adam. As soon as they get to fighting and get popular, somebody will invite them for a golf date, a football game, or a baseball game. Some is just doing it to be friendly; others is doing it to benefit themselves.

Now, Joe was to be a golfer. Chappy explained to Joe the problem with golf. He said, "When you take a golf club and swing it, you're throwing a punch off." [Golf involves a pendulum swing; boxing uses a thrusting motion.] Later, when you throw a right hand at a fighter, it's not the same. This was the truth, and Chappy knew it because he was a fighter 40 years before Joe Louis was born. He was saying you can't mix some sports. But Joe didn't listen. He played golf during the training camp.

Another thing, people started coming around that particular camp—the biggest entertainers, black and white. He was in an environment that he'd never been in before . . . and he was enjoying it. The world started changing for him. Don't get me wrong; he accepted it well. I've seen others go off the deep end with it. But it affected Joe in that fight.

It must be remembered that Louis entered boxing as a teenager, largely influenced by his family, his religion, and the poverty of his surroundings. During the early days of his career, he was molded by his trainers and managers to be a dedicated athlete. But by the time of the Schmeling fight, he had become a young man swayed by fame and fortune. He had developed his own views and was not reluctant to express them, even when they opposed thoughtful advice offered by friends. This trait—rejection of sound advice when it countered his personal preferences—was a character flaw that would haunt Louis for the rest of his life. The first victim was the theater critic and his friend, Billy Rowe.

BILLY ROWE
Syndicated Journalist and Joe Louis's Friend

The 1936 loss to Max Schmeling was the best thing that ever happened to Joe Louis. It turned him back into the Joe

Louis that was. If Louis hadn't lost, he would have wound up being an arrogant heavyweight.

I went to all your father's fights except this one. We had a falling-out at his training camp before it. I felt that he was beginning to believe his own headlines. He was taking Max Schmeling too lightly. For the first time, there wasn't the discipline that was normally in the camp. It was like a circus. A lot of theater and nightclub people were there. One day, I spoke to him about it. He told me, "If you don't like it, you don't have to come back here." So I didn't.

As a friend, I felt bad. As a person, I was insulted.

Fifty years after the Schmeling fight, Billy Conn was asked about the lesson Louis might have learned from the defeat. His response: "Sure, it was the best lesson of all. A third-rater in good shape will beat a first-rater out of shape." The knockout caused Louis to pause. Although he may have recovered physically from the fight thereafter, he never again seemed capable of fully relaxing. The realization that the heavyweight championship he wanted so desperately might be more elusive than he had thought weighed on him heavily. Nevertheless, the 1936 Schmeling bout convinced Louis's handlers of their boxer's staying power. It proved he could take a blow as easily as he could give one. He lasted twelve rounds and fought semiconscious from the fourth round to the knockout.

CHAPTER SIX

Heavyweight Champion of the World

"Today I look upon Joe Louis as an American hero. When I was younger, I was too selfish to appreciate that. . . . It was only important that he made me feel good about myself."
—John R. Thompson, Jr.

"The lonesomest spot in the world is the center of the ring after the bell has clanged to start a fight," Jack Sharkey once told reporter Frank Graham. "Your seconds climb down out of the corner—and there you are. Nobody but you and the referee and the other guy. The referee can't help you and the other guy is in there strictly to hurt you." No one who hasn't been in that spot knows what it means to be alone or afraid. When Sharkey climbed into the ring with Louis on August 19, 1936, badly out of shape, he certainly felt both.

This bout, the start of Louis's comeback from his defeat by Max Schmeling, was shrewdly crafted by his managers. John Roxborough and Julian Black didn't want a return bout against

Schmeling immediately. Looking for a safer opponent, they chose Jack Sharkey. Although he was a former heavyweight champion of the world, Sharkey was well past his prime. He was a good box office attraction, having been knocked out only by Romero Rojas, Jack Dempsey, and Primo Carnera in a twelve-year boxing career, but there was little chance that he would survive Louis's punches for long.

Before heading for his training camp in Pompton Lakes, New Jersey, Louis went to Detroit to visit his family. He was surprised when he saw his stepfather's physical condition. Prior to the Schmeling bout, no one had told Joe that Pat Brooks, Sr., had had a stroke. Several weeks later, surrounded by his family, Brooks died. Louis grieved at the loss of the only man he had ever known as father. More than 2000 mourners, including sports celebrities on hand out of respect for their fellow athlete, attended the service in Detroit's Calvary Baptist Church. Almost twice that number lined up outside in an attempt to get a glimpse of the boxer or his family.

Putting aside his sorrow, Louis got down to serious training. This time when he entered camp, he was firmly back in the capable hands of Jack Blackburn and his managers. Gone was the carnival atmosphere of the Lakewood camp. Gone were the hordes of bystanders. Gone were the extracurricular activities. This time when reporters left the Pompton Lakes camp, they had learned very little. Searching for a sparring session without the aid of signposts and guides, John Kieran, sports editor of *The New York Times*, ran into Doc Biers, owner of the estate on which the Louis training camp was located. While Louis was changing into his sparring togs, Biers urged Kieran to visit the flower garden on the property. After viewing larkspur and zinnias, Kieran asked where the boxing was.

"Oh, that's over by this time," said Biers.

"What!" said Kieran. "Without a sound? Without the clanging of the bell, the whack of leather, the whoop of the wounded and the crash of falling bodies? What an astounding change!'' Clearly, the Schmeling bout had done more to Louis's head than bruise his face.

During his training for this fight, Louis and his handlers left nothing to chance. He entered the ring totally prepared. In sharp contrast, Sharkey appeared hopelessly out of condition, showing his age. In front of 35,000 fans in Yankee Stadium (including Max Schmeling, who was in the United States, training for the proposed title fight against James Braddock), the former heavyweight champion attempted in the first round to trade punches toe-to-toe with his opponent. The results were disastrous. Throwing a succession of devastating left- and right-hand punches, Louis pounded his opponent's body and face until they were bruised and bloody. Bobbing and weaving, Sharkey changed his tactics in the second round. But Joe doggedly pursued his opponent and, with a powerful left to the face, set him on his heels. A flurry of rights and lefts slammed the former champion against the ropes, and a short right to the jaw sent him to the canvas for a nine count. Clinching his opponent, Sharkey, who was virtually paralyzed, survived the round.

Charging out of his corner at the start of the third round, the veteran threw a wild right toward Louis's jaw. It missed its target, and the Brown Bomber responded with two short, powerful rights to Sharkey's temple. Sharkey fell face forward onto the lower rope. Gamely, but futilely, he struggled to his feet by the count of eight. A left hook to his body, a right to the head, and a final left hook to his chin put him down again. While the referee counted him out, Sharkey, dazed, stared down at the canvas on his hands and knees. Louis had floored his opponent four times in three rounds, dramatically proving he had not been permanently affected by the drubbing he suffered at the hands of Schmeling in June.

His ego thus restored, Louis proceeded to rip through his

next three opponents. In September before 40,000 fans in Philadelphia, Louis fought Al Ettore, knocking him out in five rounds. Some reporters claimed that the fourth round was the best of the Brown Bomber's entire career. Opening with a powerful right to Ettore's chin, Louis stunned his opponent. Then he unleashed a barrage of punches that brought the crowd to its feet. Blood spilled from Ettore's left eyelid even before Louis put the final touch on the round—a right-hand punch to the jaw, felling Ettore for a count of nine. A left hook to the jaw finished him in 1 minute and 28 seconds of the fifth round.

Louis was confident by the time he met Jorge Brescia, a husky young Argentine, at New York's Hippodrome two weeks later. Before the bout there was still a question as to whether Joe could take a solid right punch. Any doubt was erased in the third and final round: Louis, hit hard by an awesome right delivered with all the Argentine's 205½ pounds behind it, retaliated with a series of punches in a toe-to-toe exchange. With a left hook to Brescia's chin, Joe put the Argentine onto his back, ending the fight.

The trio of recuperative bouts was completed in December, when Louis met Eddie Simms in Cleveland. The Brown Bomber took only 20 seconds to destroy his opponent with a devastating left hook. It was one of the shortest fights in boxing history.

Louis took each of these bouts seriously. Not willing to repeat his mistake, he did not underestimate any of the opponents. The only prudent course, according to his managers, was to work as hard for the Brescias as he had for the Baers and the Carneras. "Jack Dempsey had the right idea," Julian Black told reporter Edward Van Every. "There is no such thing as a sucker match. When you get into the ring, you are both even. You each have two fists and one chin."

He had earned a rest, and thus Louis visited his family during the holidays. As always, he found such sabbaticals relaxing and rejuvenating.

DELEON BARROW
Joe Louis's Brother

I never will forget one time he come to stay with me. He had a huge car and he come out to my house and got stuck. We had no paved roads then. Everybody in the neighborhood helped push him the three blocks to my house. He had a big roll of $1 bills. And when they got through, he gave everybody $3. It must have been 20 people pushing this car.

After dinner that night, I'm shooting dice on the cook stove. He says, "What are you doing?" I say, "I'm sliding the dice." Me and him started shooting the dice. I didn't have but 35 cents. I beat him out of about $5. Then he says, "I ain't going to play no more. You get the cards; let's play some blackjack." We got on the living room floor until four in the morning. I got about $30 to $40 from him. Marva came out of the bedroom and called him. Now, while he was gone, I fixed the cards. He come back and said, "I'm tired; I'm stopping. Deal it all here." That's what I wanted to hear. I dealt his cards and then I look at my hand. I done give him the blackjack! Here we play all night, I fix the cards, and I fix them wrong. He got all his money back!

I told him the story about 20 years later. He didn't do nothing but laugh.

As Louis worked his way successfully along the comeback trail, Mike Jacobs attempted to schedule a heavyweight championship fight for him against James J. Braddock. Jacobs's long-standing feud with Madison Square Garden was the least of the obstacles he had to overcome. Braddock had already signed a contract to fight Schmeling, who was now the number one contender. The bout, originally scheduled for 1936, had been postponed until 1937 because of a flare-up of arthritis in Braddock's right hand.

This delay gave Jacobs the opening he needed. He began negotiations with Joe Gould, Braddock's manager, for a twelve-round Louis-Braddock exhibition in Chicago. When the plans leaked, Schmeling took the SS *Bremen* to New York to argue his case before the New York Athletic Commission. Schmeling and Braddock were forced to put up $5000 bonds, which they would forfeit if either fought Louis before their June 3, 1937, bout. In addition, Gould signed a second contract with the Garden, agreeing to hold the Schmeling-Braddock fight prior to a Louis-Braddock match.

Nevertheless, in February it was announced that Braddock would repudiate his contract with Schmeling and in June fight Louis in Chicago. Avarice, in the end, won. Although Braddock was a more skillful boxer than some believed, he was not charismatic. He lacked the drawing power of such past champions as Dempsey and Baer. And for his part, the German Schmeling was becoming unpopular in this prewar period, despite his exciting knockout of Louis the previous year.

As a result, Gould estimated a Braddock-Schmeling heavyweight title fight would draw a paltry $200,000 gate, although a Braddock-Louis match could be expected to produce a financial bonanza. Louis was a dream for a boxing promoter—a quiet, unassuming black who always could be counted on for a crowd-pleasing spectacle. Backed by a Chicago syndicate, Mike Jacobs guaranteed Braddock $500,000. The deal was consummated when the pot was sweetened: should he lose, Braddock would receive a 10 percent split of Jacobs's share of Louis's earnings for the next decade. Lucrative for Gould and Braddock, it also was a good deal for Jacobs. If Louis won, he would have control of heavyweight boxing.

MAX SCHMELING
Former Heavyweight Champion

The winner of the Louis-Schmeling fight was supposed to fight Jimmy Braddock. I don't think, however, the New York Boxing Commission or the press wanted a German to fight

a man like Braddock. He was a very old man. His best years
were over. Everybody in America thought that I may be the
champion again. Then they thought Hitler would say, "The
title has to stay in Germany. If anybody wants to have the
title, he has to come to Germany." As a result, Joe fought
Braddock in Chicago. It all happened very quick.

Meanwhile, Louis continued to polish his skills, first in a series
of exhibitions and then in a ten-round match against Bob Pastor
and a four-round bout against Natie Brown. Ironically, Pastor,
who was considered a poor football player at New York University because he was slow, went the distance with Louis
because of his speed. He jabbed and ran for ten rounds, turning
the bout into little more than a boring track meet. Louis looked
bad, destroying the myth that he could kayo any opponent at
will. With a fourth-round knockout of Natie Brown in Kansas
City, Missouri, Louis finished up his tune-up bouts in February.

   Although Braddock was considered by some to be a capable,
determined fighter, he was 32 years old and turned out to be
no match for Louis. He had been fighting professionally since
1926 and had won both the New Jersey state light-heavyweight
and heavyweight titles. Thereafter, his track record was un-
impressive: in twenty-nine subsequent fights, he lost fifteen,
won ten, was knocked out once (by Lou Scozza in 1932), and
had two fights that ended in "no contest" and one that produced a draw.

   As a result of this lackluster performance, Braddock left
the ring for a while to find part-time work as a stevedore,
loading railroad ties on the Jersey City docks. He earned little
from boxing until he beat Art Lasky in the Madison Square
Garden elimination contest in 1935, thereby becoming the
contender for the heavyweight crown. In an upset in June
1935, he succeeded Max Baer to the title. The weapon that
Braddock used to destroy Baer was a hard, straight left to

the face. It was developed in an unusual manner: Braddock's right fist, broken in 1928, was never properly set. Although it was later rebroken and reset, in the interim the fighter had to learn to use his left effectively to earn money to support his family. When he met Baer, it had become a secret and highly effective punch. While looking for an opening for his restored right, Braddock, against Louis, planned to use his strong left hand to wear him down.

Meanwhile, at his training camp in Kenosha, Wisconsin, Louis practiced defenses against Braddock's weapons. The challenger continued to approach his training with deadly seriousness. "All of my sparring partners were willing, tough fellows," he told the press. "They were the kind of men I wanted to work with, because in training I think a fighter should 'ask no quarter'—and give none." For the Braddock fight, his managers lined up sparring partners who could best simulate the champion. Testing Louis with strong lefts and damaging rights in nineteen alternate-day sessions were Lloyd Clements, Jim Howell, George Nicholson, and Cell Harris.

Simultaneously, Schmeling was training for his doomed June heavyweight title fight against Braddock in New York. The German and Madison Square Garden still hoped the courts would cancel the Braddock-Louis fight. The charade included a weigh-in ceremony on June 3 by the New York State Athletic Commission. Schmeling attended; Braddock continued training in the Midwest for his fight against Louis.

When Louis entered the ring against Braddock at Chicago's Comiskey Park, he became the first contender to challenge the champion's title in two years. Braddock was the popular underdog, Louis the exciting puncher. Although the titleholder was kayoed in 1 minute and 10 seconds of the eighth round, he fought throughout like a champion. Dragged to his corner unconscious with his eye dripping with blood, a jagged four-inch cut under his mouth, and a slash in his ear—all requiring

seventeen stitches—Braddock, when he regained conscious-
ness, asked Gould, "Was it a good fight?"

It had been. Braddock had come out fighting. He threw the
first punch, a right that missed its target, Louis's chin, and
landed on his chest. At the end of the round, Braddock again
aimed a short right uppercut at the challenger's chin, this time
knocking him to the canvas. Too late, Louis recalled Blackburn's advice: "When you is knocked down, you stay there
until the count of nine. You can't ever get up so fast that they
can't see from the bleachers that you was down." Joe rose too
quickly and moved to the corner. Defensively ducking Braddock's punches, he finally landed a right cross and a left uppercut before the bell. It was Braddock's best opportunity of
the night. Regardless, after the round, Braddock went to his
corner shaking his head and told Gould that Louis's punches
were devastating.

The Brown Bomber's jabs began to take their toll in the
second round, but Blackburn cautioned him to take his time.
After the third round, Braddock told his corner that the
lights hurt his eyes. In fact, Louis's punches were blinding
him. Protectively, Gould told Braddock at the end of the sixth
round he was going to throw in the white towel to end the
fight. The champion angrily responded, "If you do, I'll never
speak to you again as long as I live." Gould relented, knowing
his boxer was intent on fighting to the end. Braddock was
sluggish entering the seventh round. Louis went on the offensive, throwing a flurry of jabs, but Braddock was saved by
the bell.

By the eighth round, Louis knew he had Braddock where
he wanted him. The champion was holding his hands too high,
a sure sign of exhaustion. The two boxers traded jabs, but the
champion's were weak by comparison. One of Joe's jabs landed
squarely in Braddock's face, and he quickly followed up: Louis
feinted with his left and threw a powerful overhand right to his

opponent's jaw. Braddock fell face down on the canvas in a pool of blood.

FREDDIE GUINYARD
Joe Louis's Friend and Personal Secretary

In the seventh round when Joe come to the corner he said to Blackburn in despair, "I've hit Braddock with everything I got and he still keeps coming." Chappy told him, "The same thing you hit him with last round, do it over again this time." He did and out Braddock went. That was ring-wise.

With a thundering roar, the crowd of 42,000, more than 20,000 of whom were black, rose to its feet as referee Tommy Thomas introduced Joe Louis as the "winner and new heavyweight champion." Within seconds of the radio announcement of Louis's victory, the streets of urban and rural centers throughout the world were filled with singing and shouting blacks. More than 5000 people paraded up Seventh Avenue in New York "blowing fishhorns, clanging cow bells, and beating drums." Others leaned out their windows shouting to the crowd below. "Bedlam, absolute bedlam" is Marva's memory of Chicago after the fight. The streets were clogged. Radio announcers were cautioning every five minutes or so, "If you don't have to go out, don't." Traffic was redirected from Michigan Avenue, where the Louises lived, to Indiana and Wabash, the two adjoining avenues.

"Terrified and exhilarated" was British commentator and historian Alistair Cooke's recollection of his feelings on that extraordinary night. In Baltimore's Darktown for an evening of jazz, Cooke and a friend had elbowed their way into an already packed cabaret filled with blacks. At the conclusion of the last number, they heard a high-pitched sound in the distance. As the roar approached, it became a singing and cheering. Unexpectedly, as Cooke described it when Louis retired twelve years later, in an "American Letter," published in Britain's *The Listener*, "there was a sound of doors splintering and cops barking and women screaming and men going down grabbing their toes and snarling oaths. . . . The black faces all around us bobbed and flashed. Women threw their heads back and howled great cries at the roof. People embraced and others cuffed and swung at each other." Outside the cabaret, he reflected, "It looked like Christmas Eve in darkest Africa."

On that June night blacks reigned supreme throughout the world. It was impossible to ignore the pride blacks felt in their race after the Brown Bomber so masterfully disposed of the white champion of the world. His achievement was accomplished in a quiet, self-effacing style during a racially troubled era—it was only one year earlier that Hitler had refused to acknowledge black Olympic champions Jesse Owens, Cornelius Johnson, Ralph Metcalf, Archie Williams, and John Woodruff in Germany. And the result was that Joe Louis had become a symbol of hope to his demoralized and oppressed race.

JOHN R. THOMPSON, JR.
Head Basketball Coach,
Georgetown University

No one had more impact on me in terms of giving me encouragement and motivation, giving me hope and self-respect, than Joe Louis.

I can't remember when I first learned of Joe Louis. He was part of my upbringing. My mother and father used him as a role model for me, and I continue to pass many of those stories along to my children and the players I coach.

Although today I look upon Joe Louis as an American hero, when I was younger I was too selfish to appreciate that. I didn't care what white people thought. It was only important to me that he made me feel good about myself. Today I appreciate the tremendous obstacles a black person had to overcome in the 1930s. His style—modesty, dignity and courtesy—were just as courageous in his era as that of any black militant person today.

For his time, Joe Louis communicated as loudly as Jesse Jackson, Martin Luther King and Malcolm X did in their time. The bravest people in our society were Uncle Toms because they had to suppress their true feelings. Joe Louis sensed the pulse of society and knew what was needed. He thereby enabled me to win the NCAA [National Collegiate Athletic Association] basketball championship against the University of Houston in 1984. He enables me now to say what I think. While he could have selfishly looked after Joe Louis by being more outspoken, he pulled us all with him by keeping quiet and subjecting himself to whatever humiliations he had to subject himself to. Whether he carried his role consciously or subconsciously, the pain from the abuse he received must have been real.

Most whites in the 1930s, and to some extent today, relegated black ability only to the athletic field. In an environment where there were no political or professional heroes, sports figures assumed an image-building role that was psychologically extremely important to the survival of an oppressed people. And Joe Louis—at the pinnacle of a popular and highly respected sport—was king.

ANDREW YOUNG
Mayor of Atlanta

My daddy, an avid boxing fan, was a dentist in New Orleans. A lot of his patients were boxers. Some had difficulty paying their bills. One pretty good lightweight, Eddie Brown, in payment would take me to the gym and work out with me. That's how I became a Joe Louis fan.

Dr. Martin Luther King had a very similar kind of love affair with Joe Louis. Our view of boxing was that it was a science of self-defense. My daddy had me taking boxing lessons because he said if people know you know how to fight, you don't have to fight. Martin always said that he opposed aggressive violence; he opposed retaliatory violence. He did not put boxing in that category.

Joe Louis probably launched an era where white Americans began to concede a certain level of physical superiority to blacks. That is bad, too, because I don't think that Joe Louis was superior because he was black. He just happened to be an individual with a very quick set of reflexes and a unique set of mental and physical capabilities.

CHAPTER SEVEN

"Ma, We Win"

"You could almost say Joe Louis fought the war in advance."

—Andrew Young

After winning the Braddock fight, Joe Louis promised that he would be a fighting champion. "I will fight whenever and whoever Mike Jacobs wants me to" was the way he put it. Louis was the first black champion since Jack Johnson, and felt he had to remain in the public eye to maintain the stature befitting his championship. Of course, he had a fairly extravagant lifestyle that had to be supported, too.

Louis lived up to his word, becoming the most active champion in the history of the division. Two months after he was crowned, he fought British heavyweight champion Tommy Farr in Yankee Stadium. The fight against Farr—a substitute for Max Schmeling, who turned down Jacobs's proposed 20 percent challenger purse—was a coup for the promoter. The German, still rankled by being passed over by Braddock for the heavyweight title bout, had originally been scheduled to fight Farr, the winner to be acclaimed by Europeans as the new

93

heavyweight champion. Had that fight proceeded and the German won, a Schmeling-Louis rematch would have been difficult, if not impossible, to arrange. But Mike Jacobs, a consummate tactician, again outsmarted Schmeling. He guaranteed Farr $60,000, twice the Schmeling offer, for a fight with Louis. Farr readily accepted.

Meanwhile, before Louis went into training, he fulfilled another promise—one that he had made to his Detroit boyhood friends. Traveling for a month throughout the South, he played softball with the Brown Bombers team. Louis chose not to value personal gain over a promise or lasting friendship. This meant passing up a boxing exhibition series Roxborough had organized, which would have been worth approximately $200,000 to him. In stark contrast, the receipts from the softball season totaled only $61,000—for the *entire* team.

Finally, Louis entered his Pompton Lakes training camp, but how to prepare for the bout was something of a puzzle. Tommy Farr, an erstwhile Welsh coal miner, was unknown to American fistic fans. He had never fought in the United States, and only recently had attracted attention on this side of the Atlantic when he outpointed Max Baer. Farr's boxing skills didn't appear to be a match for Louis's—he had only a solid left jab and a bobbing and weaving style that could be confusing to an opponent. But he had courage, or what fight fans call "heart." Unintimidated by the new champion's punching power, Farr firmly believed in his own strength, youth, and resourcefulness.

If few experts thought the Welshman would offer much of a challenge, Louis and his trainers weren't taking any chances. Since none of them had personally observed the Welsh boxer in a match, Louis trained as if he were due to fight three different men on August 26. The first hypothetical opponent (impersonated by sparring partner Pal Silvers) attempted to force Louis to lead and constantly backpedaled. It was not a very exciting spectacle for the more than 1000 fans, 95 percent of whom were black, to watch—but it was a good training exercise for the boxer. Silvers was followed by sparring partners George Nicholson and Tiger Hairston, who had the assignment of carrying the fight *to* Louis. Finally, Marty Gallagher, using his natural style of boxing, worked in close on Louis's body. He shoved, pushed, and butted; the champion, in turn, practiced getting his sparring partner at a sufficient distance so he could land punches.

Meanwhile, in an attempt to learn more about Farr's style, Roxborough invited the boxer and his manager-trainer Teddy Broadribb to visit Louis's training camp. Broadribb accepted and watched the champion in a sparring session. Louis's managers had hoped the invitation would be reciprocated. It never was, but it is doubtful whether it would have been helpful, anyway. Certainly Farr would have masked his true strategy, just as Louis had during Broadribb's visit. Other visitors to the Champ's camp included Max Schmeling and Max Machon, his trainer. Louis, frustrated in his attempts to meet Schmeling in the ring, had to be content with posing for pictures with the German.

Two weeks before the match, the sparring sessions intensified. Louis worked out with his partners every Tuesday, Thursday, Saturday, and Sunday, for a total of fifty-four rounds of boxing. Hindsight suggests that he may have peaked too early. Foul weather postponed the outdoor bout in Yankee Stadium for four days, to August 30. "I never like those postponements," Blackburn commented after the fight. "I point my man for a certain date, get him just right for the night he's to go—and, naturally, you can't keep him at the perfect edge for four more days."

In any event, Farr turned out to be a tougher competitor than anyone ever suspected. He went the full fifteen rounds with Louis, winning five rounds on the scorecard of one judge, six on another's, and one on the referee's. Although Louis kept his title, his reputation was tarnished by this bout. "Farr presented what should be final proof that Louis is not a great fighter by going the derby distance against him without a right-hand punch and with only cleverness, courage, and a fair sort of straight left," reported *The New York Sun*'s Wilbur Woods after the fight. Many of the 37,000 in attendance concurred, booing at the conclusion of the bout the announcement of "winner and still champion."

Louis failed to knock Farr down, rarely used his celebrated left hook, and infrequently found an opening for his right. The bout consisted mainly of jabs from both sides: The champion's punches were extremely powerful, fast, and accurate, leaving the Welsh boxer bleeding profusely from two cuts over his right eye, and another under his left, and injuries to his nose and mouth. Farr's jab was weaker (more of a "flip than a jolt," said one reporter), although in the eighth round it did cause a lump under Louis's right eye that caused him problems throughout the remainder of the fight.

The seventh round, when he traded his jabs for heavier artillery, was the only truly outstanding one for Joe. Scoring repeatedly, he pounded Farr's head and body with left hooks and short rights. Many in the crowd thought the fight was finished, but, to Farr's credit, while bleeding profusely he remained standing. The challenger also stayed upright after a stinging right to his jaw almost lifted him off his feet in round five. It was the best single punch of the fight.

This bout attracted worldwide attention, however, a phenomenon that persisted throughout Louis's career. Needless to say, the British were particularly interested. At 3 a.m. they listened to the blow-by-blow account over the airwaves. Bonfires were lit on the ridges in the Rhondda Valley in Wales, where Farr had grown up. Meanwhile, 500 Welsh miners and their wives and girlfriends listened to the commentary in the village Assembly Hall, while an additional 5000 heard it via loudspeakers outside. One reason: Tommy Farr was only the fifth British subject to fight for the heavyweight crown; only Tommy Burns and Bob Fitzsimmons had held it.

CLIFF SHUTT
RAF Flight Sergeant during World War II

I was stationed at the RAF base Catterick in the County of Yorkshire, England, from the beginning of 1937 until the out-break of the war. At that time my hometown was Darlington, about fourteen miles' distance in the County of Durham.

Between 1937 and November 1938 (when I married), I played "hooky" from camp whenever a Joe Louis fight was broadcast. You were not allowed out of camp after midnight, but I used to sneak out the back way. I went into town to sit and listen. In the 1930s, radio broadcasting normally ceased at midnight. Whenever Louis was fighting, the broadcasting facilities reopened about 2:30 a.m. in order to relay the fights live. I was glued to it. Fortunately, it never went more than two or three rounds because that gave me time to get back to camp in darkness.

The Tommy Farr fight stands out. Here we were faced with an awful dilemma. Tommy Farr was British, albeit a Welshman. National pride was at stake, but nobody (except the Welsh people) wanted to see the great Joe Louis beaten. As it transpired I believe honors were even—at least the British had produced a fighter who could go fifteen rounds with the "great man." I don't think any of the British public —except maybe a handful of loyal Welsh—had any real doubt about the outcome.

Yet, white American fight fans, still concerned that the black heavyweight titleholder might turn out to be another Jack Johnson, had not embraced Louis. Summing up the attitude of most white fans after the Braddock fight, one reporter said: "The next six months tell the story. If Joe Louis forgets his resolve to be an ambassador of goodwill for his race and wipe away the stigma that Jack Johnson brought on colored champions, he'll never make the grade." Few blacks had any such doubts. Every Louis victory, in their opinion, was an opportunity to rejoice.

JOHN R. THOMPSON, JR.
Head Basketball Coach,
Georgetown University

My favorite Joe Louis story was told to me by my father. He worked at Standard Marble & Tile Co. and my mother was a domestic. At the time, they had an apartment in the basement of the home in which my mother worked. The people, who were white, invited them upstairs to listen to that fight. When Joe knocked the fighter out, however, the people jumped up and turned the radio off. They were very disturbed, so my mother and father quickly said good night and went downstairs. The minute they got downstairs, they yelled like hell in celebration of the win.

After I was born, they moved to public housing in southeast Washington, D.C. My players laugh at me when I tell them that even a black baby wouldn't cry in that housing project when Joe Louis was fighting. But it was true. The projects were that quiet during a fight. And I always remember when it was over, what happened. Everybody would come into the street . . . beating pans with wooden spoons and yelling and hollering.

I remember when Joe spoke at the end of a fight—it was the only thing my mother was critical of regarding him. He would say, "Ma, we win." Affectionately, my mother would say, "Poor Joe," referring to his grammatical error.

But she accepted it from Joe Louis. My mother, who was
not a sports fan, had a tremendous amount of admiration
for Joe Louis.

Acknowledging the difficulty he had had in hitting the Welshman with a right, Louis said: "He fooled me. He was one tough
guy, with a peculiar style. He didn't look too effective, yet he
was puzzling and his punches were annoying." But that didn't
impress the champion's critics. "Louis was gun-shy. Schmeling had written with a hot iron the fear of a right hand across
his brain," *Liberty* magazine's Jack Tully said. Even former
champion Jack Dempsey, who was never a Louis fan, predicted
the champion's early demise. Yet, more than forty-five years
after the fight, recalling the cracking of his nose in the fourth
round, the plucky Welshman spoke respectfully of his opponent. "My nose still starts to bleed when I hear the name Joe
Louis," he said.

Normally such a gallant effort would have resulted in a
rematch, but Farr's lackluster follow-up bouts took him out of
contention for the heavyweight title. Meanwhile, three days
after the Louis-Farr fight, Max Schmeling agreed to a rematch
against Louis the following June. The deal came in the wake
of intense negotiations and shrewd maneuvering by Mike Jacobs: the promoter threatened an elimination tournament beginning with a Braddock-Baer match to find the next contender.
In the end, the German settled for the typical challenger's
purse—20 percent of the gate plus a percentage of the radio
and movie rights. Jacobs anticipated a financial bonanza. "I
can see those senators, governors, and mayors chasing me for
a crack at the bout," he predicted. "They'll be in a line from
here to San Francisco." Few cities, however, did come up with
suitable bids, and eventually the fight was booked for New
York's Yankee Stadium, the site of the first Louis-Schmeling
bout.

For a while, then, Louis put thoughts of boxing aside. He spent the remainder of the year playing softball with the Brown Bombers and visiting Hollywood, where he made a small-time film, renewed film-star acquaintances, and played golf with the likes of Lou Clayton (of Clayton, Jackson, and Durante), Bob Hope, and Bing Crosby.

In any event, 1938 began with two warm-up bouts for the Schmeling fight. In February, Louis fought Nathan Mann, reported to be a pawn of racketeer Dutch Schultz, in New York's Madison Square Garden. In the third round Mann was knocked to the canvas three times. The last, a result of one of Louis's solid left hooks, ended the bout. Next, Louis took on Harry Thomas in Chicago in April, knocking him out in five rounds, three rounds fewer than Schmeling had needed to do the same job the previous December.

After a brief sojourn to attend the 1938 Negro Elks convention in Washington (President Roosevelt heard that Louis was in the Elks parade and sent his car to take him to the White House for a visit), the champion was ready to start training for his long-awaited revenge bout with Schmeling. "I want to fight Schmeling more than he wants to fight me," he told reporters as he signed the fight contract in the State Athletic Commission offices. "If I didn't have the title, he wouldn't have anything more to do with me *inside* the ring."

MAX SCHMELING
Former Heavyweight Champion

To get the championship, I had to fight Joe Louis again. The American press thought that this fight would never be. They thought that Schmeling in 1938 would not get permission from Hitler to go to America. But Hitler didn't care. This wasn't his business, you know. His business was as a politician.

"There ain't going to be any decisions in this fight," Louis declared before the fight. One hundred and twenty-four seconds into the first round, not one of the 70,000 fans viewing the fight (a $1,083,530 gate)—or the millions of people listening to the broadcast, in English, German, Spanish, and Portuguese—would have disputed his claim. The Detroit slugger coldly and carefully annihilated his opponent. Wasting neither energy nor emotion on facial displays or unnecessary moves, he delivered more than forty calculated, almost deadly, blows to the German's head and body.

As they had after the Braddock fight, with this victory blacks everywhere celebrated exuberantly. In Harlem, empty streets turned into a multicolored carnival at 10:03 p.m. Impromptu parades, with revelers marching with a goose step and salutes mocking the Nazi regime, started throughout the city of New York—and the rejoicing was echoed in towns and urban centers throughout the country.

ANDREW YOUNG
Mayor of Atlanta

You could almost say that Joe Louis fought the war in advance. He helped to defeat the Hitlerian concept of a master race with his victory over Max Schmeling.

During the war, when it was necessary for all Americans to pull together, Joe Louis joined the war effort. He was one of the heroes that united the country. Going into the Army was his way of saying to black and white Americans, "We need to get into this fight. We can win."

President Roosevelt said, "The only thing we have to fear is fear itself." We sometimes forget the context in which that was made—at a time when Americans had never been threatened. It was made after Pearl Harbor, at a time of very low national self-confidence. One of the things that we

drew on was the Joe Louis experience. We said, "You really
don't have to be afraid of the Germans. They are not a
super race. Joe Louis has already proven that."

Louis, too, was euphoric about his quick knockout. The victory
was more important to him than his percentage of the proceeds
($351,622) from the $1 million gate. Joe, Marva, and manager
Julian Black and his wife sailed elatedly on the *Normandie* for
a European vacation on July 5. Prior to leaving, Louis attempted to see Schmeling in the hospital where he had been
sent as a result of the blow Joe had delivered to his lower back.
Barred from doing so by Schmeling's managers, he sent a telegram with his regrets for the injury (a broken vertebra).

Actually, many Germans didn't learn the results until the
day after the fight. When German reporters saw the tide going
against their countryman, they pulled the plug on the radio
connections going into Germany. And later, the Nazis edited
the fight films to blame Schmeling's loss on the blow Louis had
thrown to his back. Rebuffed, and disgraced in the eyes of his
countrymen, Schmeling tried for a comeback, returning to the
United States after defending the European championship successfully in 1939. Mike Jacobs hoped that two or three warm-
up fights would ready him for a rematch against Louis. The
war in Europe, starting in September, destroyed all such plans.

After the Schmeling fight Jacobs had gained control of all
boxing in New York: Col. John Reed Kilpatrick, president of
the Madison Square Garden Corporation, had appointed him
its promoter. Yet with his growing power and wealth, Jacobs
seemed to become greedier. He no longer wanted to share the
proceeds with the three journalists—Ed Frayne, Bill Farnsworth, and Damon Runyon—who were instrumental in the
formation of the Twentieth Century Sporting Club. He found
ways of disposing of them, one by one.

Meanwhile, Louis signed a contract to fight John Henry Lewis, the light-heavyweight champion, for a January 1939 bout. This was entered into with some trepidation by both Jacobs and Louis. The promoter was fearful that two black boxers wouldn't draw; the champion did not want to fight a friend who weighed only 180 pounds and had already lost the lateral vision in one eye. But at the insistence of Lewis's manager, Gus Greenlee, and with constant pressure from the sporting press, the Louis camp relented.

To minimize his friend's anguish, Joe hoped for a quick knockout. But the bout, ending in 2 minutes and 29 seconds of the first round, was shorter than even Louis anticipated. In the single round, Joe knocked his opponent to the canvas three times. Referee Arthur Donovan, after the third knockdown, saw Lewis's arm draped across the lowest strand of the ropes, stepped between the fighters, and halted the slaughter.

In fact, the end of the fight came with the first, powerful right-hand punch the champion landed. "I'm bigger, heavier and can hit harder. Why shouldn't I have knocked him out?" Louis asked reporters after the fight.

Regardless of his friendship with his opponent, once Louis accepted the fight, it became a job, and in the ring, he instinctively went for the knockout. However, Louis's concern for Lewis outside the ring, as with all his friends, was unshakable. Near the end of his career, Lewis asked the champion to attend one of his bouts to help build the gate. Joe agreed, going one step further. Unbeknown to Lewis, he asked his personal secretary, Freddie Guinyard, to station a person at each entrance to the stadium to count attendees. When Guinyard asked why, the Champ responded, "So Henry gets every penny from the promoter he deserves."

Louis concluded his trio of one-round knockouts when he met Jack Roper, an experienced 36-year-old heavyweight, that April in Los Angeles. This bout differed from the others in one way: Roper came within a hair, or more precisely a left hook, of an upset. A powerful punch that landed on Louis's nose and mouth momentarily stunned the champion. But then, missing a left, Roper was unable to follow up effectively. Louis regained the advantage and threw a volley of body blows that sent the challenger stumbling toward his corner. A final left and a right put the veteran down. Roper's kneecaps hit the canvas with a thud. Unable to move his temporarily paralyzed legs, he was counted out by referee George Blake. "Roper hit me harder than any man since my first Schmeling fight," admitted Louis afterward, nonplussed that he had come close to losing his crown. Nevertheless, the support and affection of his fans never wavered.

JIM COX
Freelance Journalist

Joe Louis was one of the heroes of my youth. Since there was no television and since it was during the Depression, we used to spend a lot of time in the local parks. The morning after Joe Louis won a fight, we'd (the white kids) be confronted in the park by 3000 little black boys looking for a fight. They'd want to beat up some white kid. It meant that much to the blacks.

I went to a Catholic grammar school in the late 1930s. I can remember a nun asking our current events class to name three American bombers. One kid stood up and said the Martin bomber. Another kid raised his hand and said the Northrup bomber. Then everyone was stumped. A buddy of mine said, "I know . . . Joe Louis." The nun asked what he meant. He said, "He's the Brown Bomber."

Two months later, when he met "Two-Ton" Tony Galento, a rotund New Jersey tavern owner, Louis again learned how perilous the boxing game could be. The fight, considered by some to be one of "savage fury and methodical butchery," was one of the most thrilling title struggles in boxing annals. Galento staggered the champion in round one, but found himself on the receiving end in the next. With grim determination, he fought back in the third to floor Louis with a left hook that appeared merely to graze his jaw. Only the third man to knock down the Champ—Schmeling did it twice and Braddock once—Galento thrilled the New York crowd with his punches. In the opinion of referee Arthur Donovan, Galento came closer than anyone did to dethroning Louis. "When Galento knocked Louis down, I could see that the champion was badly hurt, even though he jumped onto his feet without a count," he said. "If Tony could have landed another left hook, he would have won the title."

That opportunity, however, quickly evaporated. Ignoring the advice of his handlers and buoyed by his success in the third round, Galento attempted to slug it out with Louis in the fourth round. He was battered to a pulp with left hooks and right crosses. "I got a little careless and he nailed me," Galento later explained. An exhausted and dazed Galento clinched with the Brown Bomber, only to be flung back and subjected to more battering. Amid an outpouring of pleas to "Stop it!" from ringside fans, Louis continued to fire punches until the devastated boxer clinched again, causing referee Donovan to stop the slaughter.

Although he was left with two swollen and bloodied eyes, a battered nose, and a split lip at the end of the bout, Galento became a hero—and a most sought-after prizefighter. He received radio, movie, and fight offers from around the country and from Europe. Unable to explain the acclaim for such an unlikely hero, reporter Frank Graham merely said, "Prizefighting is a very funny business."

CLIFF SHUTT

The sportswriters at home were publishing tidbits and quotations attributed to "Two-Ton" Tony Galento. Prior to the bout, they referred to him as "Roly-Poly." They said he trained on beer and cigars and was quoted as having said in reference to Joe, "I'll moider de bum." The British were at fever heat. They could hardly wait to see (or hear) Galento get his comeuppance. How they reveled in Joe's victory!

The Galento fight, which attracted almost 35,000 fans to Yankee Stadium, was the first large gate Louis had had in a year. The Lewis and Roper fights made the Louis camp little more than $70,000; the Galento bout, $114,000. So, to maintain his standard of living, the champion had to continue fighting. But the more he fought, the more he was away from home, increasing the strain on his marriage. Six- to eight-week training periods were interspersed with recreational activities that did not include Marva—trips with male companions or discreet liaisons with other women.

VERNON E. JORDAN, JR.
Former President, National Urban League, Inc.

When I was in college, I caroused a bit with a waitress in Atlanta named Elsie. She was older than I was. She was sort of crazy and well known around town. One night I said to her, "You've had a lot of boyfriends. Who's the most exciting man you ever met?" She said "Joe Louis." But it was the way she said JOE LOUIS. The body language was there. And could she generate body language. She was quite something in those days. The ladies who sit in the same pew as my momma in church would call her a hussy. Our generation would call her VERY SEXY.

As an investment—and as a recreational outlet for Marva—Louis and Roxborough bought Spring Hill, a 477-acre tract twenty-two miles north of Detroit in MacComb County, Michigan. Containing a clubhouse, riding academy, and accommodations for 100 guests, the property was half farmland—on which Joe planned to breed Hereford cattle for exhibition purposes—and half timberland. After the Galento fight, Louis and Marva spent some long-overdue time together at Spring Hill. He went into training for a rematch with Bob Pastor in September, after which he immediately returned to the Michigan estate.

Since Pastor had gone a full ten rounds with Louis in 1937, Jacobs scheduled a twenty-rounder for the Detroit bout. But Louis had no desire to fight for twenty rounds and, unlike previous occasions, Pastor did not intend to backpedal around the ring. The challenger came out slugging, only to be knocked down three times in the first round. Fighting on instinct, in the tenth round he was knocked down a final time. The referee stopped the bout, "saving my life," said Pastor after the fight. "I couldn't see out of one eye, and he was hitting me pretty well. He was a terrific puncher."

Despite the victories, some boxing observers thought Louis had lost the invincibility of his youth. "He is not as good as they rate him," said Galento after his bout. "He can't take a punch." Former champion Dempsey acknowledged Louis's competence, but was quick to point out his flaws: "Joe Louis is a good, game fighter who boxes better than many critics think and punches like nobody's business. But his jaw is weak and eventually a puncher—a good, rough, tough guy who can take a punch and keep on punching himself—will take Louis's heavyweight title."

Disagreeing vehemently, referee Arthur Donovan contended that Louis had "not slipped a whit and could remain champion as long as he wished, and the draft board permitted."

Faithful conditioning, superlative weapons of attack (a short right, a left hook, and a straight left), and his ability to take a punch were three factors that Donovan felt made the boxer preeminent. *The Ring* agreed with Donovan. In 1939, for the third time in six years, it named Louis the number one man in pugilism for his "public relations and fine influence on the sport." His closest rival for the honor and distinction was Billy Conn, the light-heavyweight champion. Louis edged out Conn by six votes.

Conn's record—and his second-place finish in *The Ring*'s tally—hadn't gone unnoticed by Mike Jacobs. The Irish-American fighter was already under contract with Jacobs, and by the end of 1939 had been anointed by him as the heir-apparent to Joe Louis. Except that he needed a little more experience and weight, Conn had all the qualifications: He was young and classy looking, had the Irish gift of gab, was charismatic, and, most importantly, was a talented boxer. "Conn," according to *New York Post* reporter Jack Miley, "had plenty of moxie. He'd fight Louis tomorrow if they'd let him, and he is one of those natural-born crowd-pleasers who come along once in a ring generation." The stage was being set for an epic heavyweight bout in 1941.

"He Can Run, But He Can't Hide"

"In the thirteenth round, I made an awful mistake. I didn't listen to the guys in the corner."

—Billy Conn

By 1939, the heavyweight champion had pretty well depleted the list of potential rivals. Only half-facetiously, one reporter said, "If Louis continues to fight himself out of competition, he will end up having to fight his own shadow." To pick up some of the slack, the boxer did things like stepping into the ring as referee, adding a new facet to his career. After overseeing two amateur boxing events in Madison Square Garden, Louis lauded the experience: "Refereeing is better than fighting . . . at least better than fighting every night."

Meanwhile, Jacobs concentrated on finding opponents who might challenge Louis. He tapped Arturo Godoy of Chile for a bout in February 1940, raising the fears of Johnny Ray, Conn's manager, for his own boxer's future. Ray was

109

worried Godoy might take the title away from Joe, thereby beating Conn out of a championship bout. "Louis is a great puncher, but it's a lot easier to figure out how to fight a Louis than a Godoy," the manager explained. "Move only a little when Louis positions you and he does not know how to shoot." Telegraphing the strategy Conn would use against the Champ the following year, Ray added, "You can keep him drawing a bead on you all night, if you keep him on the move."

Godoy, however, used a different strategy to befuddle Louis. He remained in the crouched position used by Galento in his bout with the Brown Bomber. As a result, the champion couldn't knock Godoy down, much less knock him out. When Godoy darted, Louis's timing was thrown off. When Godoy clung to his opponent, Louis's punch was defused. And when Godoy hugged the floor, Louis seemed helpless. To add insult to injury, in the fourteenth round, the South American, while clinging to the champion, planted a kiss on his cheek.

Although Louis had landed many clean, hard punches for ten of the fifteen rounds, it was a lackluster fight and the Madison Square Garden crowd received the news of the decision in favor of Louis with a mixture of catcalls and boos. Louis emerged from the fight unbruised; Godoy had two swollen eyes and was bleeding from a cut under his left eye and from his lips. Regardless, the champion's invincibility was again brought into question. This time, referee Arthur Donovan agreed: "Joe was really bad in this fight with Godoy. He was listless, seemed to have his thoughts somewhere else."

Godoy's success with Louis galvanized the heavyweight division. "We're loaded to the barrel now," proclaimed Mike Jacobs. "The day before yesterday, it looked as if we'd never find anybody to stand up against Louis; and now, because of what Godoy did, I can put the champion in against any one

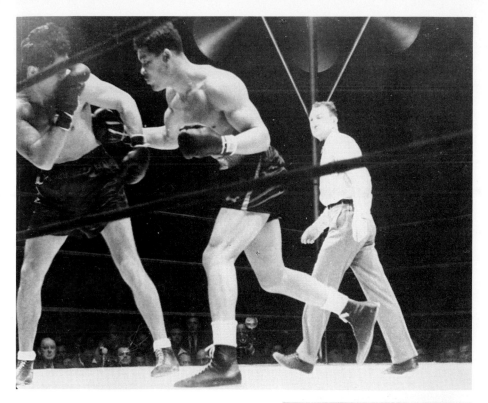

Joe Louis landing a right to the body of Max Schmeling in their second fight, June 22, 1938. (*Wide World Photos*)

A title defense and first-round knockout that resulted in Joe Louis's becoming an American hero. (*Laurie Minor, Smithsonian Institution; donated to the Smithsonian by Mrs. Julian Black*)

Louis taking the count from referee Arthur Donovan in his first fight with Max Schmeling in 1936. (*UPI/Bettmann Newsphotos*)

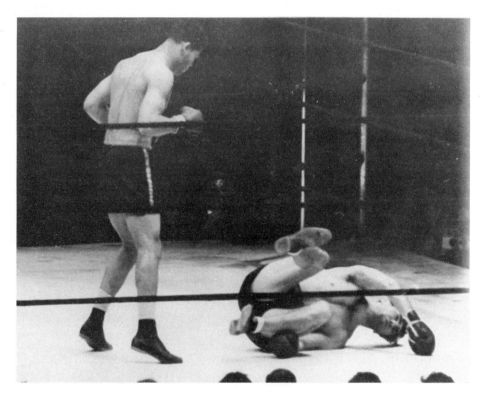

Joe smashes Schmeling to the canvas in the first round of their second bout. (*AP/Wide World Photos*)

This is the towel thrown in by Max Schmeling's handlers in his return match with Joe Louis at Yankee Stadium, New York City, June 22, 1938, and thrown out of the ring by Arthur Donovan, Referee, because it is a rule of the New York Boxing Commission that seconds cannot throw a towel in the ring to stop a fight. This towel was thrown in during the first minute of boxing in the first round.

Even the towel could not save Max Schmeling the night of June 22, 1938. (*Laurie Minor, Smithsonian Institution; donated to the Smithsonian by Mrs. Julian Black*)

The right hand of Joe Louis, "winner and still champion," is raised after the June 22, 1938, one-round knockout of Max Schmeling. (*UPI/Bettmann Newsphotos*)

Joe's grandmother, Victoria Harp Barrow, was half Cherokee and the descendant of a chief. She and her husband, Lon Barrow, were both plantation slaves. (*Eulalia Taylor Barrow*)

Joe's father, Munroe ("Mun") Barrow, was 6 foot 3 inches and weighed 200 pounds. Four of his seven children were Susie (left), Alvanious, baby deLeon, and Emmarell (right). (*Eulalia Taylor Barrow*)

The room in which Joe Louis Barrow was born, outside LaFayette, Alabama; now owned by Turner Shealey, Louis's 86-year-old cousin. (*Barrow family photo*)

Joe Louis's mother, the woman who provided the Champ with the foundation of life. (*Eulalia Taylor Barrow*)

A contemplative Louis before a training session. (*Barrow family photo*)

The young Joe Louis with mentor and trainer Chappy (left) and manager Julian Black (right). (*Barrow family photo, compliments of L. L. Foster*)

JOE LOUIS' CHICKEN SHACK
Compliments of
The Home of Detroit's BEST Fried Chicken & Bar-B-Que Ribs
8549 12TH ST. DETROIT TYLER 4-8579

A promotion photo for the patrons of Joe Louis's first restaurant. (*Eulalia Taylor Barrow*)

Joe Louis—his impact spanned the globe. (*Barrow family photo, compliments of The Chicago Defender*)

The Barrow clan happily celebrating the Primo Carnera win on June 25, 1935. (Left to right) deLeon, Emmarell, Lonnie, Eulalia, Vunies, and mother, Lillie. (*deLeon Barrow*)

Louis always enjoyed the center of the ring, whether he had an opponent or not. He was always a crowd pleaser. (*Barrow family photo*)

Joe watching a Brown Bomber baseball game and finishing a Coca-Cola. To his right, friend and personal secretary Freddie Guinyard; to his left, bodyguard Carl Nelson. (*Barrow family photo, compliments of L. L. Foster*)

When in the West, do as the cowboys do . . . (*Barrow family photo, compliments of Wide World Photos*)

In California, the Champ would diversify his training regimen, but wood chopping was more for the cameras than for training benefits. (*Barrow family photo, compliments of Wide World Photos*)

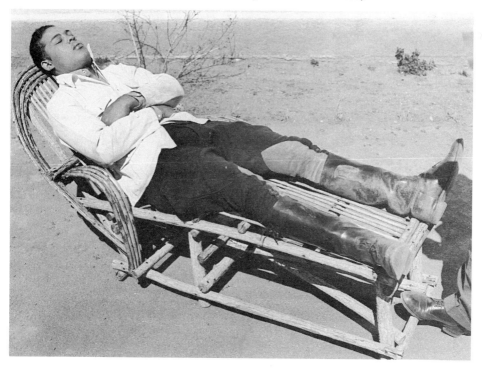

Louis could sleep anywhere, any time of day. (*Barrow family photo, compliments of Wide World Photos*)

The Champ taking a rare opportunity to give direction to his trainer, Jack Blackburn. (*Barrow family photo, compliments of Wide World Photos*)

Marva riding Joe's horse at the farm in Spring Hill, Michigan. (*Barrow family photo*)

Joe and Marva attracted crowds whenever they traveled. (*Barrow family photo, compliments of Adams Foto*)

The Champ and Marva returning to New York on the *SS Queen Elizabeth* after a visit to Europe. (*Barrow family photo*)

Joe and Marva enjoying an evening out at a nightclub. Note that the Champ is drinking none other than Joe Louis Punch. (*UPI/ Bettmann Newsphotos*)

Billy Conn starting to rise after slipping to the canvas in the first round of the championship fight, June 18, 1941. (*UPI/Bettmann Newsphotos*)

Marva Louis during her singing career. (*Barrow family photo*)

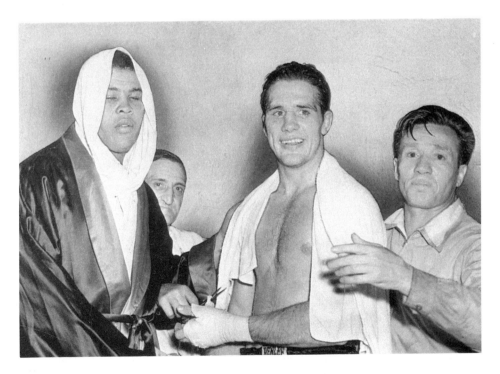

The winner and still champ, Joe Louis, looking a great deal worse than challenger Billy Conn, whom he knocked out in the thirteenth round of the 1941 fight. (*Billy Conn*)

Louis visits the troops on Kiska Island, part of the Aleutians chain, during the spring of 1945. (*Howard Sigel*)

Private Billy Conn reminding Corporal Joe Louis that he was winning through twelve rounds of their 1941 fight. (*Billy Conn*)

Louis and his mother, Lillie. (*Barrow family photo, compliments of Paul Cannon*)

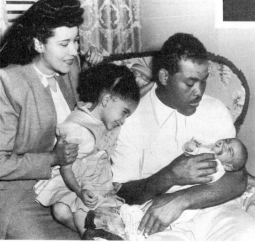

Marva, Joe, and 4-year-old daughter Jackie say hi to Joe, Jr., on his arrival from Mexico City, where he was born. (*Barrow family photo, compliments of Associated Press*)

Joe Louis and golf professional Ted Rhodes introduce 2-year-old Joe, Jr., to the game of golf. (*Barrow family photo*)

The Champ takes his son, Joe, Jr., and daughter, Jackie, to Miami for a little fun in the sun. (*Barrow family photo*)

Joe, Jr., challenges his dad to a little "sandy" roadwork as Jackie looks on. (*Barrow family photo*)

Jersey Joe Walcott winces under a hard right from the Champ in the first round of their title bout at Madison Square Garden, December 5, 1947. (*Bettmann Newsphotos*)

Louis flanked by friend and companion Leonard Reed (on his right) and trainer Manny Seamon (on his left). (*Barrow family photo, compliments of Hutcherson Photo*)

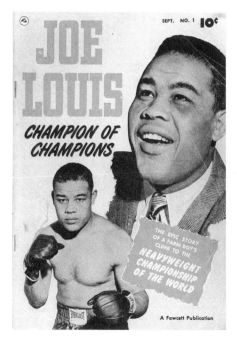

Joe and his trainer, Manny Seamon, check the gloves in preparation for another title defense. (*Manny Seamon*)

Joe Louis even reached the comic books. (*Laurie Minor, Smithsonian Institution; donated to the Smithsonian by Mrs. Julian Black*)

In his last professional fight, Joe taking a right hand from Rocky Marciano, October 26, 1951, in Madison Square Garden. (*UPI/ Bettmann Newsphotos*)

Joe Louis's feelings are revealed in his dressing room with his trainer, Manny Seamon, after his defeat by Rocky Marciano. (*UPI/Bettmann Newsphotos*)

The Champ and Max Schmeling on the south side of Chicago during the 1955 reunion. (*Max Schmeling*)

Joe Louis and his second wife, Rose Morgan, drink a toast of champagne after their wedding, Christmas day, at the bride's home in St. Albans, New York. (*UPI/Bettmann Newsphotos*)

Joe and his third wife, Martha, in March 1959, a year after their marriage. (*UPI/Bettmann Newsphotos*)

Joe Louis is shown as autograph hunters converged on him after he defeated Don "Cowboy Rocky" Lee in his debut as a pro wrestler, March 16, 1956. (*UPI/Bettmann Newsphotos*)

The 1966 happy reunion in Hamburg of two heavyweight world champions. (*Max Schmeling*)

"Joe, I forgot to tell you . . . there are no speed limits in Germany." Louis and Schmeling arriving at Max's home outside Hamburg. (*Max Schmeling*)

Max and Joe still competing . . . this time, Max himself is throwing in the towel. (*Max Schmeling*)

Joe giving Max a few pointers on golf. During the 1987 interview with Joe, Jr., the 82-year-old Max said he would take up golf when he felt he wanted to slow down. (*Max Schmeling*)

Going to rest—Army pallbearers carry the casket of Joe Louis to his final resting place at the Arlington National Cemetery. Louis's widow, Martha, walks behind the procession. (*AP/Wide World Photos*)

of nine contenders." Jacobs chose to match the champion against Johnny Paycheck, a Des Moines boxer, in New York in March.

Paycheck was considered a fair boxer. He won the International Golden Gloves heavyweight championship in 1933 and since 1938 had twenty-three knockouts in thirty-three fights to his credit. Nevertheless, he entered the ring a ten-to-one underdog. Neither his stand-up boxing style nor his lack of confidence, readily apparent from his pale face when he entered the ring, gave him much of a chance against the Brown Bomber. When the fight began, reporter Frank Graham suggested that the only injury Paycheck would get would be rope burns from circling the ring so close to the apron.

In two rounds, Louis floored Paycheck three times. The first two knockdowns were in the first round—one from a right to the chin and the other a result of a left hook. For both, Paycheck took a nine count, the last as the bell sounded for the end of the round. When the fighters reentered the ring for round two, it was clear that the end was imminent. Although Paycheck continued to backpedal, when the Brown Bomber finally caught up with him, he landed a long right to the chin to put his opponent down for the count. In the entire fight, the challenger threw only one feeble punch.

Jacobs was ridiculed for staging such a "fistic fiasco." As a result, he agreed, at a cost he estimated to be $25,000 per year, to set up a fight club in which contenders would have to demonstrate their abilities before being awarded a Madison Square Garden main event. "Never again," promised the promoter.

A month later Louis went into training for a June rematch against Godoy. The champion had every intention of maintaining his record of knocking out every opponent who had previously gone the distance with him. "Joe gonna get to Godoy fast this time. Believe me," said trainer Jack Blackburn.

"Joe kin whip'em in the body fast, like that blitzkrieging business and bring his guard down. And he kin hurt him by hittin'
him on the haid. Don't mean the top of the haid. That's too
solid. But around the temple, that's the place."

As in all of Louis's previous camps, this strategy wasn't
readily apparent to the casual observer. Most of the Champ's
sparring sessions seemed rather boring to all but the partic-
ipants. "He's one of the really good ringsters who never leave
their fight in the training ring," commented boxing writer Lester Rodney. "He carefully and scientifically brings his punches,
defense, and footwork to a proper edge by a lot of rounds of
actual sparring." Rarely did he knock down a sparring partner. Instead, throughout a session he would issue instructions:
"Throw some more rights." "Shorten your jabs."

On June 20, in front of 28,000 fans at Yankee Stadium,
Louis dropped Godoy to the canvas three times before referee
Billy Cavanaugh prudently stopped the bout at 1 minute and
24 seconds into the eighth round. At the bell for the first round,
the Chilean instantly revealed his strategy. He planned to stay
close to Louis—to avoid being caught with a solid punch and
to punish the champion's body with blows to the rib cage.
But Joe hammered away close in, too, firing a series of damaging, short punches to Godoy's head. The challenger finished
the first round with a cut above his left eye, which the champion repeatedly reopened throughout the match. For six rounds
the bout proceeded with Godoy's throwing lefts to Louis's
chest and the champion's responding with short left and right
punches.

Louis floored Godoy—it was the first knockdown of his
career—with a left hook in the seventh round, just before the
bell sounded. Outraged at being knocked down, Godoy came
out for the eighth swinging. In response, the Brown Bomber
landed a series of punishing lefts and rights to his opponent's
jaw. One right finally stopped the Chilean dead in his tracks.

Rising at the count of eight, he was dropped again by a volley of lefts and rights. Referee Cavanaugh stopped the fight, but a battered Godoy, still battling, had to be restrained forcibly by his handlers.

FREDDIE GUINYARD
Joe Louis's Friend and Personal Secretary

I always sat in the opponent's corner because there are so many tricks in a fight the average person would never know anything about. Everybody put cocoa butter on their face, for instance. It's done today. It would turn the complexion of your skin. Joe and I are dark complexed and you couldn't tell. When you hit it with a leather glove, it'd slip off. That's what we had to watch out for.

I remember such a situation in the Arturo Godoy fight. Al Wiley, Godoy's manager, had on a big sweater and he had cocoa butter in his pocket. He was putting it on him and I told the referee. Wiley said, "I ain't got nothing. He's crazy." So the next time he come to put it in his pocket, I took it out and threw it under the ring. He reached in his pocket to get it. He looked right down at me and said, "S.O.B."

Although boxing was important to Louis, it was by no means his whole life. One anecdote, in particular, provides a measure of the man's values. Publicist Harry Markson once asked the fighter rhetorically, "The greatest thrill of your life, Joe, must have been the night you knocked out Jim Braddock." The Champ responded, "No, that wasn't it." Markson continued, "Then it had to be the night you knocked out Schmeling in one round." "No, let me tell you," Louis said. "I have a sister, Vunies, who went to Howard University. I put her through school. On the day that she graduated, I attended the graduation exercises with my mother. After the ceremony, my mother, my sister, and I walked across the Howard University campus arm-in-arm. That was the greatest thrill of my life.''

VUNIES BARROW HIGH
Joe Louis's Sister

Joe was as proud of me as I was of him. At the time, most of the black kids in Detroit went to Miller High School. My sister, Eulalia, and I went to Cass, a predominantly white school. It was quite an honor to be accepted to Cass. Joe was very proud of that. When I graduated with honors, Joe took me with him to California as a graduation present. We went to Los Angeles and San Francisco.

He paid for my college education at Howard University. He also paid my tuition for me to get my Masters at the University of Michigan. When I decided not to get my Ph.D., he was disappointed. Joe created quite a noise when he came to my graduation at Howard. He was in training for a fight so he just came the day of the graduation and left. He had a convertible. I asked him if I could drive it home to Detroit. I was quite popular with that car that summer.

Between the Godoy and Paycheck bouts, Louis began paying closer attention to Billy Conn. "He's fast, no doubt about that, and he has good timing. But he'd punch a lot harder if he punched straighter," commented the champion when he visited the younger boxer's Grossinger's training camp prior to the Conn-Pastor match. He elaborated on his critique by explaining, "He swings wide, awfully wide, with his left hook, and he only punches from the elbow. If he hit straighter the punch would come from the shoulder—and that's where you get power." Although this visit was the first encounter with Conn

that Louis recalled, the challenger fifty years later vividly remembered an earlier meeting.

BILLY CONN
Former Light-Heavyweight Champion

The first time I met Joe Louis I made $20. See, I got a job
putting resin in the ring at Duquesne Gardens in Pittsburgh
when Joe's fighting Hans Birkie. I put the resin box in Joe's
corner and I was going back to the dressing room. He turned
to his manager and said, "Give that kid $20." I was eighteen
at the time. [Conn later earned $500,000 from his two fights
against Louis.]

Louis was impressed with what he saw at the Conn training
camp, and he told reporters his future opponent had fighting
spirit. "Didn't know he was so rough," the Brown Bomber
said. "The boy likes to fight; I can see that." He was also
encouraged by his growth into the heavyweight class, telling
New York World-Telegram reporter Lester Bromberg, "Looks
bigger than in his first fight in New York. You say he's 22;
when will he stop growing?" Louis knew that Conn worked
hard—boxing six to ten rounds a day—and that he was fast.
Predicting Conn would make Pastor miss a lot, he said, "He's
in fast and gets away fast."

Regardless, the brash young boxer showed little respect for
the Champ. "Louis has lost his punch. I saw him twice—once
with Paycheck, who got up twice after taking two-second counts,
and the other time with Godoy. You can't convince me that
he is really hitting the way he used to do," Conn declared. The
Pittsburgh boxer had the temerity to think that he could beat
Louis, but the experts knew he would need more than audacity
to capture the title the following June.

While Jacobs continued his search for opponents, Louis turned his attention to his second love, golf. Playing every day, he told reporters that he planned to build a course at Spring Hill, his Michigan estate, and hoped to schedule a National Negro Championship there in the future. "I ain't saying I'd have a chance of winning," the Champ said, "but it would be good to see members of my race having a real championship." While attending the National Amateur Championship at the Winged Foot Club in Mamaroneck, New York, in September, he challenged Bing Crosby, who was playing there, to a game. "We could make it a three-way match. We could box, play golf, and sing," he ribbed reporters. "I reckon my extra weight would give me the duke in boxing. Bing would whip my ears off when it comes to vocalizing, specially if the rules called for staying in the right key. But in golf I might have a chance. It might be pretty equal, if Bing would give me a couple of strokes."

Louis also took time off to support Wendell Willkie's campaign for President—"Because he promises my people better jobs." Public speaking, a new role for the boxer, was one he didn't relish, but Joe, born a Republican and a Baptist, respected his heritage. Over the next several months, he toured the country speaking out for the ill-fated candidate.

By the late fall, Louis was aching for some action in the ring. "Man, I sure wish there was someone for me to fight," he told one reporter. "Funny thing, when I was a kid I was lazier than a hound dog. Just wanted to lay 'round all day, fill my stomach with grub and lay in the sun. Now that I got plenty of money and could be lazy, I don't want to be." Jacobs finally responded with a series of matches, one a month, leading up to the much-ballyhooed Louis-Conn fight on June 18, 1941.

Jack Miley of the *New York Post* first referred to Louis's schedule as the "Bum-of-the-Month Club" when he faced Al McCoy, a light-heavyweight, in December. That fight was followed by meetings with Red Burman in New York in January,

Gus Dorazio in Philadelphia in February, Abe Simon in Detroit in March, Tony Musto in St. Louis in April, and Buddy Baer in Washington, D.C., in May. "When he gets his Bum-of-the-Month Club rolling," said Miley condescendingly, "Louis is going to cover more towns than the Ringling show. The way he buffets 'em about, Louis could play five shows a day and get himself some real money."

The "bum-of-the-month" accusation was probably unfair. The boxers Joe fought during those months were good competitors—certainly they were among the best the division had to offer at the time. Louis just made them *look* bad. In truth, some of these boxers gave him a good run for his money. Consider McCoy, kayoed in six rounds, who used the bobbing and weaving style that the champion found so difficult to attack, and Al Simon, who lasted thirteen rounds.

Then there was Buddy Baer, Max's brother, the tallest opponent (at 6 feet 6½ inches) Louis had ever fought. Unlike Primo Carnera, Baer was well proportioned. He also was a good puncher and could take punishment—which is exactly what it would take to knock out the Brown Bomber. Louis, aware of these attributes, fought a cautious fight, staying in close, refusing to exchange swings at long range. From the first round—when a series of three punches ending in a left hook connected and sent the Champ through the ropes onto the apron—he didn't take any unnecessary chances.

Louis's cunning—as well as his punching power—began to pay off in round six, when he dropped Baer twice. The crowd was roaring when the challenger rose the first time at the count of eight. Louis didn't hear the bell and floored him again. Baer, unconscious, couldn't respond to the bell in the seventh round. Ancil Hoffman, Baer's manager, and Ray Arcel, his trainer, pleaded with referee Arthur Donovan to disqualify Louis for hitting their boxer after the round ended. Instead, Donovan, Jacobs's employee and a Louis fan, making the most difficult decision of his career, disqualified Baer for not responding to the bell.

Although the validity of the Donovan call may be questioned, it was a good fight for Louis. According to one reporter, he showed a "well-rounded performance with touches of cunning and generalship" that weren't usually necessary for him. A superb shift in strategy really won the fight: When Louis's left hooks were blocked he went to the jab, forcing Baer to move his right guard. The Champ then responded with a left hook to the jaw that sent Baer spinning.

SHIRLEY POVICH
Sportswriter, The Washington Post

Joe could be knocked down because he was always on the attack and could get surprised. He wasn't a ducker or a bobber or a weaver, but a stand-up fighter. Braddock decked him before losing; Schmeling knocked him out in the twelfth round of their first fight; Jersey Joe Walcott put him down twice; Tony Galento sent him sprawling; Tami Mauriello shuddered him; and Buddy Baer sent him to the canvas.

I also remember his strength. I was at a training camp once and met a sparring partner named McCarthy, a big Boston Irishman. His first name was Jack. He says, "Listen, Shirley, I'm as big as Joe Louis, but he is the strongest man I've ever known." I said, "Why do you say that?" He says, "You know, we get in the ring, it's time to break it off. We clinch a little bit. I've pinned his arms underneath me. His arms are between my shoulders. He lifted me up stiff-armed and deposited me over here three feet away just as a matter of course. Lifts me up! I didn't think anybody could ever do that."

While Louis fought frequently, Conn took time off from the ring after defeating Pastor. He had relinquished his light-heavyweight championship title, which he had held for almost two years following his victory over Melio Bettina in July 1939, in order to challenge Louis. His May fight schedule consisted of one exhibition tune-up: a fight against Buddy Knox witnessed by 27,000 people at Forbes Field in Pittsburgh.

THE REVEREND JERRY MOORE
Nineteenth Street Baptist Church, Washington, D.C.

In 1941, talk regarding the "Great White Hope" had emerged again. A lot of people were comparing Billy Conn with the great Jack Dempsey. If Billy Conn could do his thing on Joe Louis, it would reestablish the supremacy of the white man. This was unspoken, but you could feel it everywhere. I thought prejudice was beginning to rise again. I dare say there wasn't a black person in America that wasn't praying the Brown Bomber would knock Conn out.

At the time, I was living down south in a little town called Minden, Louisiana. It was 29 miles east of Shreveport. Discrimination there was so rank you could cut it with a knife and serve it up on a platter. Somehow in those precious years blacks felt that, putting it frankly, every time Louis beat up a white man, it was a vindication of their self-worth. Best of all, he could do it legally!

Boxing experts immediately began taking sides as to whether the lethal puncher or the master boxer would win. The odds makers favored Louis, but there were many who sided with Conn. One was Al McCoy, who had fought both opponents (losing a decision to Conn). "Conn is a much better boxer and faster so he's much harder to hit than Louis. Joe hits harder, I suppose, but he never hit me with the punches Conn did," he said. Responding to such comments on Conn's speed, Louis reportedly said, "He can run, but he can't hide."

If Conn used his head, Louis believed that he could be the toughest opponent he had ever faced. Nevertheless, before the fight, he told the press that Conn's temper would get the better of him. "I know Billy will fight like a cornered cat when you hurt him," he said. "He ain't got any better sense. I mean he just naturally likes rough going and forgets to box." On the other hand, Conn recalls that his plan was to make Louis lead and to keep moving out of his reach: "My strategy was not to let him hit me. If they can't hit you, they can't hurt you. Keep your hands up. Move. Mix them up. If you keep backing up, they'll follow you."

While the two fighters trained, Mike Jacobs concerned himself with ticket sales. He priced ringside seats at $25 and for the first time since the Louis-Schmeling rematch built extra ringside seats. Jacobs expected 54,000 fans at New York's Polo Grounds, totaling a $450,000 gate. On the morning of the fight, however, he was unnerved by his boxers' weights. Louis, at 199½, was below 200 pounds for the first time in quite a while; Conn, meanwhile, was a lithe 169 pounds. To make it appear to be a more equitable match, the promoter announced to the press that Conn weighed 174 pounds. Although Louis had successfully achieved his objective of not appearing as a heavyweight bully against the slight Conn, he had become dehydrated in the process. Once before—for the 1936 Schmeling bout—that had proved disastrous for Louis.

Regardless, Louis appeared unconcerned. At the weigh-in sportscaster Don Dunphy, about to announce his first boxing match, wished Joe well. Louis reciprocated, "Good luck to you, too." Dunphy remains amazed by the graciousness of the champion: "Knowing how important this bout was to me, he took time out from his own thoughts to think of me. I have always remembered that."

Louis's composure usually prevailed before a match. Hours before a fight, he would climb onto the dressing room table and fall asleep. When he awakened, he would nonchalantly say, "I've got to get to work." In the ring, however, Louis was deadly serious. He rarely showed emotion and was very difficult for his opponents to read. Some boxers thought Louis was taught restraint by his trainers. In truth, it is a family character trait. None of the Barrows smiles or shows emotion readily.

But Louis was human and he did get nervous. Yet only his closest friends could tell that. In mentally preparing for a fight, two to three days before the bout Louis would stop speaking to the press, the public, and even his managers. He would converse only with friends of long standing.

FREDDIE GUINYARD

To get what you wanted from Joe you had to talk to him in a special way. If a sportswriter, for example, took to him directly—start asking something about a fight—he'd get the hunch of the shoulders. If he'd go sit and talk to Joe about golf, baseball, or football and every now and then throw in what he'd really want to know, he'd get his story. Joe was always this way.

In the ring I told him, "Look, ole buddy, I got a date up in Harlem. Let's get this over right quick." Mr. Black told me to cut out this foolishness. Jack Blackburn walked over to me several fights later. He said, "Did you talk to your man yet?" I said, "Mr. Black told me not to say anything." He said, "I'm the boss in this ring." So I continued to tell Joe something to ease the tension.

On June 18 challenger Billy Conn entered the ring first. Dressed in a white robe, Conn danced up the steps, ducked under the ropes, bowed to his cheering section, and crossed himself before moving toward the center. The Champ, wearing his familiar blue robe with red trim and a towel draped over his head, appeared in the opposite corner half a minute later. Eddie Joseph, the referee, was in the center. The stage was set for the match of the decade.

Louis started out fast, stalking his opponent; Conn was cautious, using his left to jab and dancing backward out of the champion's reach. He was so hesitant in round one that he slipped, falling to one knee in an effort to avoid a right. The second round, a replay of the first, saw the challenger jabbing but mostly receiving Louis's punches. In round three, Conn finally seemed to come alive. He managed to get through the Brown Bomber's defenses, feinted with a left, and threw a solid right off Louis's chin, followed by a left, a right, and another left to the face.

Retreating in the fourth round, Conn still landed some solid blows. Once he suddenly stopped dancing backward and unleashed a straight left and two rights to Louis's jaw. The champion was momentarily stunned. In characteristic response to the setback, Louis retaliated in the next three rounds. By the end of round five, the Brown Bomber had Conn retreating. A right to his opponent's chest, a left hook to his head, and a final fusillade of blows to the body had the young boxer staggering and bleeding from cuts over his right eye and on the bridge of his nose.

The tide changed in the eighth as Conn began to score. Firing a left to Louis's face, a series of blows to his head, and a solid right to his chin, he staggered the champion. Just as the bell rang, the challenger stunned the titleholder again with a left hook to the face. More than the damage he inflicted, the round provided Conn with renewed confidence. He drilled Louis in the ninth with his right, drew blood with his left jabs, and shook the champion at the bell with a left hook to the body. In the middle of the round, Billy cockily told Joe, "You've got a fight tonight." Louis responded, "I knows it." No other opponent ever had the impudence to speak to him in the ring. It unnerved Louis.

Conn held the advantage convincingly through the next two rounds. In the tenth, he fought toe-to-toe with the champion, giving as much as he received, if not more. Once, in a corner, Billy slipped but got up without a count. In the eleventh, the challenger was all over Louis, hitting him with every punch in his arsenal—left hooks to the head, straight lefts, and rights to the face. It was in the twelfth, however, that the most damage was inflicted. After Louis cut Conn under the eye with a left, the challenger suddenly fired a full left hook to the jaw, staggering the Champ. Louis clinched to avoid falling, but Conn continued pummeling his body with punches. The scores for the first twelve rounds on the judges' cards were seven-five, seven-four-one, and six-six, favoring Conn.

Louis, dazed when he went to his corner between rounds, was told by Chappy what he already knew: "You're losing. You gotta knock him out." In his corner, the confident challenger impatiently told Johnny Ray, "I can take this sonuvabitch out this round." His handlers told him, "No. Stick and run. You got the fight won. Stay away, kiddo. Just stick and run, stick and run. . . ."

FREDDIE GUINYARD

Chappy, at this point, was the only one that really wasn't shaking out of his boots. Mr. Roxborough, Mr. Black, myself, everybody was saying, "Oh my God, he's way behind. What's he going to do?"

But Joe would notice every move a fighter made. Every step backward, front, or side Joe watched. Billy had him seven rounds out of thirteen when he made a move he had previously made. Joe saw the opening. Instead of stepping back, he stepped forward and hit him with a left. Both Chappy and Joe had noticed this flaw in previous rounds.

Louis entered the thirteenth round determined and desperate; Conn opened it up overconfident. Leaving his original fight plan in his corner, he fought the Champ's fight instead of his own. This was Conn's downfall. He went too close to the Brown Bomber once too often. A powerful right connected with the challenger's jaw. His knees wobbled, and Louis, the consummate tactician, swept in for the kill. He shot two rights to the chin, two lefts to the head, a left, and a final chopping right—ending the fight. Conn was down and out in 2 minutes and 58 seconds of the thirteenth round.

BILLY CONN

In the thirteenth round I made an awful mistake. I didn't listen to the guys in the corner. They were telling me, "Just stay away from him. Keep boxing. You're way ahead of him." I said, "I'm going to go out and knock him out." Instead, I got knocked on my ass. I couldn't knock anybody out! He didn't hurt me, but that was the first time I was knocked out. The first telegram I got from a guy after the fight summed it up, "Remember what I told you. When you lose your head, your ass goes with it." He was right.

If it was a twelve-round fight, I would have won it. I said to Joe later, "Boy what a bad break I got with you. I could've won the championship, kept it for about six months, went around the corner and tell all the guys I'm the heavyweight champion, and then let you win it back." He looked at me and said, "You had it for twelve rounds and you couldn't keep it. How the hell were you going to keep it for six months!"

Joe and I were watching the films of that fight once. I

walked out of the room and told him, "Call me if the ending changes." Joe's comeback: "Sorry, Billy, the ending didn't change."

"I couldn't get started against that fast Conn," Louis admitted in his dressing room after the bout. But the Champ knew it was his opponent's impatience and his Irish temper that cost him the title. In response to his actions in the thirteenth round, Conn issued the classic line: "What's the sense of being Irish if you can't be dumb every now and then?" Deep in his heart, however, he knew it was something more: by the thirteenth round, he was extremely tired and bruised. "Listen. Sometimes it may look as though that guy ain't punching at all. But everything he lands on you hurts, and don't let people kid you about it," Conn explained.

Billy was upset by his loss. In an interview more than forty-five years later, Mary Louise, Conn's vivacious blonde wife, points to the photograph in the picture gallery of their Tudor home in the Squirrel Hill section of Pittsburgh, which shows tears in her husband's eyes after the fight. Although Conn insists the fight was just another bout, Mary Louise's explanation is different: "Billy just had too much to win for. His mother was dying of cancer." Maggie Conn, an Irish immigrant and Billy's beloved mother, died just a few days after the fight. "She held on to see me leading Joe Louis in the stretch," the former boxer recalls. The couple, at his mother's insistence and against her father's wishes, married the day after the funeral.

After the fight, Louis was stunned by a family calamity of his own. Marva served him with divorce papers in Chicago on the grounds of cruelty. She said he had hit her twice, and although her husband denied the charges, she received $200 per week in temporary alimony. When the case reached the court in the middle of August, the couple went into a private room and emerged smiling. Reconciled, they spent the next several weeks at Spring Hill on a second honeymoon and attended a horse show in Cleveland, where Louis had three show horses entered. In an effort to keep Marva pleasantly occupied, when Louis entered training camp later that fall, he sent his wife along with Russell Black and Wilelmena Roxborough, his managers' wives, on a cruise to Bermuda.

MARVA LOUIS SPAULDING
Mrs. Joe Louis (1935–1945, 1946–1949)

The only prejudice I ever experienced was when I took that cruise to Bermuda with Russell Black and Cutie Roxborough. We were all fair-skinned blacks, who in a white environment were often mistaken for Caucasian.

We had a marvelous time on board the ship, and when we arrived at the Princess Hotel in Bermuda, they sent people over to get our trunks. We spent seven days at the hotel, where we were assigned a table and had a welcoming party, a lovely policy they had for all new guests. One day when I was on the elevator without my friends, a group of men said to me, "We know who you are. You think you are traveling under an alias. We are going to have you evicted."

When I returned to my room, I received a call from the management. "Marva L. Barrow? Are you the wife of Joseph L. Barrow?"

I said, "Yes."

"Is Wilelmena Roxborough the wife of one of the managers of Joseph Louis Barrow?" the manager asked.

I said, "Yes."

"Is Russell Black the wife of another manager?" the manager persisted.

Again I answered, "Yes."

"Well, ladies, I'm sorry, but we do not cater to Negroes,"

he responded. "I will send up someone to help you pack. You'll have to move."

I hopped in a taxi and went to the American consulate. After some discussion between the consulate and the hotel, we were extended the same courtesies we previously received. There were certainly advantages to being Mrs. Joe Louis!

"No fightin' in August!" was Louis's ultimatum to promoter Mike Jacobs; instead, he spent time with Marva and played golf. At the Rackham Golf Course, a municipal course in Detroit, he hosted 186 black golf players at the Joe Louis Open, which had a $1000 winner's prize. Although his scores in his own tourney were unimpressive (eighty-eight in the first round and eighty-one in the second), he had shot a seventy-nine in the opening round of the National Negro Amateur two weeks before. With lessons from such pros as Bermudian pro Louis Corbin and Washingtonian Clyde Martin, he was considered an above-average golfer. His long ball was going 300 yards, but he said, "I have trouble with my left hook and just ain't got that delicate touch around the greens."

The respite was insufficient. With his marital problems, concerns about the change of his draft status from 3-A to 1-A, and exhaustion from the string of monthly bouts he had just completed, Louis refused to proceed with the September Lou Nova fight. After neither Black nor Roxborough could prevail upon him, Mike Jacobs flew to Chicago and later Detroit to try to change the Brown Bomber's mind. He succeeded, but with the concession that the fight be postponed ten days to September 29. As a result, the event had to be moved from Yankee Stadium to New York's Polo Grounds.

Immediately before the Nova fight, Louis said he was ready to serve his country if the army called. The army didn't call, but Billy Conn did. It was the start of a lifelong friendship between the two fighters, enhanced in their later years by their mutual fondness for games of chance. Reportedly, Conn greeted Louis with the words "Hello Corporal."

Louis answered, "Hello you movie actor." (Conn was in Hollywood filming *The Pittsburgh Kid*.)

"I want to be sure you take good care of Nova," continued Conn, who was looking forward to a rematch.

"You bet I'll attend to that, movie man," promised Louis.

Studying under a guru who taught him yoga and encouraged him to eat health foods, Lou Nova claimed to have a "cosmic punch" which would knock out the Brown Bomber. Although former heavyweight champion Jim Braddock said, "I wouldn't trade a good stiff clout on the whiskers for all the cosmic and dynamic junk in the world," the Champ didn't underestimate Nova. He realized that one punch from such a hard hitter could be his demise, and Louis had no intention of entering the army as anything but the heavyweight champion. "That'll be the big thing," he told reporters. "There's never been a heavyweight champion in the army before. That's me." The Louis-Nova bout, fueled by the publicity of the "cosmic punch," drew the fifteenth biggest crowd of all time—56,000 customers—bringing the gate to more than $580,000.

Except for one flurry of activity by Louis in the fourth, the fight was rather dull for five rounds. The Champ stalked the challenger around the ring to boos from the crowd and encouragements for more activity from the referee. Louis was sizing up his opponent and waiting for the opportunity to land a knockout punch. It came in the middle of the sixth round when Nova lowered his left, giving the Brown Bomber an opening. The Champ's right floored Nova for the count of nine. After Nova regained his feet, Louis by one ringside reporter's count hit him twenty-one times, driving the challenger from one corner of the ring to the other. After a final left hook left the cosmic puncher bloodied, referee Donovan stepped between them to stop the fight.

While Louis was waiting to be drafted, he went on an exhibition tour in the West for the army. He visited six or seven army camps and was found to have a superb positive influence on the troops. In St. Louis, he visited Count Basie in his hotel suite. Seeing ten pairs of shoes in the Count's closet and being mischievous by nature with a great sense of humor, Louis couldn't pass up the opportunity to play a prank on his friend. He took the left shoe of each pair back to Chicago with him, leaving the famed bandleader to fend for himself. Afterward, he and Marva went to Hollywood for a short holiday of golf and visits with friends. Some of Louis's rekindled relationships were with women friends. One woman, it was becoming readily apparent to Marva, could not adequately meet her husband's physical or psychological needs.

Meanwhile, Jacobs scheduled a rematch with Conn for the summer of 1942. Considered a great morale builder for the troops, it was expected to be a $1 million-plus gate. Louis was to receive an estimated $680,000; Conn $340,000. The younger boxer's temper, however, interfered again. A few months before the bout, Conn broke his hand in a fight with his father-in-law, Greenfield Jimmy Smith, at a christening party for his firstborn son, Tim. His father-in-law, a wealthy sportsman and onetime bootlegger who had never approved of the marriage with his daughter, provoked Conn unmercifully. The enraged boxer released a left hook—injuring his hand when Greenfield ducked and the punch caught him on the top of his skull. To add insult to injury, Billy broke a window with his right hand, cutting himself. Thereafter, every time Louis saw Conn, he'd say: "How are you getting along with your father-in-law? Does he still kick your ass?"

The rematch, however, was postponed indefinitely by Secretary of War Henry Stimson when he announced that Joe

Louis, by then in the service, would be allowed no more commercial fights for the duration of the war. The secretary disallowed the 1942 fight and future wartime bouts when he learned that a condition of the so-called charity bout was that Louis and Conn would receive $135,451.53 to pay their debts ($59,805.50 owed by Sergeant Louis to Mike Jacobs; $34,500.00 owed by Corporal Conn, also to Jacobs; and $41,146.03 owed by Sergeant Louis to John Roxborough).

When the fight was canceled, even Louis questioned whether he would return to the ring after the war. "It depends on how I feels when I gets out," he told reporters. "This war changes a man. You get to looking at things different. I can't tell how carrying a gun and thinking about getting ready to kill a man will affect me. Maybe I'll fight again. Maybe I won't."

CHAPTER NINE

Silent Revolutionary

*"You dummy. You made a big mistake. The phrase
is 'we're going to win because we're on God's side.' "*
—Billy Rowe

"Louis," Billy Rowe said, "gave action to the words of other
people. Singlehandedly he cleaned up boxing, reviving interest
in the sport, which had diminished in public favor after the
retirement of Jack Dempsey." According to some boxing experts, until Louis appeared on the scene, boxing was ruled
more by fixers than by referees. The sporting public believed
in the champion and the legitimacy of his victories. At the same
time, he opened the sport to blacks and, often unconsciously,
made inroads against discrimination in society at large. For
instance, Louis would never stay in a so-called white hotel.
Instead he went to the south side of Chicago and similar black
neighborhoods in other cities. When asked why, he'd simply
say, "I'll only stay there tonight if my colored friends can stay
in the same hotel tomorrow night."

Rowe, covering for the *Pittsburgh Courier* Louis's exhibition tour for the armed services prior to his induction, asked

for his views on the segregated state of the armed forces. After thinking about it, the Champ said, "No comment." Rowe was speechless. But the boxer continued, "When you gets to a telephone, I want you to call Uncle Mike and tell him I accepts his proposal to fight a charity bout for the Navy Relief Society." That was an extraordinary statement. The navy allowed blacks to serve only in messboy capacity. The words were Louis's way of putting the armed services on the spot. "There's lots of things wrong," he said. "Anybody knows that. But Hitler ain't going to fix them."

VERNON E. JORDAN, JR.
Former President, National Urban League, Inc.

While some blacks believe that every black with a name should be out there carrying the banner, I believe that there are many ways to do that. Joe Louis carried it the best way he knew how—by using the skill with which he was endowed. In that sense, he was a leader.

Joe Louis was an American hero, especially during the war years. But while white Americans loved him and cheered for him, he was still a black. And the rules applied to all blacks. They cheered for him when he went into the Army, but he went into a segregated Army. He fought to make the world safe for democracy, but in a segregated situation. The people that were cheering for Joe Louis were the same people who when Lena Horne went to Arkansas to sing for the troops put the German prisoners in better seats than the black enlisted men. There were many contradictions at that time.

Still, some blacks disagreed with Louis's position, denigrating him and his views and calling him an "Uncle Tom." A statement was released by a congregation of black intellectuals in

New York saying that not all blacks were "wholeheartedly and unreservedly supporting the present war effort." In response, Louisville's black weekly, *The Louisville Leader*, wrote an editorial that summarized what probably was the position of most blacks: "There is more than one way by which we may be triumphant in our quest for victory, and there is more than one course which we may follow in the fight to reach a desired goal—and between Joe Louis and the Negro leaders assembled in New York we take the boy who got his training in the cotton fields over and above the men who sat at the feet of the masters in education."

At the same time, Rear Admiral Adolphus Andrews, commandant of the Third Naval District, announced that Louis would become the first heavyweight champion in the history of boxing to put his title on the line for charity. In addition, Jacobs agreed to contribute his services as promoter, the Garden remitted half the rental, and Buddy Baer, the challenger, contributed 2½ percent of his 15 percent purse. The money, more than $88,000, went to the Navy Relief Society, an organization providing emergency financial services to naval officers, enlisted men, and their families.

In this twentieth defense of his title, the Brown Bomber faced Buddy Baer, who had knocked him to the wide apron of the Griffith Stadium ring in Washington, D.C., the previous May. No one expected the fight to be an easy one. Baer was big, tough, and, as he had proved in his previous bout against Louis, not intimidated by the champion. The risk of losing the title was a legitimate one. No one could have expressed it better than *New York Times* reporter John Kieran, when he said: "Win, lose or draw, Joe Louis now moves into a class by himself in heavyweight history. . . . This 'beau geste' crowns it all."

As the boxers sat in their respective corners at Madison Square Garden on January 9, a host of dignitaries was introduced. But the glory of the evening went to Joe Louis. At the conclusion of his speech, Wendell Willkie—mispronouncing Louis's name—said, "Joe Louee, your magnificent example in risking for nothing your championship belt, won literally with toil and sweat and tears, prompts us to say, 'We thank you.' And in view of your attitude, it is impossible for me to see how any American can think of discrimination in terms of race, creed, or color."

The fight turned out to be a rout, equal in some reporters' minds to Louis's 1938 Schmeling knockout. In front of some 18,500 fans, the champion demolished the gifted 26-year-old Baer in 2 minutes and 56 seconds of the first round.

At the bell, Baer rushed the champion, throwing a right to his body. From then on, though, it was all Louis. Two left jabs to Baer's chin, a brutal right cross, and more than a dozen blows to the head staggered the challenger. Fighting back weakly, Baer was dropped by a right cross for a nine count. Then a left hook, a right cross, and a right uppercut to the head dropped the unsteady challenger for the second time. Rolling over twice, he groped for the rope to pull himself up, but it was too late. The referee had reached ten.

"I can't say it was my best fight ever, but I sure felt I was right at that weight," said the Bomber afterward. He was fighting at a record-high 206¾ pounds. Heavier by 43¼ pounds and standing 5 inches taller, Baer agreed, "He's the best. Why didn't he put on that weight long ago?" Senator Prentiss Brown (a Democrat from Michigan) the next day on the Senate floor commended Louis for his exemplary citizenship, sportsmanship, boxing abilities, and clean living—which "are now crowned with supreme generosity."

Almost as the Senator spoke, Louis joined the army. (Months before, he had turned down a commission as lieutenant-commander in the navy, saying he didn't want special consideration.) Minutes before the Baer fight he had received his orders to report to his local draft board in Chicago. Roxborough concealed them from Louis until the next day, whereupon he, Julian Black, Mike Jacobs, and John Roxborough went to the Selective Service Board Number 20 in New York to request a transfer. On January 12 Louis went to Fort Jay, on Governors Island in New York, for a physical examination. As might have been expected, he passed. "This will be the biggest fight," he said to reporters in his last interview before becoming a $21-a-month private in the army. "I hope I can do as good for Uncle Sam as I did for Uncle Mike."

Two days later, accompanied by Black, Louis went by limousine to Camp Upton to be inducted into the army. Mike Jacobs followed in his car, and a chartered bus filled with reporters followed the promoter. The cavalcade met the 11:55 a.m. train arriving from New York with other inductees. Leaving his car, Louis marched with the other young men into the camp, where they were separated into two lines: the boxer was put in the black line and later assigned to the black barracks. When reporter Billy Rowe turned to leave, Louis—referring to the segregated quarters and mess facilities—said, "This is the real battlefield."

FREDDIE GUINYARD

Joe Louis's Friend and Personal Secretary

Joe was nervous when he joined the Army. After he was inducted he said to me, "You'll be here pretty soon." To make me know he was nervous, he repeated himself a little later. I said, "My God, leaving his friends has got to him." I felt the same way he did, but I tried not to show it.

Several weeks after he was inducted, Louis received the Boxing Writers' Association Edward J. Neil Memorial plaque, an award presented to the "boxer who has done the most for the sport during the year." The previous December the writers selected him unanimously. Jack Dempsey, the former heavyweight champion; Billy Conn, ex-light-heavyweight titleholder; and Henry Armstrong, who once held the featherweight, light-weight, and welterweight crowns at one time, had received the previous awards. In the opinion of sportswriters, no other heavyweight boxer had equaled Louis's accomplishments of the previous twelve months. He had defended his title seven times over six months, knocking out all his opponents, and through his conduct both inside and outside the ring had set an excellent example for youth and athletes alike.

VERNON E. JORDAN, JR.

In the Atlanta public housing project in which I grew up in the late 1930s, University Homes, the names Joe Louis and Franklin Roosevelt were of equal importance. As a boy, Joe Louis's name evoked pride, reverence, hero worship, and achievement.

I remember one particular Negro History Week, a big event at my elementary school. My best friend, Frank Hill, was selected to play Joe Louis in the school play. I was selected to be William Grant Steel, the symphony conductor. I can vividly remember how jealous I was of Frank. While Steel was an important Negro, he wasn't a hero to us. When Frank went out on the stage in boxing trunks, tennis shoes, and boxing gloves, the kids in the auditorium cheered. When I went on the stage as William Grant Steel, there was silence.

Looking back on it, I see that Joe Louis made us feel pride, feel our blackness, allowed us to believe that every-thing was achievable if you worked for it. Despite the system, we could believe that there were no limits if you put forth a lot of individual effort.

Private Joe Louis Barrow received his award at ceremonies at New York City's Ruppert Brewery, wearing his khaki uniform. Although former heavyweight titleholder Gene Tunney was also honored for organizing boxing activities in the navy, this was Louis's night. He not only received the Edward J. Neil Memorial plaque and *The Ring*'s trophy as Fighter of the Year that night but felt the love and affection of all in attendance.

Former New York Mayor Jimmy Walker, emphasizing the particular responsibilities and pressures on a black fighter, said: "Joe Louis, your personal conduct puts you far above the average. . . . I think you have been wisest of all with your comments after fights. . . . You fought your way to the championship and refused to talk your way out of it. . . . On January 9 you took your present and future into your own hands . . . all your assets . . . and bet them all on patriotism. . . . No wonder you won! . . . I know you'll be a good soldier. . . . You have made everyone proud to be an American. . . . You have placed a rose on Abraham Lincoln's grave." The 250 individuals present rose in support of those words.

But if Walker took the honors for oratory that evening, Louis's simple comments won the hearts of those who were present. "I never thought I'd ever feel as good again as the night I won the championship," he said. "Tonight I feel better than ever in my life. I thank you for all this, and I hope I never will do anything that I'll be sorry for."

Private Barrow returned to Camp Upton to complete his basic training. At the army's insistence, he was granted an exception so he could be near his temporary training camp at Fort Dix, New Jersey. The Champ was preparing for his upcoming fight against Abe Simon on March 27 for the Army Emergency Relief, a fund to benefit families of all soldiers.

When reporters arrived at the training headquarters, possessing the necessary two highly prized passes (one signed by the Post provost marshal and the other by the Army Information Service), they heard strains of "Things Ain't What They Used to Be" from a standard-issue phonograph. As one observed, "things ain't." Trainer Jack Blackburn, for the first time in Louis's professional career, was not at Louis's side, for example. He was in Provident Hospital in Chicago with pneumonia. This didn't make things any easier for the champion. Not only that, less than four months earlier, Dr. Chester Ames, a black Detroit physician who had been with Louis since he left the amateur ranks, had died. More than offering medical expertise to Louis, Dr. Ames had understood the champion's emotional and mental makeup. He whisked him away from crowds when necessary and advised his managers on when he should and shouldn't fight. Louis, losing first his left and now his right hand, spoke with Chappy daily by telephone. "Chappy says I'll win in the third round," the Champ said. "Well, I'll have to make good for Chappy because it will make him feel better."

Although the rest of the Brown Bomber's regular training team was present—Bill Bottoms, the cook; Jimmy, the waiter; manager John Roxborough; assistant trainer Manny Seamon; Freddie Guinyard, the personal secretary; and Walter St. Dennis, the press agent—Corporal Bob Sherman, who was teaching Joe the art of war, was also in attendance. In addition to the usual boxing training routines, Louis could be seen being put through his paces on drill grounds two hours every day, on the rifle range, and in sessions on the use of the gas mask.

Among those who received passes to Louis's training camp were 1900 soldiers from the base, a dozen boxing reporters, Boxing Commission Chairman John Phelan, Boxing Commissioner Bill Brown, and Captain Dorsey Owings of the Army Morale Division. The routine and many of the observers might have changed, but the Brown Bomber had only one thing on his mind. "I want to win this fight for the army *and* for Chappy," he told reporters.

The odds were in his favor, but were not quite as lopsided

as Chappy had predicted. Even money said the champion would win inside five rounds; two-to-one that Louis would win inside ten; and three-to-one that he would win in a fight that didn't go the full fifteen rounds. The odds makers remembered that Simon had lasted thirteen rounds against the Brown Bomber the previous year.

On March 10, a few weeks before the bout, Private Louis was asked to attend a Navy Relief Society dinner and show in Madison Square Garden. After a host of dignitaries offered prepared remarks, the titleholder unexpectedly was asked to say a few words. Though unprepared, Louis's words were succinct—and memorable. "I have only done what any red-blood American would do," Louis concluded to a standing ovation. "We gonna do our part, and we will win, because God's on our side." On visiting the publicity department of the Twentieth Century Sporting Club earlier in the day, Louis declined publicity director Harry Markson's offer to write a few lines for him in case he was called upon to speak at the rally. His celebrated ad lib that evening causes Markson even today to lament that he "hadn't been the author of that line."

BILLY ROWE
Joe Louis's Friend and Journalist

"How'd I do," said Joe after his speech before the Navy Relief Fund bout. I said, "You dummy. You made a big mistake. The phrase is 'We're going to win because we're on God's side.'" Joe said, "Well, I guess I blew it."

Your dad went to his hotel to go to bed. The next morning I went to the hotel to pick him up for breakfast. When I knocked, he opened the door and threw the newspapers in my face. "Who's the dummy, now?" he said. His phrase "We'll win because God's on our side" became one of the slogans of the war.

Joe could be profound about many things, but especially

race relations. He wanted blacks to have exactly what everybody else had. He wanted Americans to be Americans. We had a conversation once about the words "Negro" and "colored." "There is pride and purpose in a race, but what is there in a color," he said. At that time, propaganda made most people anti-African. Joe thought that most Negroes didn't want to be African because they didn't want to be under the control of the "white Tarzan." He always had some off-the-wall way of saying something that was profound.

Prior to the fight Louis bought $2500 worth of tickets at various seat prices and gave them to his fellow soldiers. Needless to say, he had a strong rooting gallery at Madison Square Garden that night. And in his corner he had Larry Amadee, John Henry Lewis's former trainer; Julian Black; and new trainer Manny Seamon, who had permanently replaced Chappy.

The first round was slow. It took almost 1½ minutes before the first blow, a right by Louis, landed. Quickly following up with lefts and rights, however, the Bomber dazed Simon. In the second, Louis maintained his momentum. A left hook sent the challenger flying into the champion's corner, lefts and rights spun him into the ropes, and a right to the head floored him. The wobbly challenger was saved by the bell. Joe tried to end the fight in round three, as Chappy had predicted, but when he saw he couldn't, he slowed the pace and waited for an opening. A low blow by Simon gave the round to Louis. Recovering in round four, Simon scored with flicking left jabs and a blow to his opponent's stomach. Nevertheless, the tide changed in the fifth round. Louis landed a solid right to the challenger's jaw, knocking him to the canvas. Again at the count of five, Simon was saved by the bell.

The challenger was dropped to the canvas again in the sixth round. Edging his way to the ropes by the count of five, he reached one knee by seven. By nine, Simon's hand was off the ropes and he was almost erect. By ten, he was upright. Regardless, he was counted out by referee Eddie Joseph. Joe Louis had won his twenty-first championship bout—for the army and for Chappy. And more important, by fighting an intelligent and crafty match on his own, Louis proved he was not Blackburn's puppet.

His army career enlarged Louis's circle of influential friends. One, Boston Celtics basketball player Ash Resnick, was inducted into the service with Joe on New York's Governor's Island. Although Louis went into Special Services and Resnick into the Air Force, Resnick subsequently became Louis's employer (at the Thunderbird Casino and later at Caesar's Palace in Las Vegas), golfing partner, and constant companion.

Another individual who played a key role in Louis's life was Truman Gibson, a black Chicago lawyer. During the war, Gibson, a civilian aide to the secretary of war, was responsible for guiding the War Department's policies toward black soldiers and civilians involved in the war effort. The two had met previously when the lawyer was an associate in the law firm retained by Julian Black to handle his personal affairs. On occasion, the then-unknown fighter would accompany Black to the firm. He and Gibson were about the same age, and they would chat while Black and a senior partner conducted business.

TRUMAN GIBSON
Louis's Attorney

When I think back on my first recollections of Joe sitting in my law office I remember him eating apples and always reading something. Although he was quiet, he would occasionally say something which would let you know he knew what was going on around him.

After basic training—with Gibson's assistance—Louis was transferred to Fort Riley, Kansas, home of the last horse cavalry unit. At least once a week, Joe called Gibson about blacks' problems at the base. On more than one occasion they involved Jackie Robinson, who was also stationed at Fort Riley. Louis, through Gibson, helped Robinson and several other blacks eager but stymied in their quest to enter Officer Candidate School (OCS) to get their commissions. Shortly thereafter, Louis again called for Gibson's assistance. It seems that while in OCS, Robinson verbally lambasted a white drill officer who called a black soldier a "stupid nigger son of a bitch." Several expensive gifts for the commanding general later, Robinson was able to complete OCS successfully.

Louis and Robinson, then known only as a former football star from UCLA, teamed up to achieve several successes on segregation issues at Fort Riley. One instance stands out. The black section of the segregated canteen, much smaller than the white part, always seemed to have long lines. Louis and Robinson exerted pressure on the base commander, Robinson was made morale officer, and more seats in the canteen were given to blacks. It was a small—but significant—victory for the times.

Years later, writing about his hero worship for Louis, Jackie Robinson said: "I sincerely believe it was his worth and understanding, plus his conduct in the ring, that paved the way for the black man in professional sports. . . . My love for Joe Louis goes much beyond what he did in the ring, or even his desire to right an injustice." Louis, in turn, respected the man who broke the color barrier in baseball for his outspoken efforts on behalf of blacks. "Jackie didn't bite his tongue for nothing," he told reporters admiringly. "I just don't have the guts, you might call it, to say what he says. And I don't talk as good either, that's for sure. But you need a lot of different types to make the world better."

Louis was well aware that many blacks thought he didn't do all he could have for the civil rights movement. But he also knew his limitations. "Some folks shout, some holler, some march, and some don't," he explained without animosity toward those who belittled him. "They do it their way; I do it mine. I got nothing to be 'shamed of. I stand for right and work for it hard 'cause I know what it means not to have the rights what God give us."

TRUMAN GIBSON

I know what Joe did and experienced during the war. He had a great capacity for feeling. He was a deep person and he resented the way Negroes were treated. You have to live through it to know what black soldiers put up with during the war. Every bus driver in the South was deputized and armed. His sole mission in life was to make Negro soldiers get to the back of the bus. It might be only a slight exaggeration to say more Negroes were killed by white public bus drivers in the South than were killed by the Nazis.

In fact, that was the end of Jackie [Robinson]. Jackie was commissioned and sent to Camp Swift in Texas. One day, he was going from town back to camp. The bus driver saw him and told him, "Okay, nigger, get to the back of the bus." When Robinson momentarily hesitated, the driver pulled a pistol. It was a fatal mistake. Jackie, who was hotheaded, took the pistol, broke every tooth in the guy's mouth with it and had it in his head he was going to kill him. After that incident, the U.S. Army (honorably) discharged Jackie for the good of the service.

Louis saw all of these things and burned inside. He never accepted special treatment, was always available for exhibitions, and bought his fellow soldier gifts—not the least of which was Jackie Robinson's OTC graduation class's uniforms. He was involved to an extent that few people realized.

When the champion's training was completed, he joined the

Special Services Branch. A troop of champions including Louis, Sugar Ray Robinson, and Bob Montgomery, a lightweight champion, was organized to tour army bases in the United States, England, Italy, the Aleutians, and Africa. Louis became Gibson's eyes and ears on segregation issues as he traveled the world. From Fort Bragg, North Carolina, he called Gibson to report that blacks were not allowed on the same buses as white soldiers. The call resulted in a series of discussions that brought to an end bus segregation at military posts, camps, and stations. Later, Louis and Sugar Ray Robinson created a cause célèbre regarding segregation at Camp Sibert, Alabama. And from England, Louis relayed to Gibson the news that blacks were not allowed in movie theaters. An investigation resulted in the integration of the theaters.

BOB HOPE
Entertainer and Boxing Fan

Joe's path and mine crossed during World War II in London, while we were both entertaining the troops overseas. He was well received by the enlisted men.

Billy Conn and I were touring together when we met Joe. (I had met Billy in Nuremberg. He said, "Get me on your show, will you?" I happened to meet the General who headed Special Services a few minutes after I had spoken with Billy and asked him if I could use Billy in a boxing routine that I had in the show.) Joe said to Conn, "Keep your nose clean; we're going to make a lot of money in the next fight." He did, and they did.

In private life, when he was under the direct influence of his managers, Louis avoided racially embarrassing situations. But now that he was on his own, his brooding nature emerged.

Louis, in a significant way, changed during the war. For instance, once an airline delayed a plane for him when he was late reaching the airport from an army exhibition in Oklahoma City. As Louis walked up, a white businessman was complaining to the pilot, "What nigger is so important that I have to be late for my appointment?" Seeing the heavyweight champion, he apologized, but Louis pushed his hand away, looking at him in disgust. His experience in the army had crystallized his views. He truly realized how much he represented all blacks.

RACHEL ROBINSON
(Mrs. Jackie Robinson) Chairperson,
Jackie Robinson Development Corp.

During the War, I was a student at UCLA during the day and worked as a riveter at Lockheed at night. One day I received a call from a Joe Barrow who said he was an Army buddy of Jack's and he was going to come by and "honk at me." I was a little bit snobbish at the time and I was offended at the expression. So when he arrived on the front steps, I was still in the bathtub. My mother came flying through the door. "You won't believe who's on the front porch. Joe Barrow is JOE LOUIS!" I was stunned, embarrassed, but most of all thrilled.

It just served to illustrate what I thought he would do— not make a big appointment and have me waiting on the front steps for him. It was the modesty and simplicity of it which impressed me.

Louis's military record was indisputably impressive. In addition to contributing the purses of two heavyweight championship bouts to service charities, he put on close to 100 exhibitions for the troops and traveled more than 70,000 miles visiting soldiers at countless bases and hospitals around the world. During these boxing and physical fitness tours, he spent the day shaking hands, giving speeches, and boxing with his former sparring partner, First Sergeant George Nicholson. As the tour wore on, he became more and more comfortable as a public orator. Louis was gracious, warm, and good-humored with his fellow soldiers, who threw endless boxing questions at him. The most frequent queries, according to *Life* magazine, were "How much do you weigh?" (Answer: "Just 215 pounds, 10 pounds over my fighting weight.") And "Who was the hardest puncher you ever fought?" (Answer: "Baer, but he never hit me.") For his contributions during the war, the champion, when he was discharged, received the Legion of Merit medal "for exceptional meritorious conduct."

TRUMAN GIBSON

After the war, I went to New York to tell Joe he was to be discharged from the service. I met him in Mike Jacobs's office and drove with him up to camp, but still hadn't told him he was about to be discharged. About halfway up, Joe stopped the car. He said, "Guys are getting out now. There's $10,000 in it for you if I get out now." Mischievously, I said, "I tell you what you do, Joe. Meet me in Mike's office at 9:30 tomorrow morning and we'll talk about it."

The next day we met in Mike's office and I told him that as of 9:00 that morning he was ex-Sergeant Joe Louis Barrow. (P.S. I didn't collect the $10,000.)

During his four years of army service, Louis grew as an individual. Even though he was guided in his responsibilities by the army, he was forced to think and to act on his own. He was comfortable with himself for the first time. Yet while he was establishing a new life—and position in American history —the underpinnings of his prewar life were disappearing. Even though he was unaware of it at the time, this period was to prove disastrous to his future. Indeed, when he left the army, he did so without some of his closest advisers and his wife— and irrevocably in debt to the Internal Revenue Service. Life would never be the same for the champion.

Louis's foundation actually began to crumble with the death of Chappy in 1942. He received the news on the rifle range at Camp Upton and cried for the first time in his life. "All that I am as a fighter, a champion, I owe to Jack Blackburn. He was teacher, father, brother, nurse, best pal to me, and I'll never get over his going away from here. I'll be only half as good as I was. Oh, they say I'll forget Chappy as time goes on, but I know different," Joe told reporters. "He was my sparkplug for nine years."

Meanwhile, there were losses of a different kind. In 1943 John Roxborough, the closest of his managers, was sent to prison for two years for his involvement in the numbers racket. For appearance's sake, until he was released, Roxborough refused to have Louis meet him at the prison. For the same reason, he decided not to manage the champion in the future. During the war, Louis also separated from his friend and personal secretary, Freddie Guinyard. As he had with Billy Rowe, Louis dismissed his assistant for interfering with his free-spending ways.

FREDDIE GUINYARD

With Mr. Roxborough in prison, Chappy dead and Mr. Black in Chicago, I felt a responsibility to Joe. Mr. Jacobs gave us a certain amount of money to run the training camp. Every time someone had to get something, I had to sign the check. Joe kept asking for money, I kept signing and he kept losing it on the golf course. I understood what Joe was doing. Golf is like pool. You keep playing because you think you can beat your opponent in the next game.

I spoke to Joe. I said, "You're here to train. Not to play golf." He wanted to know how the hell I got so smart all of a sudden. We had a little argument. He said, "It's my money." Being from South Carolina, I was stubborn. I signed the balance of the checks, got in my car and come back to Detroit. I went up to the prison and spoke to Roxborough. He told me, "Freddie, you and Joe come off the coal pile together; you help him get back there." I shouldn't have done it, but I couldn't turn around now.

But even after I was in Detroit in my own business, Joe would tell fellas in the Army in Europe, "I'll see what my buddy can do for your people over there in America." Then he called or had somebody from Washington call me to take care of this or that for him. He said, "Don't tell them I did it." But it was his thought, his heart, his manner that made him do things for people. He spent a lot of money that way and he never got a nickel's worth of credit for it.

As for Marva, she was finally fed up with Louis's womanizing and flamboyant lifestyle, and in 1945 she filed for divorce. As part of the settlement, she received 25 percent of his future purses, instead of a previously agreed-upon flat payment of $25,000. Julian Black had refused to lend Louis the money, thereby precipitating the permanent split of the boxer and his manager, and the final settlement with his wife.

By 1946, there was no one around Louis who could provide him with sound, sensible advice and have any chance of the champion's accepting it. On the other hand, Mike Jacobs, a shrewd businessman, gave Louis all the money he requested. Jacobs knew that if he kept the boxer in debt, he would have to continue to fight for him. In the final analysis, Louis's managers Roxborough and Black did not take advantage of him, as many think; when it came to spending money, Louis was his own man.

CHAPTER TEN

Aging Fighter

"I thought I won it [the 1947 fight] very big."
—Jersey Joe Walcott

It took only two years to transform Joe Louis from a poor man to a rich man. And perhaps the speed with which he gained both fame and fortune explains the way he chose to live. "If you dance, you gotta pay the piper," he once reflected. "Believe me, I danced and I paid and I left him a big, fat tip." Money, Louis felt, existed for only one purpose—it was to be spent. He became well known for his extraordinary generosity, and even when he had no cash on hand, he would borrow money from one person to give it to another with the idea that "I didn't have nothin' once."

MARVA LOUIS SPAULDING
Mrs. Joe Louis (1935–1945, 1946–1949)

When we were first married, your father was very cautious with his money. It stemmed from his childhood. He said when he was a youngster, his family was so poor that they didn't have proper clothing or heat in the house. His pants were so ragged that when he went to Detroit's Brewster Gym, he kept his back to the wall. He told me he was never going to be poor again.

His first investments were the best investments he made. With his early paychecks, he bought his mother and his sisters houses in Detroit. It was a great shock to me when he changed. The more fights he won and the more important he became, the more sycophants he attracted. To me, they were just leeches. Your father supported them in a very expensive, first-class way.

Although Louis's total career earnings topped $4.6 million, he died owing the Internal Revenue Service more than $1.25 million. It took time, but when Louis finally realized the bind he was in, he hired Truman Gibson as his personal lawyer and adviser and Ted Jones as his accountant. The two quickly discovered that Louis's tax problems stemmed from two sources —inappropriate deductions and an improperly structured settlement agreement with Marva. Both problems were created by individuals employed by Mike Jacobs.

During the war, Louis spent something like $250,000, mostly on gifts for soldiers. Following the advice of Nathan Ellenbogen, Mike Jacobs's accountant, these were itemized as business deductions, which were subsequently disqualified by the IRS. Meanwhile, Jacobs repeatedly extended credit (some say more than $150,000) to Louis, who spent the money freely. Jacobs in this way made all the fighters he promoted beholden to him. He kept them in perpetual servitude. Indeed, when Louis was asked why he borrowed so much money from the promoter, he shrugged and said, "Just because it was there. It was really more than I needed." Gibson concurred with Louis's assessment. "Joe was a chemist where money was concerned. He could absolutely destroy it.'' Louis expected his managers to come up with as much money as he wanted, whenever he asked for it. He went deeper and deeper into debt, eventually reaching the point where no amount of future earnings could possibly cover it.

Meanwhile, Sol Strauss, Jacobs's lawyer and later his successor as promoter for Madison Square Garden, drew up Joe and Marva's divorce agreement. The contract read that payment was ''in lieu of alimony.'' As such, it was taxable to Louis. If it had stated ''in lieu of alimony *and* support,'' the sum would have been taxable to Marva.

By the time Louis was discharged from the army, he owed the IRS a deferred tax bill of $115,000, plus more than $150,000 to Jacobs and $40,000 to Roxborough. Therefore his advisers scheduled a rematch against Billy Conn. Louis was four years older and out of condition, as was Conn, and had an entirely new backup team. Marshall Miles, approached by Louis in 1944 to manage his boxing affairs, had grown up in the numbers racket in Buffalo. Manny Seamon, an assistant trainer under Chappy, became his trainer. Formerly responsible for selecting sparring partners at the Louis training camps, Seamon had previously trained lightweight champion Benny Leonard.

Prior to the Conn fight, Louis signed a contract to make a publicity tour, which turned out to be both physically and psychologically draining. Although Joe Louis could stand up for the rights of blacks in the army, he didn't have the same authority or power in the civilian world. His managers, moreover, preferred not to make waves.

MARSHALL MILES

Joe Louis's Friend and Manager

I was introduced to Joe by Roxborough in 1931. He asked me to come to Detroit from Buffalo. He wanted to introduce me to the next heavyweight champion of the world. I laughed at the thought.

I officially became Joe's manager thirteen years later. As soon as he got out of the Army, because he needed the money, he made a deal to go on a publicity tour with a band for 30 days throughout the South. He made $1000 per stage appearance. When he told me about it, I tried to get him out of it. He wouldn't go for it because he said he'd throw the whole band out of work if he reneged. Occasionally on that tour, we had racial trouble in the hotels we'd stay in. In Texas, the manager of the hotel we were booked in met us at the airport. He says, "Mr. Miles, all I ask of you is that you don't use the dining room." They gave us a whole floor and set up a dining room in one of the suites for us.

After that tour, Louis began training in earnest for the Conn fight. But the dedication and intensity he had shown in previous camps were not apparent. Nor was he the same fighting machine physically that he had been. Louis now weighted 240 pounds. His jowls were puffy. His previously solid-as-steel muscles were soft. And it was difficult for him to get the weight off before he could even start boxing. Every day Seamon would bathe the Champ in epsom salts and hot water. He'd do roadwork in the morning and take long walks in the afternoon. To warm up for the Conn match, Louis went on an exhibition tour through the Northwest, and between November and December 1945 he fought nine exhibition bouts.

But the change was not only physical—there was an alteration in attitude. Something clearly had happened to the heavyweight champion during the war. Marva believes it may have been the constant traveling to perform exhibitions for the troops. Others suggest it was the lack of a demanding athletic regimen. But Freddie Guinyard thinks the reason lies elsewhere.

FREDDIE GUINYARD

Joe Louis's Friend and Personal Secretary

Marshall Miles called me from the Pompton Lakes, New Jersey, training camp two weeks before the Conn fight. He said, "I can't do anything with Joe. He plays golf; sometimes show people come around here and he stays up until eleven or twelve o'clock. And I think he misses you."

I went down. I spoke to him casually to find out what was bothering him. It was financial. Mr. Jacobs had loaned him some money. In addition, his debt to the IRS had risen from $69,000 to over $100,000. In return for money he owed Marva, he had given her part of his boxing contract. He had lost a lot on the golf course, and he had given a lot of his money to friends. So when he got a fight, he owed the fight already. When you're paying off from behind, you're always in trouble.

From the start, Joe could always get money from Mr. Jacobs. I remember the first time. The promoter had come out to Detroit to see Mr. Roxborough and Mr. Black. When he was getting ready to leave, Joe asked him if he could ride to the airport with him. Joe took his coat and put it over his arm and helped him into the car. When he got to the airport, he asked if he could borrow $10,000. Mr. Jacobs gave it to him readily. Laughingly he said, "I can hold my own coat for ten grand!"

At the urging of managers and friends, Louis finally concentrated on his training and entered the June 19, 1946, fight at 207 pounds, only 7 pounds heavier than he had been for the 1941 bout and determined to win. Conn himself was 14 pounds heavier. Indeed, although Louis was able to get into reasonably good shape considering his four-year layoff, his handlers knew Conn was in trouble. They had sent informers into Conn's training camp during the previous months to check on his condition, and the reports indicated that he was overweight and that his reflexes were considerably slower than they had been.

Despite all this, the eagerly awaited rematch made ring history: ringside seats in Yankee Stadium went for $100 and the gate of 45,000 fans hit almost $2 million. Not only was this the first major athletic contest after World War II, it was the first televised boxing event. Fans who had been deprived during the long war years were ready—and unabashedly enthusiastic.

JIM COX

Freelance Journalist

I was crossing the country with a trainload of U.S. soldiers coming back from San Diego to Virginia to be discharged during the Louis-Conn fight. At every little town, we'd lean out the window and shout: "Who won the fight?"

For this fight, Manny Seamon had developed a strategy in training camp that Louis successfully transferred to the ring. "You will become the boxer," Seamon advised, "and take the play away from him." Louis, carrying out the plan, surprised Conn, a notoriously slow starter, by coming out boxing. He threw jabs to his opponent's head and quickly had him back-pedaling. Conn found he didn't have the speed of his prewar days, and as a result, his dancing lacked the confidence of the 1941 bout. Before the second round, Seamon reminded his boxer, "Stick to our plans, Joe. You already have the upper hand by showing him that you can box . . . and keeping up with him." That round went as the first. Conn just didn't have the power or the speed.

Flicking jabs and left hooks, Conn tried to pick up the pace in the third round. Although his punches didn't have much power, he won the round on points. From the fourth through the eighth, however, it was all Louis. The Brown Bomber continued to play his opponent's game: jabs to the head, hooks to the body, and an occasional right cross. In desperation, Conn tried a Max Baer tactic in the fifth. He stopped and started to move his arms like a windmill. Joe ignored his opponent's clownish antics and continued his punishing boxing. Twice— in the fourth round and again in the sixth—when Conn slipped, Louis, always the sportsman, backed up and let the challenger regain his footing before proceeding.

Pelted by jabs in round eight, Conn was backed against the ropes. Louis pursued his advantage, throwing a left and an overhand right. Staggered, Conn clung to the champion in an attempt to remain upright. It was useless. Louis backed away, and after a right uppercut and a left hook to the jaw, Conn fell on his back. Always game, Conn attempted to regain his footing but, spent, fell back to the canvas.

ADELE LOGAN ALEXANDER
(Mrs. Clifford L. Alexander, Jr.)
Joe Louis's Fan and Admirer

During those years, my family lived at 555 Edgecombe Avenue in New York City. It was the same building in which Joe had an apartment. We would see him going in and out of the elevator, and he would always say hello. As Cliff once said, Joe was "hometown." Although he came from Detroit, New Yorkers, because he often fought here and had a residence here, thought he was ours.

I was eight years old at the time of the 1946 Louis-Conn fight. I remember because I won the family betting pool and because I got to stay up late to listen to the fight. Because I was eight, I picked the eighth round for Louis to knock out Conn. Everybody said, "The child wants that round. Let the child put her quarter on that round."

When Louis was asked in his dressing room whether he was as good as he used to be, he answered with restraint, "I don't know. I wasn't tested." For his part, Conn called the bout a "stinkeroo." Johnny Ray, his manager, cried. He was more depressed at that moment than his boxer because he was the first to realize that Conn was finished.

Years later, Conn remains realistic about his role relative to Louis's in boxing history. As a guest of Pittsburgh Steelers owner Art Rooney, he once visited the football team's locker room. When Conn was introduced to a group of white players, they politely said hello, clearly not impressed by the individual before them. With his usual Irish blarney, he shouted over to a group of black players, "Do you know who Joe Louis was?" As they all nodded, he turned back to the white men and said sarcastically, "And you sons of bitches don't know me."

Although the Louis-Conn rematch had the second largest purse in the history of boxing, the champion's share went to the repayment of debts. The IRS received back taxes, Mike Jacobs was repaid his loan, and Marva was paid one-third of the manager's percentage. (A trust fund for daughter Jacqueline was created with her share of the proceeds.) Of the $600,000 purse, Louis had little left—and still had not paid taxes on the income just earned.

Three months later—Louis had taken time off to remarry Marva—the champion was lined up against Tami Mauriello, a journeyman heavyweight from the Bronx with twelve losses on his record. Louis was up to 212 pounds by this time, and he was not in top condition for the fight. Mauriello took advantage of this by starting out aggressively. In quick succession, he feinted with his right, started a left hook, and plowed an overhand right into Louis's jaw. A suddenly excited audience saw Louis thrown against the ropes. Mauriello, sensing that the champion was dazed, threw another right and a left uppercut. Louis, on the defensive, clung to his opponent until he recovered. Then with a left hook he knocked the challenger down. Another left hook and a glancing right sent Mauriello to the canvas a second—and final—time. Louis, in reaction to the knockdown, allowed himself a smile in the ring for the first time in his professional career. "The fight was the last time I really felt like my old self. I had complete control, energy, power," he later explained.

DON DUNPHY
Radio Broadcaster

Joe may have been slightly lucky this time. Mauriello was a very slow-moving heavyweight. After your dad pushed him into the ropes, Mauriello was almost like a kid who in desperation backs up and fires a punch. He released a tremendous right-hand shot that drove Joe completely across the ring to the other side against the ropes.

Prior to the Mauriello meeting, Louis and his managers agreed that the proceeds of the fight would be used to pay his IRS debt. No one was to be paid expenses. The bout brought Louis approximately $100,000, which was left with Jacobs until January when the taxes were due to be paid. When Miles asked for the money, however, he found that the promoter had allowed Louis to withdraw all but $500 of it. The boxer had invested $40,000 in the Rumboogie, a Chicago nightclub owned by a friend, and freely spent the remainder.

MARSHALL MILES

I can't say that Mike Jacobs was detrimental to your father's career. He got him the title. But he got a little greedy. He never did give your dad anything. He wrote down every

nickel that Joe got from him during the war and made sure
he was repaid.

We got beat out of a lot of money in Joe's later fights.
Jacobs put in extra seats ringside. We had to pay 40 percent
of the cost of building them. We never did get the benefit
out of those seats.

Louis spent the remainder of 1946 and much of 1947 traveling
on an exhibition tour throughout Central and South America.
He was an accomplished showman and much in demand for
such exhibition work. He generally was paid $10,000 a city,
plus expenses. Marva started the tour with him, fell in love
with Mexico City, and remained there for the birth of their
second child, Joe Louis Barrow, Jr. During this fifteen-month
layoff from boxing, the Champ also bowled a lot, averaging
around 165 but occasionally reaching the 270s, and played golf
as often as possible. Sometimes he'd fill a car or two with golfing
buddies and their caddies and drive hundreds of miles for a
golf game. By this time, he was scoring fairly consistently in
the low 70s.

That year, Joe Louis Enterprises was formed to help deal
with his tax situation and future earnings. At Louis's suggestion, Truman and his associates negotiated with Madison Square
Garden to obtain the exclusive right to certain fight films. Joe
Louis Enterprises produced the fight films for the first and
second Walcott fights, for instance. Not only did the deal bring
in significant income, it also provided Louis with a substantial
tax write-off.

Meanwhile, Mike Jacobs had suddenly become ill and transferred his promoting responsibilities to Sol Strauss, who happened to be his cousin. A lawyer with limited experience in
the fight game, Strauss learned quickly and became a fair and
effective promoter. His first responsibility was to find Louis

an opponent. This wasn't as easy as it sounds: the Brown Bomber, in combination with the war, had decimated the heavyweight field. Among the opponents Sol considered were Joe Baksi and an unknown, Jersey Joe Walcott. He discussed the options with Louis, but neither, in the champion's opinion, had box-office appeal. Not making any inroads, Strauss finally said, "Get me right, Joe. I'm not trying to sell you anything."

Louis smiled and said, "Mr. Strauss, you ain't got nothing to sell."

Eventually, Strauss and Louis settled on the black fighter, Jersey Joe Walcott, who happened to have served for a time as one of the champion's sparring partners. Born Arnold Cream, he had been impressed by a slight, 5-foot, 1½-inch fighter from Barbados named Joe Walcott when he was a youngster. So when Arnold Cream went into the ring, he adopted the name, prefixing it with that of his home state.

Louis's impoverished heritage hardly exceeded Walcott's humble beginnings. A native of Merchantville, New Jersey, he worked, in his words, "at every filthy job from cleaning cesspools on up to earn a living. And I never did a wrong thing." Walcott's poverty resulted in his fighting many bouts on an empty stomach. Some experts go so far as to claim that his three knockdowns—by Abe Simon, Al Ettore, and Tiger Jack Fox—were the result of starvation rather than lack of ability. He was intensely religious, was married, and had been educated by a Baptist minister's daughter.

SUNNIE WILSON
Joe Louis's Running Buddy

Walcott was Joe Louis's sparring partner. He knew damn near everything that Joe would do. Walcott needed some help. He had a nice family and Joe was a kind-hearted young man. He agreed to give him a chance to make a few

bucks by fighting an exhibition, which Joe did for many of
the poor fighters. But remember that in an exhibition fight,
if you knock out the champion, you become champion. There
is no such thing as an exhibition fight in reality. I don't think
Joe took the Walcott fight seriously. Joe didn't train too much
for it. He thought, "I'm not going to hurt my sparring partner."
His sparring partner sure hurt him though!

Walcott entered the December 5, 1947 bout against Louis un-
disturbed by the press. The reason: his managers barred journalists from his training camp. They feared that the typical
questions asked of a Louis challenger—"Are you afraid of the
Brown Bomber's jab?" "How many rounds do you think you
will last against the Champ?"—would rattle their fighter. But
Walcott probably wouldn't have been intimidated anyway. As
a Louis sparring partner in years past, he felt he had outboxed
him while warming him up for the 1936 Schmeling fight. He
later told reporter Lewis Burton: "I went around thinking to
myself, but not daring to say it to others, 'Louis is champion,
but I can whip him.' "
     When Louis weighed in at 211¼ pounds on the morning of
the fight, he and his handlers were uneasy. The champion had
expected to be 3 pounds heavier, but by neglecting his water
intake and his diet in the last three days, he had dehydrated
his body. In reality, Louis went into the ring weak against a
finely tuned, aggressive fighter who was determined to win the
heavyweight title.
     The champion's shaky condition showed up immediately.
Although Louis was initially the pursuer, Walcott scored points
and finally won the first round by flooring him with a solid right.
Louis was not physically hurt, but his pride was wounded.
Rising quickly, Joe tracked his opponent more cautiously through
the next several rounds. But in the fourth round, Walcott nailed

the Bomber again with a right to the jaw. This time Louis was hurt and took a seven count to try to recuperate. Throwing a flurry of rights and lefts, Walcott pursued his dazed opponent.

One brief moment in which the Champ seemed to recapture his past glory came in the ninth round. When Walcott was against the ropes, the Bomber hit him with everything he had, pouring lefts and rights into his body. Surprising Louis—and many who saw the fight—the 33-year-old challenger took everything Louis gave out and at the end of the round began punching back. Sitting behind Walcott's corner, Marshall Miles, Louis's manager, heard Walcott's handlers tell him he had the fight won, coaching him to stay away for the last three rounds. It was the wrong strategy. Walcott's running tactics lost him the championship title. Briefly, as sportswriter Arthur Daley reported, Walcott had found the "secret that had eluded Conn. He not only ran but was able to hide." In the end, however, the champion found him—and won by a decision.

Nevertheless, it was not a well-received victory. To boos and catcalls, referee Ruby Goldstein announced a split decision in favor of Louis. The two judges, Marty Monroe and Frank Forbes, voted for Louis; referee Goldstein, once an acclaimed boxer himself, voted for Walcott. "Some will agree with me; some won't," the referee later told reporters, "but it appeared to me that Louis was in the same position as any other man who stays away from his trade too long. He wasn't sharp and he was missing punches he wouldn't have missed had he been boxing more often." Some took this criticism one step further: Joe Louis was on an irretrievable decline. Too often, Louis saw an opening, had his fist arched and ready, but released it too slowly. The Brown Bomber's reflexes simply weren't there anymore.

Although the decision remains in Louis's column in the record books, it was highly controversial. Some blamed it on the New York scoring system in which the judges count round by round and point by point. It was on the basis of one judge's counting (he gave Louis more rounds and Walcott more points, then gave his vote to Louis) that Joe Webster, Walcott's manager, issued a protest to the New York Athletic Commission after the bout.

Louis, disappointed by his performance in the ring, told Walcott that he was sorry. He was referring to his poor showing, but Walcott took it to mean that the champion thought his opponent had won the fight. To this day, Walcott insists that he won the title that night.

JERSEY JOE WALCOTT
Former Heavyweight Contender

Like thousands of people who saw it, I thought that I won the fight. I thought I won it very big. But out of my respect and admiration for Louis, I never felt bad about not getting the decision. He was such an idol to the world. I think that anyone that dethroned him would be the most hated guy in the world.

Although Louis now wanted to retire, he knew that he couldn't go out on this sour note. Going to Chicago for a prescheduled exhibition bout with Bob Foxworth, he left Sol Strauss in New York to negotiate a rematch with Walcott for the following June. A last-minute sticking point was Joe's insistence that a third fight be scheduled if he should lose the title. "Is Louis going to retire or isn't he?" Walcott demanded. Louis insisted that he still planned to retire, "win or lose," but wanted the clause inserted anyway. At one point during negotiations at the Twentieth Century Sporting Club, Walcott reportedly stood in the middle of the room and said he would not budge until the picture of his moving to a neutral corner over a prone Louis was hung on the walls along with the other Louis photographs. Walcott won that one.

Learning that Louis was to make an appearance at the Club Ebony, Walcott rushed up to Harlem. Although he waited for four hours, in the end he missed the Champ by ten minutes. Louis, hearing of the incident, uncharacteristically challenged: "He'll have to sign in two weeks or he's out." He threatened as replacements light-heavyweight champ Gus Lesnevich, if he retained his title after a fight with challenger Billy Fox, or the winner of the heavyweight bout between Joe Baksi and Gino Buonvino.

Eventually, Walcott and Louis ironed out their differences and an exhausted Champ, a small entourage (including his wife, Marshall Miles, and Manny Seamon), his car, and a well-stocked food pantry that included more than 300 steaks, sailed on the *Queen Mary* for a twenty-six-day boxing exhibition trip to Europe. In London, he was scheduled to box three times daily at the Health and Holiday Exhibition, for a total of seventy-eight bouts. He had been promised $80,000 for his efforts. But the exhibition had financial difficulties and he had to settle for $40,000. Louis, however, was enthusiastically greeted by the British, who had avidly followed his boxing exploits for years at 2 or 3 a.m. over the airwaves.

Louis moved on to Paris and was equally well received. Crowds in the streets would chant, "Joe Lou-ee" and "Champion le boxe." The Champ also put on boxing exhibitions in Brussels and considered doing so in Sweden until he learned that they wanted to pay him in ice skates rather than cash. After the tour, the entourage returned to New York in April so Louis could begin training for the Walcott rematch. But Europe had turned out to be an expensive trip for the Champ. And his relationship with Marva had become even more tenuous when his extramarital affairs continued in Europe. The enormous outlays he made for gifts to apologize for his indiscretions burned a large hole in his already tattered bank account.

MARVA SPAULDING

Joe hired a guide for me in London and Paris. In London she took me to the museums and to the shops. In Paris she arranged for me to visit the top designers.

I loved perfume, so Joe bought me a German trunk and filled it with perfume. Each perfume was in a crystal bottle, many of which were encrusted with semiprecious stones. When we returned and were going through customs, an official asked to look into a second trunk, one I hadn't seen before. It, too, was filled with bottles of perfume. I turned to Joe and said, "Why the second trunk? Do you plan to supply all the chorus girls up and down Broadway with perfume?"

Jersey Joe Walcott approached the June 25, 1948, rematch at a psychological disadvantage, if he cared to look at it that way. When he entered Yankee Stadium, the site of six of Louis's heavyweight championship bouts, he would face a man who had improved his performances in rematches against all nine opponents he had met previously. In addition, Walcott was up against the most popular boxing champion since Jack Dempsey. If the championship mantle had passed to Walcott on that evening, it would have created as great a commotion as when John L. Sullivan lost to James J. Corbett.

Walcott was able to ignore all this. By the time of the rematch he had come a long, long way from his sparring partner days. He dressed conservatively but stylishly. He drove a Cadillac and provided well for his family, who lived in a ten-room house in New Jersey. More importantly, he approached the fight with a positive mental outlook. Although he was bitter about the conclusion of the 1947 bout, by the following June his attitude had turned to grim determination. Walcott had emerged as an intelligent, assured challenger.

Nat Fleischer, editor of *The Ring*, suggested that Walcott had reached the peak of his fighting form in the first Louis match. "The fact that he is just an ordinary fighter, and that his performances, prior to the night he scored two knockdowns over the champion and almost won the world heavyweight crown, lacked the sensational, made his fistic exhibition in the first Louis battle stand out," said Fleischer. "It was by far his best work in more than a decade of ring fighting." The questions remaining were: Could Walcott regain this peak in the rematch? Even if he could, was that sufficient to beat Joe Louis?

Although the fight was postponed for two days because of rain, more than 40,000 fans arrived at the stadium on June 25. Entering the ring at 214 pounds—and stronger than he was in the first fight—Louis proposed to box his opponent until he tired. He waited for the challenger to lead. But Jersey Joe planned to stay outside Louis's reach. The result was a lackluster fight with only occasional touches of brilliance. In the third round, in an exchange reminiscent of the first fight, Jersey Joe sent the Bomber to his haunches with a left and a short right to the jaw. Taunting Louis throughout the bout, Walcott bobbed and weaved, walked away grinning, and pounded his gloves together. In the eighth round, a revived Louis let loose a long left hook and a series of left jabs. Walcott no longer jeered. Referee Frank Fullam tried to make the bout into a fight with a challenge to the fighters in the tenth: "Hey, one of you get the lead out of your ass, and let's have a fight."

FREDDIE GUINYARD

Chappy taught Joe to keep moving and to touch a fighter to distract him. If a fighter starts to throw a punch, if you touch him on the shoulder, the chin or any place, he can't throw it. He's got to start over again. You're taking him out of his rhythm. But he could never get it across to him until Joe saw for himself in the Walcott fight.

You know what Chappy told me once when we were talking? He said, "Freddie, Jack Johnson would have whipped Joe every night of the week because he moved. I hate to say this, but that's what would've happened." Then when Walcott made a monkey out of him [Joe], by this fast moving and shaking, I saw what he was talking about. A moving target is harder to hit than one standing still.

But Walcott, making the same mistake as Conn did in the 1941 fight, then started to play to Louis's strength. In the eleventh, he moved to the ropes and dared Joe to hit him. Responding, the Champ threw three solid rights to his jaw. Although "the challenger looked like a doll out of which sawdust has run," according to ringsider British journalist Peter Wilson, he quickly recovered. Rebounding off the ropes, he shot a left and a right to the Bomber's jaw. Angered, Louis threw two final punches, a left and a right, dropping Jersey Joe to the canvas. Watching Walcott get only to his knees by the count of seven, Louis could see by his expression that he wasn't going to make it.

"In that last blazing, vicious, man-killing half-minute he [Louis] redeemed his and Walcott's version of a world's heavy-weight championship from being a cheap, tawdry, prize-money scrap," wrote Wilson, describing many observers' feelings. Then in typical dignified Louis fashion, the Champ made the long-awaited announcement from the ring. "This was for you, Mom," he said. "This was my last fight." Afterward, Joe explained his decision to reporters: "Five years ago I would have come out in the first round and got it over in a hurry, but I am not the fighter I was." It took Louis, surrounded by thirty policemen, more than a half hour to enter his hotel that evening. Half of Harlem was outside waiting to hail its champion.

CHAPTER ELEVEN

"Covered with Rust"

"I cried like a baby when your father was knocked out by Marciano."
—John R. Thompson, Jr.

By 1948, Louis truly wanted to retire from the ring. Asked after the Walcott fight whether he considered himself the heavyweight champion until a new titleholder was selected, he emphatically responded, "I am an ex-boxer." And once he did hand up his gloves, he immediately received a number of interesting business offers—from Chrysler, Buick, an oil company, and an insurance company. Marva encouraged him to accept the insurance offer and form The Joe Louis Insurance Company, and he did. Its offices were established on Sixty-third and Maryland Avenue in Chicago, but as in the past, Louis lost interest just as the business was becoming successful. He stopped going to directors' meetings. Eventually the company was sold and the name was changed.

"After he retired, I think he never became involved in a

successful business venture because he thought business was too quiet. He just couldn't get into it," explains Marva. Before the war, under the guidance of John Roxborough and Julian Black, Louis invested only his name. After he separated from his managers, he began investing his own money as well, in what turned out to be a host of wayward ventures. Among them: the Brown Bomber bread company in New York; a mechanic's training school in Chicago for underprivileged children; a soft drink company, which manufactured Joe Louis Punch.

More often than not, Louis invested to help out one or another of his cronies, not for any financial return. In this regard, he knew what he was doing, but he just didn't take into account the personal downside risk. Joe couldn't believe he would ever want for money. His philosophy was "I'll do it my way; I'll find out." But being obstinate cost him a lot of money.

Take the Rumboogie, a Chicago cabaret. Louis became part owner through the back door. He lent a friend, Charlie Glenn, money to get started. Then, after he and his personal secretary, Leonard Reed, returned from his European exhibition tour in 1948, they visited the cabaret. Reed bragged to Louis about the money he had saved from the exhibition tour and said, "I'm going to take my $18,000 and I'm going to buy me a house." Louis plucked the $18,000 check from Reed's hands and went to talk to Glenn. Returning a few minutes later, he announced to his astonished friend, "You and I now own the Rumboogie." Shortly before they were to depart on an exhibition tour to South America, Louis told Reed to "turn the cabaret over to his stepbrother, Pat Brooks." Pat was a nice fellow but could neither read nor write. Although Brooks was tutored for weeks on how to run the club, a few weeks after he became manager, the cabaret was bankrupt.

After the war, Louis joined journalist Billy Rowe in starting a New York public relations firm, contributing Louis & Rowe

Enterprises' first account, the publicity for the Louis-Conn fight. Mike Jacobs paid the firm $10,000, plus rent, for its efforts. Louis, however, made only brief appearances at the firm's West Fifty-seventh Street offices and was paid only when he contributed.

In the 1940s, Joe gave his name to a friend's milk company. For many years, The Joe Louis Milk Company was a fixture in Chicago; indeed, after the owner, Jess Thornton, died, the business was successfully continued by his wife, Helen. However, enormous debts incurred by her second husband caused her eventually to close the company. Such bad luck also dogged another venture, this one with Sugar Ray Robinson and Freddie Guinyard. The trio bought a distributorship for a Canadian beer, Canadian Ace, Louis and Robinson getting 49 percent and Guinyard 51 percent. But the venture, like so many others, was doomed. One reason, according to Guinyard: Canadian Ace was considered by many consumers to be the "worst beer in the world."

LEONARD REED

Joe Louis's Friend and Personal Secretary

Nobody really swindled Joe out of anything. Joe was a giver. Joe was not a consumer; he wanted to give. He was always helping people, expecting nothing in return.

Why was I with Joe? Why did I stay with Joe? Why would I have done anything that Joe wanted me to do? In 1935, I was sick with pneumonia. I said out of the clear blue sky, "I'm going to give up this business [owner and manager of the Plantation Club, a black-and-tan nightclub in Detroit]." Joe said, "If you do, what are you going to do?" "Open a Chicken Shack," I responded. Joe said, "Here's $10,000. It will take $5,000 to open and another $5,000 to back it up, wouldn't it?" He just laid the $10,000

on my bed. That's how we got in the Chicken Shack
business. No paper, no writing, no nothing. We split everything equal. We were partners. Shortly afterwards, when
I got hurt in an automobile accident, Joe again came to
my rescue.

   He did [Frank] Sinatra a favor, too, and I guess Sinatra
felt that Joe came to his rescue once and later helped
Joe. In 1947 or 1948, Sinatra wasn't doing too well. He
was in the boxing business and had a young fighter out
of Chicago. Sinatra was having a fight in Los Angeles
and the pre-gate wasn't doing so well. When Joe met him
in his office on Sunset, he asked him if he would do a
two-round exhibition or referee a bout prior to the fight.
Joe asked him to check his schedule with me. I said, "Okay.
Sing a song I've written and I'll fix it up for you." Sinatra
agreed.

While spending time on such varied entrepreneurial activities,
Louis also attempted to resuscitate his floundering marriage.
This time, however, it was beyond repair. Marva tied up his
earnings from the Walcott fight, and Louis had to find a
way to pay off his back taxes and finance his standard of
living. His advisers did so by scheduling a series of exhibition bouts that took the Champ into the South and to
Kingston, Jamaica. Quietly, Marva went to Mexico to obtain
a divorce.

   While the exhibition series took care of his immediate financial needs, Joe began to rethink his long-term prospects.
In consultation with his legal adviser, Truman Gibson, he con-
ceived the idea of forming a boxing organization that would
compete with Mike Jacobs's Twentieth Century Sporting Club.
Working with Arthur M. Wirtz and James D. Norris, a Chicago business team that financed the operation for 80 percent
of the return, Louis formed the International Boxing Club (IBC)

to promote and televise fights. Within a week of the signing, the IBC obtained the Gillette bouts (the Friday Night Fights) and subsequently introduced the Wednesday Night Fights, offering the first telecast of boxing from the Midwest to the East.

TRUMAN GIBSON
Joe Louis's Attorney

I remember Joe's meeting in Florida with Jim Norris, which set the ball rolling for the formation of the International Boxing Club. A friend called Jim at 3:00 in the morning and told him to have Joe come out the next morning. Jim had a place on the golf course in Coral Gables, Florida. They hit golf balls for three hours, then talked business.

We proposed a reverse elimination tournament for the heavyweight title, where the winner of the first fight would meet the next contender. The winner of that fight would meet the next boxer, and so on. Norris said, "I like it, but you have to talk to my partner, Arthur Wirtz."

We flew to Chicago, got grounded in Cincinnati, and had to come up by bus. Arthur, an imposing 6-feet-6-inch guy, said, "I like it, but I have to talk to my partner, Jim Norris." I thought this was a runaround, but Jim, who doesn't fly, arrived by train the next day. The deal was hashed out in one day.

Prior to the venture's reaching its peak, however, Louis, because of his financial situation, had to sell his interest early to Norris. Thus, he never realized the full profit potential of his investment.

In launching the IBC in March 1949, in Miami, Florida, the Champ actually made two announcements, via National Boxing

Association Commissioner Abe Greene. First, he formally announced his retirement from the ring, officially ending an extraordinary boxing career spanning eleven years and eight months. He had defended his title twenty-five times, significantly more than any other heavyweight champion. "I have held the championship for a long time and I won it in the ring," Louis said. "I expected to lose it the same way I won it. However, things have developed so that I think I ought to stick to the retirement announcement I made some time ago."

Subsequently, Commissioner Greene also announced Louis's formation, along with Wirtz and Norris, of the International Boxing Club. It would handle the elimination tournament to determine the next heavyweight champion. In June the IBC proposed to match Jersey Joe Walcott against Ezzard Charles, the victor by decision over Joey Maxim. The winner of that bout would meet either Lee Savold or Gus Lesnevich in the fall. Louis was paid $350,000 by the IBC for giving up his title and signing the contenders, and an annual salary of $20,000.

"I really hated to do it," Louis told reporters after these announcements. "It meant so much to me. But I can't take it back now . . . I know, at least, my mother will be happy with my final decision." The ailing Mike Jacobs's organization was dealt a deadly blow. When Joe told Uncle Mike, he graciously put his arms around him and said, "Joe, I ain't got a kick coming. You were always great with me." But his Twentieth Century Sporting Club would never recover from its loss of Louis as its primary fighter. The IBC paid Jacobs $150,000 to step down from his position as promoter for Madison Square Garden.

Louis filled up the months before the eventual heavyweight title fight by going on an exhibition tour. He traveled to Nassau, Havana, Cuba, and various southern cities in the United States. In June he returned to watch the Charles-Walcott fight. It was held in Chicago Stadium, which Norris owned.

DON DUNPHY
Radio Broadcaster

A couple of days before the fight the sportswriters were asking him, "How are tickets going?" The usual promoter's response would be "Oh, wonderful. I've got orders from Chicago, New York and so on." Joe, new to the promotion game and perpetually honest, said, "I don't know. We ain't sold none yet." He fractured everybody.

Ezzard Charles won the fifteen-round decision, but the lackluster event left him a contested winner in the view of most boxing experts. Although Charles was recognized as heavyweight champion by the National Boxing Association, he was still considered only a contender by the International Boxing Union and the British Boxing Board of Control, which recognized Lee Savold. While Charles attempted to fight his way to worldwide recognition, Louis fought in a series of exhibition bouts from October 1949 until April 1950.

With the Internal Revenue Service hot on his tail, Louis could no longer rely on exhibition pay or business ventures to support him. Joe had to reenter the ring. Important as his personal financial needs were, however, finances were not the only factor forcing him back into boxing. Louis's colleagues at the IBC, Wirtz and Norris, encouraged him to return to the sport because they couldn't build a gate on the appeal of the current heavyweight contenders. A fight between Louis and Charles thus was scheduled for September 1950.

Prior to the Charles fight, Joe's financial predicament became even more heated—former manager John Roxborough faced off against his current advisers, Truman Gibson and Ted Jones. Roxborough, still owed money by Louis, filed suit in a New York court demanding 25 percent of Louis's purse from the bout. His case rested on the fact that Louis's finances had

been mishandled since 1947 by Jones and Gibson: (1) Funds
from the 1947 Latin American exhibition tour were used to buy
a trade school, rather than to pay taxes as presumed; (2) Louis
did not file a tax return in 1947; (3) Louis should not have been
advised to return to boxing; (4) Canadian Ace Brewery, of
which Louis was a partner, was allegedly being operated by
mobsters; (5) Gibson and Jones participated in Louis's business
ventures. Gibson and Jones argued that Joe's financial problems occurred before they became his advisers. His 1950 income was expected to be about $40,000 from business ventures;
his debts, $208,000 in back taxes and $5000 a year until 1955
for child support.

Amid all these financial problems, Louis prepared to face
Ezzard Charles on September 27 in Yankee Stadium. "I didn't
want the fight," Charles said later. "Joe was my boyhood idol.
But my manager, Ray Arcel, said that if I wanted everyone to
consider me the champ I'd have to fight Joe. I signed, but I
wasn't happy about it." Louis had had a long layoff—except
for exhibition bouts—and so had Charles: he had been out of
the ring for eight months because of an injured heart muscle.

Louis began training at Pompton Lakes unenthusiastically,
only six weeks before the bout. It was difficult for him to return
to the strenuous routine of training camp. Running and sparring
came harder. He wasn't in the ring by choice, and he was
fighting not only Charles but the age-old ring adage "They
never come back."

The former champ's shortcomings were clear in the tale of
the tape. Louis was 36; Charles was 29. Louis was also 32½
pounds heavier than his previous fighting weight and, in boxing
performance, only a shadow of the former Brown Bomber. Not
only was Charles lighter, he was quicker—and desperate to
retain the title against the aging former champion. Still, Louis
entered the ring a two-to-one favorite. Jersey Joe Walcott was
among those who picked Louis to knock out Charles. "Charles

doesn't belong in the same ring with Louis if Joe hasn't lost too much from his long layoff. I fought my worst fight against Charles and almost beat him," commented Joe's erstwhile competitor.

Louis started the fight by stalking his opponent, showing the only trace of his former championship style he would display in the bout. Charles darted around Louis—hooking, jabbing, and landing lefts to the Champ's body. When there was an opening, Louis was slow to respond, causing his long-time boxing friend Sugar Ray Robinson to scurry to his corner after the fifth round. "Joe's got to keep sticking with that left hand," he advised. "He's got to take the play away from Charles and keep him off balance."

But Louis simply didn't have the power or the stamina. "I knew from the seventh round on that I couldn't do it," he told reporters afterward. "It wasn't a case of reflexes or anything; I just didn't have it." Charles noticed Louis's hesitancy, too. "After the eighth or ninth round," he later said, "Joe began to falter. I started dreaming. 'Could this be the great Joe Louis?' I wanted to win, but I didn't want to knock him out."

Louis was not about to make it easy for Charles, however. Something of his old championship form came out in the tenth round, when he released a blazing left hook to Charles's jaw. The Cincinnati boxer's knees buckled, and the Bomber followed up with a left hook and a right to the head. Charles clinched but was repeatedly battered by short lefts and rights to the head. "I knew I won that round, but I never really had him hurt real bad," Louis lamented afterward. But Charles's corner was briefly worried after that barrage. Contrary to previous round warnings, "Move around" or "Hands up," before Charles went back into the ring still slightly dazed, his seconds advised, "Get close and hold."

Louis later told reporters that he never felt defeated, not even in the fourteenth round when Charles had him on the ropes after a series of blows ended in a crippling right to his jaw. Pursuing his advantage, Charles threw a succession of punches to Louis's head and body. Somehow, Joe remained standing, finishing the round with a solid right to his opponent's jaw. After his close call in the fourteenth, a weary Louis had to be assisted by his trainer and manager to reenter the ring for the final round.

Mercifully, Charles allowed his opponent to finish the fight on his feet. Repeatedly, he fired lefts and rights to Joe's head and body. And with Louis against the ropes, he released a final series of punches as the bell sounded. As the fifteen-round unanimous decision was announced in Charles's favor, Louis wept.

SHIRLEY POVICH
Sportswriter, **The Washington Post**

"I would someday like to be like Tunney. Beat somebody and retire," Joe once told me. "I'm going to retire with at least $1 million when I'm 30." But they moved him back in. He represented a box office draw. The Ezzard Charles fight was the saddest fight. In it, he took the worst beating of his life—worse than against Marciano. He was battered terribly in that bout.

After keeping reporters waiting more than ten minutes outside his dressing room, a crushed and defeated Louis let them in. His left hand was submerged in a bucket of ice. Sporting a tightly closed and discolored left eye, swollen lips, and body bruises, he refused to denigrate the victor. "No, I wouldn't say Charles is the best fighter I've ever faced," said Joe. "But he's a good fighter, good in all departments." He announced "positively" his retirement from the ring.

Charles indicated that he had been wary of the former champion throughout the fight. And the marks he showed gave testimony to the fact that the old Brown Bomber still had something left. Charles's left eye was battered closed, and his right eye and cheek were puffed out of shape. "Joe was always dangerous, and I did not want to take any unnecessary chances," he said in his dressing room. "Why, when I felt his left jab in the early rounds I could understand why he became the heavyweight champion of the world."

DON DUNPHY

Charles was a good fighter, but because he succeeded Louis, I don't think Charles was really appreciated by the people. That happens. Tunney wasn't appreciated because he succeeded Dempsey. Corbett wasn't appreciated because he succeeded Sullivan. Holmes wasn't appreciated because he succeeded Ali. I don't think the public can have a new idol every year.

Louis's purse exceeded $150,000, but the IRS refused to accept it in lieu of back taxes due. (Truman Gibson had attempted to negotiate a settlement with the government based on the receipts from the comeback bout and Louis's inability to earn "that kind of money" any longer.) So Louis's retirement announcement was once again rescinded. Two months later, he was on the comeback trail for the second time in his career— again out of necessity rather than desire. Louis faced eight opponents over the next nine months. He beat them all, four by knockout. Most notable of these fights was his showing against New Jersey boxer Lee Savold, who was considered the heavyweight champion by the British Boxing Board of Control.

In front of a crowd of 18,000 New York fans clearly sympathetic to the Brown Bomber, Savold was knocked down in 2 minutes and 29 seconds of the sixth round. The match was all Louis from the opening bell. Savold, clearly over the hill at 36, threw only five real punches (all high, looping right hands) during the entire fight. His left fist, held unusually low, provided a natural opening for Louis's straight right and left jab. Savold's bruised cheeks and bloodied nose lent support to Louis's success.

The sixth round brought the crowd to its feet. Backed into a corner, Savold was an easy target for the Bomber's final left hook. The British champion crumbled to the canvas in a sitting position, unable to rise before the referee concluded the count.

Louis was exuberantly hailed by his fans, who had turned out en masse at Madison Square Garden after the fight, originally scheduled for the Polo Grounds, was twice postponed by weather. His dressing room, too, was packed with well-wishers, including Milton Berle and Walter Winchell. Some observers, including a *New York Times* reporter, said that the former champ still had the "strength and determination to batter out of his path any who would undertake to frustrate" his climb to the top again. Others, more realistic, knew that Savold wasn't a worthy adversary.

Indeed, the Savold fight simply showed a brief flash of Louis's former boxing skills. His true physical form was revealed four months later in his match against Rocky Marciano, a 27-year-old heavyweight from Brockton, Massachusetts. Born Rocco Marchegiano, the young boxer was only 14 when Louis battered Max Schmeling in 2 minutes and 4 seconds in their 1938 rematch. A friend, Izzy Gold, recalls listening to the fight with Rocky at a fair in Brockton. "We had about 50 cents in our pockets," recollected Gold. "And we were thinking about all that money that Louis made. We never dreamed that some day Rocky would be fighting Louis in Madison Square Garden. We had wild imaginations in those days, but not that wild."

For his efforts against Marciano, Joe was promised a $300,000 minimum guarantee, or 80 percent of the proceeds. The match was considered a mandatory confrontation by Marciano's managers, regardless of the uneven split in the gate. After all, Louis stood in the way of prestige for the boxer. Even though Marciano had won all his previous thirty-seven ring encounters (thirty-two by knockouts) and was younger by more than a decade, the former champ was still an eight-to-five favorite. When he entered the ring before more than 17,000 Madison Square Garden fans on October 26, 1951, Louis was balding and puffy, but supremely confident. He had a three-inch height and eight-inch reach advantage over the brawler from Massachusetts and far more experience. A couple of days before the bout, the Brown Bomber had knocked out sparring partner Holly Smith. He felt ready.

Louis's handlers, however, were worried. There was clearly something wrong with his right side. Although the doctors didn't find the cause, he wasn't able to hold up his right hand or use it effectively. Marshall Miles and Manny Seamon, Louis's manager and trainer, had him train indoors at night so the press wouldn't learn about the disability and tried, to no avail, to get him to use his right.

Marciano, unaware of the affliction, was fearless. From the opening bell, he pursued Louis, eventually stunning the former champ with a right to the jaw. In the second and third rounds, he crouched, not allowing the Bomber to get a clean shot at him. In the next two rounds, however, Joe's left jab scored points. By then, both fighters looked the worse for wear: the Massachusetts boxer was cut above the eye and was bleeding from the nose; the former Champ's face was swollen and red.

Louis's age began to show by the sixth. He was sluggish. Unable to take advantage of openings when they appeared, he once tapped Marciano on the shoulder rather than delivering a blow. At the end of the seventh, however, victory briefly appeared within reach. Joe staggered Marciano with a solid left to the jaw. Regardless, Marciano's youth and strength began to prevail by the eighth. He was able to get in close, take everything the Bomber threw, and then deliver his own powerful punches. A left hook finally floored Louis. Experience made him take an eight count; heart allowed him to get up. Afterward, Marciano would recall that moment. "He went down not like a young boy goes down. When a young boy goes down, he still has that hustle, that feeling inside like 'I gotta get up,' but Joe went down with a thud."

Marciano was confident as he moved toward victory. With a fusillade of punches, he drove Louis into the ropes and followed up with two left hooks. A final devastating right to his jaw lifted Louis off his feet and through the ropes onto the apron. Referee Ruby Goldstein started the final count but, sensing its futility, waved his arms, signaling the fight's end, when he reached four. Sugar Ray Robinson, Louis's longtime friend, had already reached his hero sprawled on the canvas—a sad memory for a generation of Louis fans. Holding the former champion's head in his arms, he crooned, "Joe, Joe, you'll be all right. Joe, you'll be all right, man."

JOHN R. THOMPSON, JR.
**Head Basketball Coach,
Georgetown University**

I cried like a baby when your father was knocked out by Marciano. Looking back, however, I think it was good in a lot of ways. As a young person, it showed me that Joe Louis was human. Previously, I would have told you that Joe Louis could jump off a building with a single bound. It's more realistic to the world to know that no one is immortal.

Exuberant—but not without some remorse—Marciano said after the fight, "I'm glad I won, but I'm sorry I had to do it to Joe Louis." No one was pleased to see the great former champion destroyed so decisively by this young, tough buck. But everyone knew it would happen sooner or later if he remained in the fight game. Everyone knew, including Joe Louis.

Louis also believed, however, that *losing* wasn't a word that belonged in a fighter's vocabulary. "A fighter can't think that way, and he can't talk that way," he once told reporter Red Smith. "Oh, I think I recognized it," the Champ continued. "Especially when I was just starting out and scared. After I won the title, I didn't think about it no more. Oh, I knew that if I kept on fighting, some guy would come along and take the title away from me, but not this guy, never tonight."

Yet, Louis was philosophical about the conclusion of the Marciano fight. Talking to reporters who had to bend down close to his ear while he was lying face down on his massage table after the bout, Louis looked his age. His face was badly bruised and his left hand was in an ice bucket. He felt that the better man had won the fight. Comparing Marciano to Schmeling, he said, "This kid knocked me out with what? Two punches. Schmeling knocked me out with—must have been a hundred punches. But I was 22 years old then. You can take more then than later on."

"Did age count tonight, Joe?" the reporters asked. "Ugh," Joe responded, nodding his head. But in case any of those present might have forgotten, he added a final epitaph: "I've knocked out lots of guys."

SHIRLEY POVICH

He was knocked out twice—once by Schmeling and once by Marciano. There were fifteen years between knockouts. My God, is this a man who can't take punishment? The last

time against Marciano he was covered with rust. I saw that
fight in New York. Joe didn't belong in the ring. Covered
with rust, and he's in there with the young tyke. For two to
four rounds he went very well. If he just had a little bit more
stamina, he would've done it. It was the eighth round. It was
one of the saddest things. . . .

Now, for the third time, Louis would tell his public that he
was "positively" going to retire. The difference was that this
time he had no choice. Boxing commissions in various states
began to refuse to reissue his license. "He should not take
chances of being hurt," said Joe Triner, chairman of the Illinois
Athletic Commission. "He's too great a name and too great a
former champion to be allowed to take chances. He has been
a great part of the game, but he should quit before it's too
late."

Louis wound up his boxing career in 1951 with a series of
prescheduled exhibition bouts in the United States and in the
Far East. He received hero's welcomes in both Tokyo and
Taipei, with thousands attending his arrival. The end was probably more difficult for Louis's fans than it was for the Champ
himself.

CLIFFORD L. ALEXANDER, JR.
Secretary of the Army (1977–1981)

The last fights were wrenching experiences. You did feel
sorry. There's hardly a perfect time to walk away from a
sport, and most athletes don't do it unrelated to money. As
I wrote in a piece for The Washington Post when your father
died, it happens for a variety of reasons. It is the lure of the
"good life" that makes champions spend beyond their means.
It is also the seductive siren song of the crowd: the throngs

who want to reach out and touch the champ. It's the intox-
ication of standing in the ring with hands raised in victory.

It was particularly hard to watch Joe Louis at the end
because he was our hero. A heavyweight champion at that
time was more important than any other weight class. In
addition, he symbolically did something by beating the German [Schmeling] in the ring. This kind of sporting event was
a metaphor for the actual goodness of what we as a country
stood for. World War II was a war that was far more simplistic
than wars have been probably before or since. We were
the good guys, and they were the bad guys, and here was
this man standing for that.

CHAPTER TWELVE

The Opening Wedge

"Joe probably was the greatest single factor in destroying the color line [in golf]—merely by the force of his skill and his personality."

—Shirley Povich

Louis first took up golf in the mid-1930s, and soon after it became his favorite pastime. Certainly, it suited his physical abilities and his personality. He could hit the ball a long way, yet the sport was far less physically demanding than boxing. Not only that: golf served his competitive nature and obliged his gambling instincts.

MARVA LOUIS SPAULDING
Mrs. Joe Louis (1935–1945, 1946–1949)

Ed Sullivan introduced your father to golf when we were in New York. He would come by with a book on golf and say, "Marva, see to it that he reads this." When Joe became interested, he gave him his first set of clubs and got a pro for him.

Joe loved golf. He was playing golf when both you and Jackie were born. He called me from the golf course after Jackie's birth and said, "Marva, I heard you had a baby. Well, you haven't hit the jackpot yet. Why couldn't you have had a boy?"

Golf contributed to his downfall. In one summer, he lost $90,000 gambling on the course. Players would raise their handicaps with him and bet for high stakes. When he began to lose money playing golf, I said, "I'm never going to eat golf balls. I don't think I could digest them."

Louis had a tremendous amount of patience with the game, and whereas a lot of golfers don't like to practice, he did. On the practice tee, he learned to address the ball in an unusual manner. He would place the toe of the club, rather than the sweet spot, directly behind the ball; when he swung, however, he did so with the sweet spot's moving through and making contact with the ball. When asked why he aligned the club this way, he said it helped him to avoid the dreaded shank.

On occasion my father took me to the links, one of the few places where we could be alone. I believe a special bond was created as a result of our mutual interest in the sport. At first, I just used to watch him hit the ball. The first time I did so, when I was only two or three years old, was at the Pipe of Peace Golf Course in Chicago, now renamed Joe Louis the Champ Golf Course. The very back tees, those used by professionals and low handicappers, have been renamed the Brown Bomber's tees. When I got older, he gave me some of his clubs. But it was not until my late teens that he considered me good enough to play with him.

We used to play for pride and for money; we always had a little riding on the game. I remember one time in Las Vegas when I lost $25 to him. Not having enough money on me to pay him, I said I would reimburse him when we got home. His emphatic retort was "No, you pay me now. You never make a bet on the golf course unless you can cover your bet." I borrowed the money from the pro and paid him. He didn't ask me where I got the money; he just took it. Later that afternoon, I went back to the course and repaid the pro.

He was tenacious and competitive in everything he did, and golf was no exception. During one round in Las Vegas I under-estimated his abilities. We were on the sixteenth hole and even, when he prematurely boasted, "How are you going to tell your friends in Denver that your ole man beat you?" "You haven't yet," I confidently chided him back. Spurred on by my chal-lenge, he proceeded to knock in a thirty-foot birdie putt on the seventeenth hole to my par and a seven-foot birdie to my par on the eighteenth hole. He beat me two up shooting seventy-six to my seventy-eight. I also had pressed, or doubled, the bet on eighteen. After his birdie, he smiled and said, "Son, you only have to win two holes—nine and eighteen—that's where the money is. Everything else is academic."

The gambling aspect of golf was just as intriguing to Louis as was the athletic challenge of the game. He was as well known on the golfing circuit for his risk taking as he was for his com-petence. Although the number varies, depending on who is speaking, he probably lost close to half a million dollars on the sport. Big Sam from New York, golfer Joe Inman's caddy, once told journalist Tom Callahan, "I saw the Brown Bomber in California on a golf course. He was a good golfer." "A big hitter and a good gambler," added another black caddy. "I knew him from Jackson Park in Chicago. Pretty good, but the ones he played were usually better. Joe'd stick his hand in his pocket after every hole and pull out bills sticking out every which way and hold them out for everyone to take what was coming to them. Guess Joe made a life of making other people rich."

Although golf may have been detrimental to his financial

well-being, Louis really didn't care. As often as not, unbeknown to those he was helping, he would lose a round or two for their benefit. Ted Rhoades, later an excellent black professional golfer, is an example. Early in the golfer's career, Louis sponsored him. Once in California, Rhoades asked Leonard Reed, the Champ's personal secretary, to ask Louis to lend him $200 to pay his rent. Knowing that Rhoades needed another $200 for food—and that the promising young golfer could beat him handily—Louis suggested they play a round for $400. He lost and happily paid Rhoades the money. The fledgling golfer, while keeping his dignity, paid his rent.

Typically, however, Louis's golfing bets were small ones. He felt the challenge was in the bet, not the amount.

BOB HOPE
Entertainer and Boxing Fan

Your dad was a good golfer, so it was natural that we should be introduced on the golf course. I think it was in 1939. I know it was at the Ridgewood Country Club in Ridgewood, New Jersey, however, because he almost got me.

He and Byron Nelson, the pro there, were paired against Ed Sullivan and me. Joe and I, independently, were playing a $10 Nassau. Sullivan was buttering Joe up, I guess to get him to come down and take a bow in his audience. At the first hole, Joe had a putt about a foot and a half to two feet. Sullivan said, "That's good Joe." He never asked me. So Joe picked his ball up. On the next hole, he had another short putt. Sullivan again says, "That's good, Joe." Again Joe picked his ball up. On the third hole the incident was repeated. After Sullivan said, "That's good, Joe" I said, "not for me! I want to see that putt."

Your father fell on the ground laughing. He knew he had been getting away with this and he wondered how long I was going to stand for it.

Oh, I had more fun with him. I beat him quite a bit at golf until Lou Clayton of the comedy group Clayton, Jackson and Durante gave him a few lessons. Lou was a wonderful golfer. That's about all he did after he retired. I didn't fool around with Joe much on the golf course after those lessons!

I do remember, however, that he was with me when I had a hole-in-one at Lakeside in California. Along with us were Fred Astaire and Jimmy McLarnin, the former welterweight champion. I hit a seven-iron on the fifteenth hole and it rolled in. Joe said, "Hey, that thing went in the hole."

Your father didn't talk too much on the golf course. But every time he'd miss a shot in a trap or elsewhere, he'd say, 'Oh, Joseph.' That's all. 'Oh, Joseph.' When people don't talk too much, once they say something, it's funny. He was great at those one-line understatements.

Sometimes, even when he won on the golf course, he lost financially. On one occasion at Chicago's Wayside Golf Course, Louis played Alvin James, an acquaintance who owned a small cleaning and pressing establishment. It was the kind of challenge Joe loved. On the first day, James beat him out of $10,000. The next day, Louis said, "Play you double or nothing." Louis won the round, plus a press, and ended the day ahead $17,000. When it came time to pay, short by $7000, James wrote Louis an IOU with his cleaning business as collateral.

That night Leonard Reed wanted to inspect Joe's new business. But when he told the Champ where he was going, Louis asked to see the IOU, then tore it up, telling Reed, "How's the man going to live if you take his pressing shop?" Reed, ruminating recently about the incident, said, "I know Alvin James would've collected from Joe had he won, but Joe said, 'Give him his pressing shop,' and left it at that with Alvin owing him $7000."

Louis's wry sense of humor, however, was as readily apparent on the golf course as it was elsewhere. He was known as a prankster among his golfing buddies, who never ceased to be amused at his antics.

LEONARD REED
Joe Louis's Friend and Personal Secretary

Joe and I had a lot of fun while playing golf. I remember once when we went to play in New Orleans at a course on which no blacks had played before. We waited for 45 minutes for the limousine to depart from the New Orleans airport. Joe finally said, "Go find out when we're going."

These four guys are standing around talking. One said, "You're with Joe Louis, aren't you?" When I acknowledged this affirmatively, he said, "Well, we're trying to decide which one of us can tell Mr. Louis that he can't ride in the limousine [because of his color]."

I said, "That's no problem; I'll just tell him we'll get a cab." As we were getting our bags into the Yellow Cab, the driver says to me, "I can't take Mr. Louis. I can take you, but we can't ride any colored people in our cabs." [Reed, who is black, is fair-skinned with straight hair and often mistaken for white.]

Joe jumps in a nigger's cab and just as I get in, the driver tells Joe he can't take me because I'm white. Joe stays in the cab, and I go back to the original cab and said, "Well, follow that cab." When we arrived at the Negro hotel, the reservationist says, "Mr. Reed, you can't stay here. There's no integration." Now, I get the drift. I'm going white all the way.

The hotel sends me to the Roosevelt, a white hotel. When I'm in my room, there's a knock on the door. It's the bellboy. He said, "Mr. Reed, are you colored?" I said, "No, why?" "Well," he replies, "there's a colored lady downstairs with three children. She said that she's your wife, and she's coming up if you don't come down. She's raising quite a stir." He suggested that I go out the back way to avoid trouble.

When I got down to the street via the back entrance, I saw Joe in a parked car laughing. He had paid this woman $50 to tell the hotel that she was my wife.

Although Louis didn't normally make waves regarding discrimination, golf, the only remaining segregated sport, became an exception for him in the 1950s. Incensed by the inequities faced by his black golf friends, he used the sport to make a public statement on behalf of all blacks. It was one of the few times, aside from his wartime activities, that he did so.

Louis used the 1952 Professional Golfers' Association (PGA) tournament in San Diego, California, as his vehicle. A six handicap amateur golfer, he had been invited by the tournament committee to participate in the $10,000 San Diego Open golf tournament at Chula Vista. That, however, was before the committee was told by Horton Smith, president of the PGA, that its bylaws prevented a non-Caucasian player from competing in a PGA-sanctioned event.

Louis went to San Diego anyway. "I didn't expect they'd let me play when I came down here," Louis told reporters. "But I wanted 'em to tell me personally. I want to bring this thing out into the light so the people can know what the PGA is."

SHIRLEY POVICH
Sportswriter, The Washington Post

If I ever saw Joe exercised at all, it was the time that he got turned down for the PGA San Diego Open Invitational. This was the one thing that genuinely upset him. He said to me, "I don't understand those kind of people. Golf is the only sport left. Baseball: the color line is gone. Football: the color line is gone." I don't think anybody ever unified the enemies of racism like Joe did. I think Joe probably was the greatest single factor in destroying the color line—merely by the force of his skill and his personality.

In addition to Louis, two black professional golfers, Bill Spiller and Eural Clark, had been invited. As an amateur, Joe was exempted from qualifying. Bill Spiller qualified with a thirty-six-hole total of 152 at Rancho Santa Fe, but Eural Clark, after posting a 156 at La Jolla, missed the tournament cut.

Louis took on the PGA as he would any boxing opponent —with dignity and without emotion. "Even [in] his personal attack upon Smith, the Bomber spoke in his soft Alabama tones, never raising his voice, never indicating anger either by inflection or action," said *San Diego Union* sports editor Jack Murphy. "His features were composed in the familiar expressionless mask he wore while bearing in for the kill against Schmeling and Conn and Baer. In that, he was the Louis of old. His emotions didn't betray him."

When the committee agreed to let him—but not Spiller— play Louis initially declined the invitation. His high visibility and a public statement on the subject fueled the fire. Walter Winchell on his Sunday evening show said, "I thought they shot birdies—not skunks—on the golf course." Such comments helped trigger a board meeting of the committee.

The hastily called conference included Lou Reneau of the sponsoring Chevrolet Dealers; Anderson Borthwick, tournament chairman; the PGA's Smith; and Maurie Luxford, adviser for the Open. Sam Snead was called into the committee meeting. Without even bothering to sit down, he said: "Hell, let them tee it up. They've got to beat me." And he walked out.

Another golfer, Dutch Harrison, stalked out of the meeting, saying, "If that's what the meeting is all about, the hell with them." The outcome in light of the players' comments—and Louis's determination—was predictable. It was announced that Joe Louis would be permitted to play because of his amateur status; Smith invited him to join his foursome. This time Joe agreed to play.

The policy, however, was not extended to black professional Bill Spiller. Said Smith: "In the case of Spiller, there is nothing that can be done now because he doesn't meet the requirement for a membership in the PGA under the existing rules." Smith promised to raise the non-Caucasian rule at the next meeting of the PGA tournament committee.

In this way, Joe Louis was as successful in creating an "opening wedge" for blacks in professional golf as Branch Rickey had been with Jackie Robinson in baseball. "This is the beginning of the defeat of discrimination in golf," Joe was to tell reporters.

If the members of the PGA thought that would end Louis's involvement in the issue, however, they were sorely mistaken. Several black golfers—with Louis in the lead—went on to test the PGA's segregation policy in Phoenix and in Tucson. Although they were allowed to play in those two tournaments, they were not permitted to use the dressing rooms. Louis and his cohorts changed in their cars.

Meanwhile, behind the scenes, Louis pursued other avenues. According to Billy Rowe, a journalist and a Louis confidant, Louis spoke to President Dwight Eisenhower, a member of the Augusta National Golf Club, about the problem on a number of occasions. "That," said Rowe, "is what broke the camel's back."

The non-Caucasian clause was dropped from the PGA's bylaws in 1961.

CHAPTER THIRTEEN

Affairs of the Heart

"You had no alternative but to remain friends with him [Joe]. He wasn't an ordinary person. He was special."

—Rose Morgan

Throughout his life, Joe Louis remained an exceptional individual, able to bridge the barrier between the races, an accomplishment few could match in the mid-1900s. To his public, he was the antithesis of Jack Johnson—a decent, sensitive individual who didn't arouse white individuals' racial prejudices. He was a national hero who provided inspiration for whites and instilled pride in blacks. Even Louis's friends intimate with his flaws never stopped admiring him.

Joe Louis's public image looms larger than life. Everyone liked him; many loved him. He was a man's man—strong, well connected, and fun to be around. He was also a woman's man—handsome, romantic, and a lavish spender. Louis married four times, twice to the same woman, and had numerous

affairs, trysts, and associations with unknown as well as celebrated women. He had two natural children by his first wife
Marva. Late in life, with Martha, his third wife, he cared for
two foster children and adopted four others.

Just before the Max Baer fight in 1935, Louis married Marva
Trotter. He was 21, she 19. Marva, like Joe, came from a large
family. Hers included seven sisters and three brothers. Marva
was born outside Clearview, Oklahoma; the Trotters moved to
Chicago when she was five after a flood ravaged their small farm.
The girls were close in age, making "life lots of fun," says
Marva. "There was a constant exchange of clothing, fusses,
and fights because you wore favorite things."

Marva first saw Joe in 1934 at Chicago's Trafton Gymna-
sium, where he was training. At the time, she was a steno-
grapher for the Chicago Insurance Exchange. A friend who
was taking her to lunch told her, "There's a Negro boxer in
town who's terrific. He is going to be the next heavyweight
champion of the world. Let's watch him work out." Later that
night Louis called Marva. Spotting her among the fans, he had
known he wanted to meet her.

Marva was interested in pursuing a relationship with a
man she found "gentle, handsome, and charming." Regardless, her mother was initially against her daughter's going
out with a boxer. "It was considered racy," explains Marva,
"but everyone was beginning to take chances then," so Mrs.
Trotter relented. During their courtship, however, she insisted
they be chaperoned by one of Marva's siblings. Marva also
recalls that part of Louis's entourage—at least one handler,
manager, or adviser—was always in evidence. On their first
date, dinner at a Chicago hotel, Joe seemed shy. When he
wanted to say something, he often started out by telling a
clever joke. Joe made Marva laugh. When her mother died
in 1935, he proposed, saying, "Now you need someone to
take care of you."

MARVA LOUIS SPAULDING
Mrs. Joe Louis (1935–1945, 1946–1949)

I thought Joe was magnificent when we first met. He had a beautiful body; he was graceful, almost like a ballet dancer. I liked that.

We had a short courtship, but that's the way he did things. I just learned to keep a cosmetic bag filled, a black suit with a change of blouse, a basic black dress, and lots of hats. I loved hats. In the beginning I felt like Cinderella. I was exposed to so much. It was just travel, travel, travel. It was really exciting, different, and fun.

The Reverend Walter Trotter, Marva's brother, married the couple in the apartment of a friend on Edgecombe Avenue in Sugar Hill, an elite section of New York's Harlem. Earlier in the day, Joe had called Marva from his training camp and suggested getting married before the Baer fight rather than after. Only a few intimate friends and relatives were in attendance. Julian Black was the best man; Johnnie Trotter, Marva's sister, was the maid of honor. Marva's floor-length wedding dress was Italian—of white velvet—its boat neck covered in a narrow piece of ermine. Joe, on his way to the fight, wore a sweat suit with a baseball jacket over it.

Later, as Louis became more and more of a public figure, his taste took a decided turn for the better. He had strong ideas about how those around him should act and what they should wear. He would go through Marva's closets and select the things that he liked for her. On their first trip to Europe, for instance, he suggested what she should take, from evening dresses to cocktail dresses to touring suits. She, in turn, catered to him. She bought his things—all custom-made—at Sulka's in New York. She used special Italian hangers for his suits so they wouldn't wrinkle and organized his closets and drawers methodically.

Joe loved clothes. At the height of his career, designers would give him their lines to wear. He would often change two or three times a day. He had dozens of suits and was particularly fond of two-toned shoes. A list of what he wore every day was taped to the bathroom mirror, at his insistence, so he wouldn't duplicate an outfit in any single week.

Louis also liked high-performance cars and limousines. Every October from 1935 until his retirement he purchased, or was given, one of the first Cadillacs of the model year to come off the General Motors assembly line. He bought a limousine for Marva and instructed the chauffeur never to leave her alone. Marva, craving independence, eventually was given a Ford convertible with red leather seats that she had admired. Louis's cars were kept in the same meticulous order as his clothes—polished every day by one of his entourage like fine pieces of furniture.

He was less careful, however, about many of his other personal possessions. Marva, annoyed by his proclivity for giving away his jewelry to women friends or clothing to admiring fans, counted every item she packed in his suitcase when he traveled. Nonetheless, he rarely returned from those trips with the full complement of garments with which he had left. Once she gave him a custom-designed gold watch with a solid-gold basket-weaved band; on the back was an engraved locket. To ensure that he neither gave it away nor lost it, she allowed him to wear it only in her presence; at other times, it was kept in the home vault. As a result, the watch is one of the few remaining family heirlooms.

Marva considered herself "wife, lover, confidant, friend, and teacher" to her husband. Shortly after they married, she hired, with her husband's approval, Russell Cowans, a black journalist with a master's degree in English from the University of Michigan, to tutor him. When he wasn't training or fighting, Joe was studying—reading, writing, and arithmetic—with

Cowans at night. Eventually they worked their way into a full high school curriculum. In spite of his achievements, Joe swore everyone to secrecy regarding his academic pursuits.

Louis was so magnanimous, and his accomplishments so unique for a black at that time, that he attracted a circle of people who just wanted to be near him, some to curry favor, some merely to bask in the glory of being in his shadow. Actually, he didn't have to order people to perform personal services; they did so automatically. Take valet services, for instance: every morning Freddie Wilson, his driver and companion, drew his bath and selected his clothes—to the constant annoyance of Marva.

Joe had a proprietary attitude about his wife and wanted to keep her safe; she called it "confined." For example, during one of her husband's training camps, Marva went to Indiana's French Lick Academy to hone her equestrian skills. Without her husband's knowledge, she used his personal thoroughbred for her lessons and for a Detroit horse show. When he found out, he was furious. Joe, who thought the horse too dangerous for her, swore he would "chop the animal up and make dog food out of it before he would give it to her." Eventually, seeing how skillfully she rode the horse, Louis acquiesced.

MARVA LOUIS SPAULDING

We rarely fought, but I remember exerting my independence on that occasion. After I borrowed his horse for the show, he came home and said while he was taking off his riding outfit, "Marva, you know I'm a professional boxer. If I hit you, they will put me in jail because you're an amateur." I got nervous because there was no one in the house. I picked up one of his riding boots and hit him on the head.

I was so frightened, I drove the limousine to Spring Hill [the Louis estate] without telling anyone. On the way, the wheels of the car got stuck in sand. I walked to the nearest

farmhouse, but they didn't have a telephone. I arrived at
Spring Hill late that night. Your father and an official from
the FBI were waiting for me. All your father said was "Marva,
you are so fresh. All you have to do is just be beautiful,
gracious, a good mother, and a good wife. Just be my doll-
baby." I knew, however, he was really angry because his
eyebrows went up and his jaw trembled.

Off and on during the 1930s and 1940s, Louis would go to California, occasionally accompanied by his wife. She was with him,
for instance, when Louis's fictionalized biography, *The Spirit of
Youth,* was filmed. Even though a public figure himself, Louis
reveled in meeting Hollywood stars ranging from Clark Gable
to Jimmy Durante. It was there that his discreet entanglements
with Lana Turner and Sonja Henie began, and that his torrid
love affair with Lena Horne ended. He had met her at the Cotton Club in Harlem. Louis's cronies insist that he was usually
not the instigator of these liaisons. An enormously popular celebrity in his own right, he would go into a nightclub, meet a
star, and receive from her a note with her phone number on it.
Never one to pass up a beautiful woman, he would pursue the
invitations. Marva called Hollywood a "social merry-go-round."
    As a result, Marva found her life lonely and empty. Boxing
and training kept Joe away for weeks, sometimes months, at
a time. Often for other reasons, he would disappear without
notice. For instance, once in the early 1940s, after he received
a phone call from Clark Gable inviting him to go fishing off
California's Baja Peninsula, Louis volunteered to go to the
store to buy a box of salt for Marva. A week later, without
telling Marva where he had been, he returned with the salt. He
had accepted Gable's invitation to go fishing. On the top of the
box was a peace offering: a five-carat diamond ring.
    More frequently, Joe would disappear into the black com-

munities of major cities with his cronies. There he was most relaxed, able to indulge his proclivities for nightclubbing and womanizing. The black enclaves protected his anonymity, so Louis's shenanigans were rarely reported in the press.

SUNNIE WILSON
Joe Louis's Running Buddy

Joe and I had a good time together. After the 1937 championship fight, when I was courting a little girl named Anna Lee, Joe brought Marva down to the Brown Bomber Chicken Shack which we owned. He had just bought a new Mercury and said, "Let"s try this car out." Marva and Anna Lee went into the restaurant to wait for us.

I had about $500 and Joe $1200 in our pockets. We drove to Toledo, Ohio, to see a big show with a lot of pretty girls. The next morning we followed the show to Cleveland, Ohio. We left there and went to Pittsburgh, Pennsylvania; came back to Cleveland (where we borrowed money from friends); and then followed the show to Buffalo, New York.

Meanwhile, Roxborough's worried about us, the FBI's worried about us, Marva's worried about us. See, we never called anyone. So, we looked up one morning in Buffalo and there was Freddie Guinyard. We didn't go back with Freddie. We kept on going; borrowed money and went on to Albany, New York, still following that show.

This is going on the second week now. We're tired, our money's running out, the trunk of the car is full of our dirty clothes, when we got a message that President Roosevelt wanted Joe to open up the March of Dimes campaign in Washington, D.C. So we brought more new clothes and went on our way to Washington.

Total we were gone a good two weeks. Your mother went back to Chicago. My girl didn't want to speak to me for months. Roxborough didn't want to know me and Freddie thought it was my fault. But it was Joe's fault, not mine. He kept wanting to follow that show clear to Buffalo.

The pattern the relationship would take emerged shortly after their marriage: Joe would have an affair with a girl or go off with a buddy; Marva would receive a lavish gift. After Louis and Sunnie Wilson disappeared on the trip to Buffalo, for instance, Joe gave Marva a long sable stole she had once admired. The extravagant gifts, presented in an "innocent, little boy manner," prolonged the relationship. And when Louis was home, Marva found him most attentive. "I learned to accept the absences because upon his return, it was as if the outside world didn't exist for us," explains Marva.

But inevitably, Joe's attentions would again wander. So he and Marva developed an understanding. This was the game the couple played for years: If either drove up to a restaurant or club and saw the other's car parked outside, he or she would not go in. One night, Marva, not seeing Louis's automobile, went into a club her husband was frequenting. The maître d' said: "Mr. Louis is here, would you like to join him?" "No," said Marva haughtily, "Seat me at the table next to his."

Loneliness was one problem Marva bravely confronted; Joe's adoring public was another. Crowds would follow the couple, and occasionally, when they got out of the limousine, they had to fight their way to their apartment or hotel. "Sometimes," Marva recalls, "I'd wonder how I was going to get through the day alive."

MARVA LOUIS SPAULDING

Eventually, you tire of it—the crowds knocking your hat off and pushing you out of the way to reach him. Fame is the most difficult thing that can happen to a relationship. I think a man can handle it more easily than a woman. Your life

is just not your own. You always have to be up and on the
scene. And Joe was very proud. "Oh, Marva, you're not
going to wear that. Change your clothes." You see, you
represent them, and they want you to be tops. At least,
Joe did.

You're lonely, and you have to be very careful of your
selection of friends and acquaintances. You could never go
out with somebody that wasn't a part of his entourage or
family. Immediately, the columnists would say, "There's a
separation with the Louises," as they do with most celebrities.

Marva yearned for a normal family life, in particular, children.
Her dreams were finally realized in February 1943, when Jacqueline was born. Jackie, named after trainer Jack Blackburn,
was delivered in Chicago while her father was stationed at Fort
Riley, Kansas. Joe, receiving the news of the birth of his child,
requested a one-week furlough and headed home.

When his leave ended, Louis spurned army routine for the
glamour of Hollywood. He spent the next six months filming
the Irving Berlin picture *This Is the Army*. Some sixteen Harlem
song-and-dance stars also in the service had parts in the picture.
Joe's extramarital relationships resumed. And eventually, his
continuous relationships with other women, exhibition tours
and fight schedule took their toll. Although a child had helped
fill part of the vacuum, the relationship remained aimless. My
father and mother were divorced in March 1945.

During their one-year divorce, Louis continued to woo Marva
with gifts, trips, and phone calls. He sent her to Europe. She
once met him in San Francisco, and he continued to give her
a new car every October, a tradition that persisted even after
their second divorce. One year, Marva decided that she wasn't
going to accept it; Louis called and asked why she was "walking." She said, "I'm not. I have the same car that I had last

year." "That's what I mean, Marva," Louis responded. "You're walking. I'm sending over a new car." And he did.

They remarried in July 1946. For her part, Marva explained that she did so because she hadn't met anyone who was more interesting. But his excesses and philandering continued just as before. Marva tried to console herself with a brief career as a singer. Joe objected to it, but eventually supported her—although he was on a tour of Europe when her career was launched at the Ebony Club in New York. Initially, the reviewers talked about her husband, her figure, and her fabulous clothes; eventually, she began to receive positive reviews for her talent.

Regardless, her career was short-lived. While Marva was on one singing tour, Jackie developed pneumonia. Although she couldn't cancel her contract, when it was completed, Marva ended her singing career. She turned to fashion, civic, and charitable work, activities that Louis felt were more fitting for his wife.

Marva became pregnant, and in due course I was born—the hoped-for son, Joseph Louis Barrow, Jr.—in Mexico City on May 28, 1947. She had traveled there to be near my father during his Central and South American exhibitions and stayed on for the birth. At 12 pounds I (nicknamed "Punchy") was a very large baby, but the newspapers, clearly hoping for another heavyweight champion, exaggerated.

LEONARD REED
Joe Louis's Friend and Personal Secretary

He loved your mother like no other man did, except one thing—she wasn't enough. We'd go into Chicago sometimes and he wouldn't even go home. Stay in the hotel.

I said, "Aren't you going to go see Marva?"

"No," he said, "I'm mad."

Mad about nothing. He didn't have anything to be mad about. He just felt guilty. This is how that marriage finally ended up. Marva got tired of Joe not coming home and hearing about Joe's women.

His sex drive was unstoppable. In each town in which he fought, we'd have a suite of rooms in a hotel. After a fight, he'd say: "Send in Gloria." Okay. Five minutes later. "Bearcat [Reed's nickname], send in Carmen." Now Carmen goes in. When Carmen would come out, "Send in Lydia." One, three or four girls he'd have after a fight. Each going in and staying fifteen to twenty minutes. I don't know what they were doing, but I know that I went around the hotel picking up the tabs.

He supported women around the country. I had a list of women I'd send money to religiously. I got them apartments and paid the rent so he could go there when he was in town. If he had a woman already and another one came, I'd have to take the other one out. He'd give me $100 and say, "Take her out somewhere." I had to entertain all the women that he couldn't get to.

But I know that the only woman that Joe ever really got on me about was Marva. I was dancing with her one time and I said, "You're the most gorgeous thing." He overheard me and said, "Don't ever say that to her again. Just leave her alone because that's my wife." I said, "Okay." I didn't mean nothing, but he thought I did.

Nevertheless, the second marriage was ill-fated. Soon, Marva hired an accountant and a lawyer to tie up the champion's earnings from the 1947 Jersey Joe Walcott fight, investing most of the proceeds in Chicago real estate and in a trust fund. The Barrows were divorced in 1949 for the second time, and Marva married Dr. Albert Spaulding, a Chicago internist, in 1950. Immediately after she married, Joe—who was on an exhibition tour in Australia—called, incensed. He spoke to his former wife for forty-five minutes, an exceedingly long telephone conversation by his standards, threatening in the end to take away the children. Marva still remembers his parting line: "Marva, I want him [Dr. Spaulding] out of that house by the time I get back." Louis's vigorous attempts—and those of his advisers —to end the marriage were futile and rebuffed. They were based on his belief that Marva could never belong to anybody but him.

Even after the divorce, Marva attempted, for the children's sake, to maintain something of a relationship with their father. When birthdays came, and no present arrived from my father, she asked friends from other parts of the country to send us a gift signed "from Dad." It didn't take much for us to realize that we weren't Dad's top priority.

JACQUELINE LOUIS BARROW
Joe Louis's Daughter

I remember growing up with Dad not around as much as the fathers of my friends. He wasn't there for the important events of my life—when I graduated from grammar school and high school, for example.

I remember how important my summers with him were when we were children. When he married Martha [in 1959], we'd take the Santa Fe Super Chief to Los Angeles. The first summer I learned to drive, I wrecked his car when I was hit broadside by Walter O'Malley, the son of the owner of the Los Angeles Dodgers. The Supersport was replaced by a Honda.

There were also several summer trips to New York. We'd stay at the Sherry-Netherland Hotel, taking full advantage of room service. Once you ordered a Baby Ruth candy bar. Often we'd go to Atlantic City from New York. There was one infamous $300 Yellow Cab ride from New York to New Jersey. The governess put us in the cab to meet Dad at Ma Robinson's Rooming House. I used to love the boardwalk

and eat the salt-water taffy there. But these happy childhood
family get-togethers were all too infrequent.

In spite of his forgetfulness, he was genuinely pleased to be
the father of a son and a daughter. He used to brag about us
and show off the pictures that Mother gave him. But his ap-
pearances at the Spaulding household were rare, and when he
did visit, it was little more than a day out for him. Never did
he take us to the circus or a baseball game. And at lunch or
dinner we were never alone: more often than not, we would
be accompanied by several of his buddies. Nor did he seem
comfortable conversing with youngsters whose lives he knew
little or nothing about. He did, however, insist on a solid education for his children. Both of us attended private schools—
Jacqueline was at St. Ambrose, and I went to University of
Chicago Lab and High School.

As is the case after most divorces, when Mother remarried,
our stepfather, daddy Ab, as we called him, became the dom-
inant father figure. When we were young, few friends knew
our father was Joe Louis. A schoolmate of mine, Stan Hanover,
recently recalled first learning in the sixth grade who my father
was. It occurred during the reading of a composition about
families. When it was my turn, I said, "My Dad went to a gym
and became heavyweight champion of the world." Hanover
turned to another buddy, Tim Stutzman, and said, "Who does
Joe think he's kidding? Nobody's going to believe that." "Stutz"
looked at Stan very calmly and replied, "It's true."

We were in our teens before the legendary figure of Joe
Louis took on significant proportion in our lives. But only later
did he take enough interest in us to allow us to become close
to him. "As a young adult, I realized that this was just Dad,"
reflects Jackie today. "He lived his life the way he wanted to.
He lived by his own rules." In the 1960s, Jackie and Dad
reconciled their differences and became quite close. She lived

in Los Angeles with him and his third wife, Martha, for most of 1968. When they moved to Las Vegas, she drove there frequently, and when she had a falling out with Martha, she still phoned Dad frequently. "I miss those ten- to fifteen-minute conversations," she reminisces. "We would talk about everything—what was happening at Caesar's Palace, his foster children, my life, current events." What does she think of Dad today? "I think he was terrific," Jackie quickly responds. "He had a great sense of humor, he was a very warm and generous person, and he had such a great memory I'd want him on my Trivial Pursuit team."

Meanwhile, after his divorce, Louis found it difficult to live alone. He had never previously had to fend for himself. And even though he traveled with a fast crowd and demanded his independence, he liked the stability of a home life.

CANDICE CALDWELL JOSEPH
Joe Louis's Foster Daughter

I can't imagine Daddy ever living alone and trying to conduct everyday life by himself. I don't think he was ever in a grocery store. Who would take care of his clothes—coordinate them, clean them? Rarely did he drive a car. He was a scary driver.

In some ways Dad was childlike and innocent. Although he was a grown, intelligent, caring man, most things didn't bother him. He was a good person. He would not do anything with malice or viciousness. I don't think he had it in him.

Nevertheless, it still came as a surprise to his friends when Louis married Rose Morgan, the well-to-do owner of a New York beauty salon, after a whirlwind courtship in 1955. Like Marva, Rose was an attractive, refined woman who would remain Louis's friend throughout his life. But unlike his first marriage, this time he chose a woman of independent means whose personal business affairs took much of her time and who he thought was not interested in starting a family.

He had met Rose at several events where influential blacks would gather, but it was at the opening of the Moulin Rouge, a Las Vegas hotel where Louis was host in the black section of the city, that the romance began to blossom. He followed her back to New York and shortly afterward invited her to visit him in Buffalo after a wrestling match he refereed. It was there that he proposed.

ROSE MORGAN
Mrs. Joe Louis (1955–1958)

Joe was used to people responding to his every need. I remember being invited to Buffalo before we were married. He called me on a Saturday morning. I arrived very late that night. Dumbfounded at my tardiness, he said, "Don't you know, when I say come, baby, you must come immediately?"

That was my first date with him. When he proposed to me that week I asked him how he knew he'd like to live with me for the rest of his life. He said, "Who said I was going to live the rest of my life with you?" I laughed. That sounds like him, doesn't it?

Several of Louis's friends did not approve of the match, citing the couple's differences. Regardless, Rose married him because she felt so important in his presence. She, among all women, had been able to conquer him. "You see," she said recently, "he had known an awful lot of women, and he chose me. That was truly a compliment." Joe, in turn, felt comfortable and relaxed with Rose. Conversation flowed easily between them, and the frantic pace he kept with other women was unimportant to her. He also thought, according to one person who knew them both well, that Rose was financially more secure than she actually was.

As had Marva, Rose attempted to put Louis's finances in order, but to no avail. The couple went on several quiz shows, including Dennis James's *High Finance* and *Masquerade Party*, to raise money to pay his income tax debts. But the winnings that were left after he paid the Internal Revenue Service were spent as freely as in the past on friends, acquaintances, and strangers.

Louis's spending habits quickly became apparent to Rose. Take, for instance, the day he received a large check from the cologne manufacturer of the Joe Louis perfume, "My Man." At the bank where he had gone to cash it, he met an acquaintance who complained of the need to have her teeth fixed. Without thinking, Louis dug into his pocket and handed her $200. Before he arrived home, the story had reached Rose.

The marriage lasted less than two years. At first, the good times outweighed the bad. On the infrequent occasions when they were together, they would dine in with friends such as Count Basie, the Jackie Robinsons, or the Roy Campanellas. Preferring to avoid eager photographers and fans, the couple often stayed home—talking, reading, and studying together. Although Joe was easy to live with—he'd sleep all day and they hired help to cook and clean for him—when he was ready to go out, Rose was exhausted from her business day. Louis found domestic life confining and one woman insufficient to meet his needs.

ROSE MORGAN

During the summer when you and your sister Jackie came to visit, your dad would disappear for a month. He made me baby-sit. There were occasions when he would come

into town and I wouldn't know he was there. He would go
to an apartment he had at 555 Edgecombe Avenue. After
I found this out, I took all the sheets from the apartment.
When he asked why I had taken the sheets, I told him, "You
should let me know when you're in New York."

In 1958, annulment proceedings were started. Simply, the couple agreed they were really on "two different sides of the street."
Louis was home infrequently, and Rose knew he was seeing
other women during his time away from her, in particular Martha Malone Jefferson, a respected Los Angeles criminal attorney. Even before the decree was final, Martha's attorney was
calling Rose's counsel to find out Louis's marital status. The
former champ, who was in no rush to go to the altar again,
asked that that information be kept confidential. Eventually,
Martha won him over. As he did with many of his women
friends, he took Martha to visit Marva. Marva was favorably
disposed toward the marriage. "Martha looked like a 'kewpie
doll,' " recalls Marva, "and she could help him with her legal
skills."

Martha had met Louis in 1957 while he was on a wrestling
tour, a brief career which ended when an opponent broke his
rib. She was instantly attracted to the then-balding and paunchy
ex-boxer. What she saw was a kind, generous man. "That
generosity and Joe's humility," Martha would tell reporters at
his funeral, "brought him dignity money could never buy. Joe
had so many friends, he could have stayed in a different person's house every night and he could never live long enough
to run out of places that loved him."

Martha Jefferson became the third Mrs. Joe Louis in 1959.
Marva was right—initially, Martha was good for him. She took
on the Internal Revenue Service, accomplishing what no one
else could: henceforth, Louis would be taxed only on his cur-

rent income. Although his debt was never canceled—ultimately it totaled $1.25 million—the constant hounding of Louis finally ceased. Even more than his previous wives, Martha waited on her husband hand and foot. She encouraged him to stay at home, putting television sets in each room, including the bathroom; drove him to and from the golf course, waiting there for him to finish; and refused many of his former friends entry to their house. Although she succeeded to some extent in taming him, many Louis insiders feel that in so doing she eventually destroyed the Brown Bomber. "She really cut Joe down," was Leonard Reed's recent assessment.

Occasionally, Louis would flee from the cage Martha had built around him. She didn't, however, allow this to last for long. She would use all the resources at her disposal to track him down and bring him home. Once, in the 1950s, Louis went to Honolulu with Reed for four weeks to perform their two-man comedy routine at a major hotel. Two weeks into the engagement, Martha arrived unannounced. Understanding fully her husband's sexual proclivities, she didn't trust him to be alone for long.

"I'm not a jealous or selfish person," Martha later told reporters. Whenever she met her husband in the company of other women, however, she would quickly introduce herself, "Honey, move over. I'm Mrs. Louis." She had every intention of remaining Mrs. Louis "until death do us part." Once, according to Marva, she shot Louis between the toes when he asked for a divorce.

When smothering affection, devotion, and threats didn't work, Martha turned to children to help domesticate her husband. She attempted to do this initially through me and Jackie. During the early years of her marriage Martha suggested that we move from Chicago to their home in Los Angeles. Knowing Dad's limited interest in children, Mother (Marva) was frightened by the prospects of such an arrangement. She wrote to her sister,

Johnnie, who also resided in Los Angeles, asking that she watch out for our welfare: "Martha and Joe have been here [Chicago] a week and she has worried me to death to take Punchy and Jackie to Los Angeles. She must be nuts! She is very sweet, generous, and nice, but selfish. I think her main purpose is to cement her relationship with Joe. Happiness and peace of mind come from within, and I feel it is too much of a burden to place on youngsters to assure an old man's happiness. If she can't keep him with her charm and wherewithal, I offer my sympathy."

In 1957 Martha had become the legal guardian of Candice and Amber Caldwell, the daughters of one of Martha's clients who had recently died. Although she tried to adopt the children, their mother, who was alive, never agreed to the arrangement. The children lived with the Louises in Los Angeles and later moved with them to Las Vegas. But Louis remained as distant from his foster daughters as he was from his natural children.

CANDICE CALDWELL JOSEPH

Although I called him Daddy, I was never very close to him. I didn't talk to him a whole lot. I sometimes told him what happened in school. I always, as children do, asked him for money. He never disciplined us or corrected us. Most of the time he was playing golf or he was upstairs in bed. Mommy Martha served him lunch and dinner in bed. He came down to breakfast, watching "Captain Kangaroo" every morning with Amber. Famous people visiting the house became commonplace—Marguerite and Willie Mays, Mahalia Jackson, and many boxers, among them Archie Moore, who baby-sat for us. He'd cook a feast for ten people when it was just my sister and me for dinner.

When I was an adult I asked him if he ever really felt

like he was my Dad when we were growing up. He told me,
"Not really. If you had been younger and hadn't known your
own father, I might have." This was honest, but it hurt. My
father died in 1956 and I really tried to make Joe more my
father. I wanted him to be.

As Martha's marriage to Joe teetered, she attempted to hold
on to him by adding more children to the family. In 1967 she
took in an infant. Jo-Jo was followed into the Louis household
by three other children—John-John, Joyce, and Janet. As Louis
spent more and more time away from home, Martha turned
her attention to her children. Regardless of Louis's lack of
interest in the children and his serious health problems, in 1980,
less than a year before his death, Martha initiated proceedings
for formally adopting the four children. I seriously question
whether my father was aware of the proceedings or his new
legal responsibilities; they were precipitated and shepherded
through by Martha.

Oddly enough, Louis *did* enjoy other people's children. One
explanation: without the full responsibility, he was more relaxed. In any event, Dana Resnick Gentry, Ash Resnick's
daughter, had a special relationship with "Uncle Joe." She
recalls, when she was little more than a toddler, accompanying
her father and Louis on loan-collection trips for Caesar's Palace. On one occasion, as she was waving good-bye to them at
the airport, they grabbed her out of her mother's arms and took
her on the plane with them. She still recalls some of Louis's
antics on this first excursion as a "casino collector." For instance, strolling down New York's Fifth Avenue, with the two
men each holding one of her hands, Joe and her father picked
her up into the air; placed her in a large, empty garbage can;
and kept walking. Amused, a couple of paces along they turned
around to look at the astonished child. On the golf course,

Louis would amuse the child, too. Friends recall seeing him and Resnick driving down the fairway of the Las Vegas Country Club Golf Course with Dana held upside down outside the cart in one of Louis's powerful hands.

In any event, all three of Louis's wives remained in contact with one another—and close to him—until his death. As Rose aptly said: "You had no alternative but to remain friends with him. He wasn't an ordinary person. He was special." One evening in the 1970s, Louis escorted both Marva and Martha to a New York fight. On seeing the threesome a friend asked, "Joe, how did you manage to take out two gorgeous women at once?" Louis proudly replied, "I just love both of these girls, so I thought I would do the town with them both." For the occasion, earlier in the day both women had had their hair done by Rose Morgan at her beauty salon.

CHAPTER FOURTEEN

When the Cheering Stopped

"Joe was on a roller coaster. He couldn't stand still. He always had to be moving."
—Marva Louis Spaulding

"There are some things you should never see. A great stage beauty in the morning without her makeup. A stag dying in the sunset. A great ship sinking. A great warrior succumbing to great odds. A lion wounded and at bay to the jackals. And Joe Louis in a wheelchair." Those words were written by syndicated columnist Jim Murray after he had seen Louis in Las Vegas, and they aptly reflected what many people felt about their champion in his later years. But not Joe himself. He was always content with his destiny.

Louis's decline began in the 1950s. Out of the limelight and beyond the applause of the ring, his life seemed empty. One by one, his family, his close friends, and his advisers were dying—or were estranged. In 1953, he was particularly hard hit by two losses. In January Mike Jacobs died. For all Jacobs's faults, Joe still credited him with creating his heavyweight title opportunity. Then in December Louis lost his mother. With her death, he lost his roots, his religious and structural foundation, and the stability of his family. When her small estate was settled, the Internal Revenue Service took the $660 Lillie had left her son. Shortly afterward, the IRS took the trust funds Marva had set up for their children.

Life seemed to disintegrate for Louis. His marriage to Rose fell apart. The IRS continued to badger him for past taxes, which by then exceeded $1 million. Marva, his first wife, gave him a key to an apartment she had renovated in a building he had given her when they were married. "It was for his personal use, for all he had given me," she explains. She stocked it with the finest linens and towels, furniture, and clothes. Some time later, when she checked the apartment, she was appalled at its state of disarray. Half the furnishings and clothing were gone. Women were discovered to be at the root of the problem.

Life did not improve in the 1960s. Joe's older brother, Lonnie, died and Louis-Rowe Enterprises, Incorporated, lost its account with Cuba when the United States broke off diplomatic relations with Castro. Louis's reputation, when his picture with Castro hit the front pages, was smeared.

In 1966, Joe and Martha moved from Los Angeles to Las Vegas, when Louis received an offer to join the public relations department of the Thunderbird Hotel as a casino "greeeter." A year later, he resigned and moved with friend and casino executive Ash Resnick to Caesar's Palace. The Louises moved into a suite provided by the hotel, and for a time Joe's life stabilized. This last phase of his career placed him amid the city that never slept: an environment filled with bright lights, glitter, and excitement. It suited him, and Joe quickly became one of the Las Vegas "personalities." The Louis of old was rejuvenated.

As a greeter, Joe would roam the casino gaming hall meeting

and gambling with the guests. The former heavyweight thoroughly enjoyed interacting with high rollers and being hailed as "Champ." He enjoyed, as did his "public," the immediate access to people who had admired and respected him. Being in Las Vegas placed the former boxer back in the middle of the ring; the Champ had made a comeback.

As in the past, Louis seemed to care more about the well-being of those around him than he did about his own. He merely wanted to make people happy. If that meant giving them money, he did so gladly. "Everyone took advantage of Joe because he was such an easygoing guy," asserts Resnick. "In Louis's early years when he had the money, it didn't bother him when he lost. In the later years, I used to say, 'Joe, if you were only fighting now, think of all the money you would have.' He would say, 'Ash, what's the difference? I'd just bet a little higher.' " Louis simply didn't care about money. One of his favorite lines while working with Resnick at Caesar's Palace was: "Ash, it don't look good for the ex-heavyweight champ of the world to walk around busted. I think you'd better give me a couple hundred." This would happen a couple of times every day.

ASH RESNICK
Former Director of Casino Operations,
Caesar's Palace Hotel and Casino

One day I gave Joe $100. I said, "Joe, go over to the blackjack table and bet the $100." He won. Now, he had $200. He bet the $200. He gets a blackjack. Now, he's got $500. So I said, "Joe, get away from the blackjack table. Go play craps. Maybe you'll get lucky."

About a half-hour later, I go over to the table where Joe is playing. He's got a pile of black chips in front of him. I said, "Joe, give me $5000. Let me hold it for you until tomorrow." He looks at me and says, "Ash, I held the heavy-weight championship of the world for twelve years; don't you think I can hold $5000 overnight?" Needless to say, in another hour, he was busted. And then, "Ash, it ain't nice for the heavyweight champ to walk around busted."

He really had a great sense of humor. Joe and I were pallbearers at Sonny Liston's funeral, and we were walking out of the casino and pass our friend Abe Margolies, who is shooting craps. He says, "Hey, Joe, Ash, where are you guys going?" Joe says, "We've got to go to Sonny's funeral." So Abe says, "Gee, Joe, I was just going to give you $5000 and let you take a shot in the craps." Joe, pretending to take off his jacket, says, "I'm sure Sonny will understand."

Joe loved to gamble. One day, he's playing the wheel, which goes up to 36. He's losing and getting disgusted. This sweet old lady keeps yelling at Joe, "Play my age. Play my age." Finally Joe turned around and says, "Lady, if I'm going to play your age, I gotta go to Keno; that goes up to 80."

He traveled across the United States on a monthly basis with Resnick collecting debts owed the casino, attending promotional parties, and playing in Pro-Am golf tournaments. The pair would arrive in a city, invite eight to ten individuals who owed the hotel money from gambling debts to dinner, and collect several hundred thousand dollars or more in an evening. "Joe would make collections appear more social than business," Resnick recalls. "It also didn't hurt to have a former heavyweight champion holding the money."

On one trip they had collected close to $1 million and they put the money into a small suitcase that belonged to Resnick's 2-year-old daughter Dana, who was with them. Sitting in a coffee shop, Resnick asked Louis to mind the baby and the suitcase. About five minutes later, Resnick returned to find the baby sitting alone and Louis walking out the door. Running after Louis, Resnick asked: "Joe, did you take the money with you?" Louis, nonplussed, answered: "No, the baby's watching it." He didn't think anyone would steal from Joe Louis.

Louis enjoyed his initial years at Caesar's. As financial and family obligations mounted in the late 1960s, however, his life seemed to deteriorate. Although pressures from the IRS had been nullified by Martha, Joe remained financially hampered. And Martha created a family environment with small children that did not fit his new-found independence. Louis became a confused and troubled man. One day—whether because of years of suppressed financial pressure, extramarital entanglements, or guilt during his marriage to Marva—Louis turned to drugs. He remembered the day, the year, the month, the hotel, and the room number when he was introduced to cocaine. It was by an actress who told him it would improve his sexual prowess. At first, Joe used it as a social stimulant. He became more dependent when he began seeing a funeral director from Beaumont, Texas. Often she would ask him to take some movie cassettes to friends in New York. After the Federal Bureau of Investigation approached Louis, he found out he may have been transporting cocaine for her in the cassette cases. At the urging of federal officials, he severed his relationship with the woman.

It was during these later years that Louis also began to smoke and drink, shocking family and friends. In the 1940s and 1950s, every time the Champ saw his former secretary Leonard Reed smoke, he would tear the pack and crush the cigarettes. Eventually, Reed stopped. And Louis himself never drank anything stronger than Coca-Cola. It is ironic, therefore, that the only time Leonard Reed remembers being hurt by his former employer was when he tried to get Joe to stop smoking.

It occurred on the first hole of the Dunes Hotel golf course. Louis reached into his pocket for a cigarette, astounding Reed.

Figuring turnaround was fair play, Reed took the pack from Louis, tore it, and crushed the cigarettes. Joe grabbed his pal, saying, "Don't you ever do that again." Louis was serious. Although Reed didn't test Louis's resolve on that issue again, he still wonders whether he would have been dismissed, as was Guinyard before him.

Three holes later, Reed received his second surprise of the day when Louis reached into his bag, got out a bottle of Courvoisier, and took a sip. Reed, who had not seen Louis for several years, almost cried when he realized what was happening to his lifelong friend.

In 1969, Louis was hospitalized in New York for a drug overdose. Although the connection between cocaine and mental illness was never confirmed, Joe's mind began to go about the same time. The doctors described it as paranoia. Louis was afraid that the Mafia was after him. When he was traveling, a friend or relative would have to precede him onto the plane. On one such occasion, a man approached him to shake his hand. Joe knocked him down. Similar instances occurred at the gaming tables at Caesar's Palace. In addition, he was afraid hotel rooms were unsafe. He would put the mattress and the box springs together like a tepee and sit underneath them. He'd ask for the air vents to be taped to prevent "poison gas" from entering the room. Martha would even have to taste his food to convince him it was safe. Because of Louis's growing instability, the family moved out of the hotel with Caesar's help to a private home, one previously owned by Johnny Carson.

As the incidents grew in severity, I received two or three phone calls a month from Martha describing my father's irrational behavior. I was living in Denver at the time, having moved there in 1966 to complete my last two years of college at the University of Denver. I enjoyed Denver and on graduation, even though I had grown up in Chicago where my mother and stepfather still lived, I decided to stay. My career as a banker began in December 1968, at the United Bank of Denver. As a management associate in the Trust Banking Division, I felt fortunate to be in a profession that as late as 1968 had been blocked for minorities. Denver provided an independent start to my life and the opportunity to see my father, who also lived there.

Louis's decline was extremely disheartening and painful to his family. Martha was distraught; her calls to me increased, as they did to Marva. Growing more fearful that the former boxer would hurt himself or someone else if he did not receive the proper psychiatric help, Martha convinced Joe to visit their home in Colorado, a state in which an individual can, before committing a violent act, be committed to an institution without his or her consent with the certification of two psychiatrists.

On their arrival, I called to determine for myself his state of mind. Would he tell me of the Mafia's trying to kill him? Would he describe his fears of hotel rooms, the people following him, those watching him? After several minutes of small talk, it was clear he was not going to reveal much more than his latest golf scores.

I deluded myself into thinking his mental problems were illusionary. That, however, was a short-lived hope. When I visited my father that evening, I found him in the master bedroom. Although it was summertime and still a very bright evening, the room was dark and drab. He had drawn the shades and curtains, creating a cavelike atmosphere. "I don't want them to see me here," my father responded to my quizzical stare.

"Who?" I asked.

"Never mind" was his blunt retort.

Drained and disturbed by what I was hearing, I glanced around the darkened room and noticed the disassembled desk lamp. "I had to check it out," he replied to my query about it. My heart sank. As my father buried himself in his self-made tomb, any hope I had of his avoiding psychological observation vanished.

The next day, in the guise of friends of Martha, two Colorado psychiatrists visited Louis at their home. After the visit, the doctors agreed that he should be observed further. He entered Colorado General Hospital's Psychiatric Ward on commitment papers I signed.

It was a tormenting time for me because my father couldn't understand why I had incarcerated him. "Son, how could you do that to me? What did I do to deserve that? Why didn't you talk to me about it the other night?" he pleaded. That really hurt me. I asked him if I had discussed it with him first, he would have agreed to observation. He merely shook his head in disgust and looked away. For the first time in my life, *I* had created the separation between me and my father, a split which I thought would last forever.

At Louis's insistence, he was transferred to the Colorado Veteran's Hospital. He said, "I am a veteran; if I have to be hospitalized, it will be in the one of my choice." It was the only part of his incarceration that was under his control. His stay was extended for another ninety days. Eventually we started talking. I would visit and on certain days he would be released into my custody. Occasionally, we would play golf.

Once Billy Eckstine, who had a singing date at the Denver Playboy Club, and Willie Adams, another longtime friend of Dad's, joined us. Hoping for a special reunion, I asked a friend to make arrangements for golf at Meadow Hills—then a semi-private club. What a day of stories and memories! One after another, Billy, Willie, and the Champ told joke after joke and reminisced about being on the road with Count Basie and Duke Ellington. For the first time, I felt I was a peer, and, more importantly, the void I had recently created evaporated. No one cared much about the golf that day. I don't think any of us broke eighty.

Louis's progress was positive, but not sufficient for his release from the hospital. Regardless, he eventually conned the doctors into letting him go to Las Vegas for the weekend. He never returned to Denver. Although our relationship was again relegated to infrequent talks and visits, that summer had brought a closeness that remained.

Many questioned whether Las Vegas was the right environment for the former boxer. Joe, however, remained the "Champ" there—to see and be seen by the people who meant so much to him. "After all, whose life was it anyway?" relatives would ask reporters who questioned the wisdom or the niceties of the gambling environment.

In 1977, Louis developed a heart condition called a dissecting aneurysm. His symptoms—severe back pain and high blood pressure—led to aortal fibrillation (heart irregularities). The prognosis: several days to a few weeks to live. Frank Sinatra, Louis's friend since the late 1930s, called Michael DeBakey, a renowned heart surgeon who had developed a treatment for this disorder. DeBakey agreed to see Louis. Sinatra provided his plane for Joe's trip to Houston and paid all his medical bills. DeBakey donated his services.

I recall Martha's telling me of my father's condition. I flew to Houston from Washington, D.C., where I worked for the Department of Energy, to be with him before the operation. The entire flight down I wondered whether this would be the last time I would see him. Although I arrived a day before the scheduled operation, his deteriorating condition necessitated an immediate operation to remove the aorta and replace it with a graft. I was able to spend only a few minutes with him before he was prepared for surgery.

MICHAEL E. DEBAKEY, M.D.
Chancellor, Baylor College of Medicine

When I think of the brief time I spent with Joe Louis at Houston Hospital, the qualities of honesty, integrity, drive, discipline, and dignity come to mind.

The amazing thing about your father was he never got down. He was always so cheerful and he had a lot about which to be depressed. He had a courageous approach to death. It is a part of life and he had reached the end of his time period. He told me, "If God's with us, it's going to be all right."

On his way into the operating room, he was surrounded by nurses, technicians, and doctors. One nurse asked him, "Joe, is there anything you want us to do for you?" "Yes," he said, "do what Dr. DeBakey tells you to do." Everyone got a kick out of that.

Frank Sinatra asked that Joe be protected and, of course, the Hospital wanted that too. But your father was very kind about giving autographs. He'd say, "I'd like to say hello, if anyone wants to come to see me." Frank called almost every day about him. He was very fond of your father. Everyone in the hospital was.

Recovery, including physical therapy, kept Louis in Houston Hospital for three months. In spite of intensive therapy, limited circulation to his legs resulted in confinement to a wheelchair. By then, Joe looked weak, weary, and drawn. Everyone who saw the former great heavyweight champion's being pushed around in his wheelchair at Caesar's Palace was saddened by the sight. Journalist Dave Kindred wrote about the time he saw Louis and Ali together just prior to the 1980 Muhammad Ali–Larry Holmes fight in Las Vegas. "Joe, I'm gonna put a whuppin' on him," Ali said, trying in vain to cheer his friend and mentor. "You gonna be there, Joe? Joe, I watched films of you the other night, Joe, you and Schmeling. Your combinations were something else, Joe. That one-two you hit Schmeling with in the first round, that's what I'm gonna hit Holmes with. One round, Joe, I might do it in one round. So don't be late, Joe, you might miss it."

The end so evidently imminent, Joe was incapable of responding except with a barely perceivable nod and an affirmative grunt. "You eatin' good, Joe, you eatin' good?" Kindred overheard Ali say. This time, Louis grunted a negative. Ali bent close to his friend's ear and whispered, "I'll try to come see you, Joe, before I leave. I'll come to your house."

Despite the setbacks, Joe never lost stature with his fans. When he attended fights as a spectator, the cheers were long and loud. As in the past, few fighters wanted to precede Louis into a stadium because, without even trying to, he would steal their thunder. Everyone respected the former heavyweight champion of the world—even the President of the United States.

REG GUTTERIDGE

**Boxing Correspondent,
Independent Television Sport, London**

I remember once being at Caesar's with a group of London casino operators. It was in 1976, and Queen Elizabeth was visiting Philadelphia at the time. Joe said to one of the casino operators, "Do you think the Queen would visit Caesar's?"

Well, it was very embarrassing. The Royal schedule is set ten years in advance! No one, however, wanted to say so. I said, "You never know, Joe." So Joe asks for a phone and asks the Caesar's operator to connect him with the President. Within seconds, President Ford was on the telephone. He posed the question. The President must have said he'd look into it and call Joe back.

I thought, how polite of the President. Within minutes, however, the President calls back! "Unfortunately," he says, "the Queen's itinerary has been worked out in advance."

Only Joe Louis, I thought, could call the President of the United States, get him on the phone in seconds, make a request of him, and have him respond within minutes!

During Louis's retirement, he never lost contact with his friends and erstwhile ring enemies. Louis was always able to have happy moments in spite of his up-and-down lifestyle. In 1951, he was reunited with Max Schmeling for the first time since their 1938 fight. Schmeling was in the United States refereeing a fight in Milwaukee. After the match, he drove to Joe's home in Chicago and tracked him down at the local golf course. Louis and Schmeling connected again in 1966 when the two boxers were asked by ABC Sports to sit at ringside with Howard Cosell at the Muhammad Ali–Karl Mildenberger fight in Frankfurt, Germany. Prior to the match, a German newspaper arranged for Louis to travel to Hamburg, Schmeling's home, for a more intimate reunion.

MAX SCHMELING
Former Heavyweight Champion

If I had a wish, it would be that Joe Louis were alive and that we were still friends.

There was much propaganda around our 1938 fight. The press said many bad things like "Hitler sent Schmeling over there to beat Louis to pieces." I didn't know how Joe Louis felt. My thought was that after the war was over, I would have the chance to go back to the States. The first thing I would do would be to get in touch with Joe Louis. Just have a plain talk to him. Max Schmeling to Joe Louis. That's what we did. We spent the evening in the south side of Chicago. I was the only white man in this restaurant, the Archway Lounge. I was recognized by all the colored people. This was the start of our friendship.

I saw Joe again when the *This Is Your Life* television show surprised him. I flew over to New York to be a part of the show. In 1966, we had another special time together when he came to Hamburg. I'll always remember our car ride to my villa. I was driving on the German autobahn. I was going over 120 kilometers per hour. Joe went lower and lower in his seat. Here was the fearless Joe Louis, afraid of my driving. In America, I later remembered, you have speed limits.

In the mid-1960s, Louis became an adviser to heavyweight boxer Sonny Liston. He was senior cornerman, coach, and trainer all rolled into one. In 1976 Louis briefly joined the Ali team. Ali paid Louis an advisory fee for attending his training camp. Although Joe was skeptical about his true value to Ali, he accepted the invitation from the boxer. At the peak of Ali's career, sports reporters enjoyed speculating about who would have won if the two heavyweights had met in their prime. But whatever the outcome of that might have been, Louis occasionally bested Ali verbally. Once on national television, Louis told Ali: "When I was champion, I went on what they called the bum-of-the-month tour." "You mean I'm a bum?" Ali asked. "You woulda been on the tour," chided Louis—with that classic stoic look he gave all his opponents.

Of all the men he met in the ring, Louis was probably closest to Billy Conn. They saw or called each other repeatedly from the time of the 1941 fight onward. Their mutual interest in gambling and their wry senses of humor drew them together frequently in Las Vegas in their later years.

BILLY CONN
Former Light-Heavyweight Champion

We were always good friends. We had a lot of fun. One time, when we were at Caesar's, he borrowed some money from me to play craps. He lost. He came back again and I gave him a couple hundred more. He's a high player, so it takes a while. He's not coming back. I says to some pals,

"Now if he comes back again, tell him I left." So I ducked behind some slot machines. He comes back. It's taken about twenty-five to thirty minutes. He says, "Where's Billy?" They said, "He just left." "Jesus Christ," he said, "I got $8500 for him." Boy, did I come out fast. He said, "I thought you left." "I left if you wanted some more money," I kidded him.

He always had a great comeback. One time we were sitting in the Stardust having something to eat. Clay [Muhammad Ali] comes in and sits right down. Nobody invited him. He starts telling Joe what a break he got he wasn't around in his time. He would've did this and that to him. So Joe looked up at him and said, "Listen, boy, if you even dreamt about it, you should apologize."

Joe was a great guy. He never rapped anybody. He never said a bad thing about anybody. Like one day, I was standing with him in a casino. This guy come up to him and says, "Joe, I'm hungry. I need some money." Joe had a pocketful of black chips and a pocketful of green chips. He gives the guy a handful of black chips. I said, "What the hell, you didn't even know him. What are you giving him $100 chips for?" He said, "What the hell's the difference? I'm going to get broke, anyway." So he comes down to the crap table. He gets broke. He said, "Didn't I tell you I was going to go broke?"

During this period of his life, Joe was honored frequently by the boxing world. In 1954, for instance, *The Ring* inducted him, along with Jack Dempsey and Henry Armstrong, into the Boxing Hall of Fame. He was installed in Madison Square Garden's Hall of Fame in 1968. "Joe is one of the originals," John Condon, vice president of the Hall, said during the installation ceremony. The inscription in the Garden reads: "Highly respected sports celebrity and most active heavyweight champion in boxing history, the Brown Bomber put his title on the line twenty-five times. Eight defenses were made in the Garden with six ending in knockouts. His aggressive style and punching power accounted for ten first-round victories.''

The Jackie Robinson Foundation, established in 1973, wanted to give Louis one of its first Humanitarian Awards. When he was selected, however, he was too ill to attend the dinner. Rachel Robinson is apologetic because the Robinson family didn't mobilize soon enough to help Louis. ''I wanted him to have a dignified, secure ending to his life. Like Jack, Joe did not publicize his financial problems or ask for help.'' There were many other parallels in the lives of Robinson and Louis: Both came from southern sharecropper families, headed by extraordinary women who taught humility. Both achieved their recognition through individual rather than organizational efforts, thus teaching the blacks who followed the significance of the inner resources of the individual. Both were symbols and early activists—in their own ways and in their own arenas. ''For me as a child, Joe Louis represented power,'' Rachel Robinson says. ''When he fought a white man, it represented blacks fighting back. In some ways, it was primitive symbolism.''

In 1978, Secretary of the Army Clifford L. Alexander, Jr., a black who had grown up in Harlem listening to Joe Louis fights, presented him with the army's Distinguished Civilian Service Medal. It is the highest honor the army can bestow on civilians. In front of an audience of movie stars and boxing greats at Caesar's Palace, Secretary Alexander pinned the medal on Louis's tuxedo. Ten years later, the former secretary still vividly recalled presenting the medal to Louis. It was the first time he had met the former heavyweight champion; Alexander made a few remarks and went over to put it on his coat. Joe by this time was relegated to a wheelchair, but the former secretary recalled being thrilled at meeting his hero. Alexander uses the word *greatness* to describe the former champion. ''It was a greatness with style,'' he says. ''When he boxed, he boxed with enormous style. When he won, he won with enormous style.''

Frank Sinatra hosted a benefit for Louis at Caesar's Palace in 1978. Everyone from Los Angeles Mayor Tom Bradley and Cary Grant to Muhammad Ali and Billy Conn was there. It was a big night for Joe. Max Schmeling, who flew over from Germany for the occasion, remembers the evening clearly. "It was the last time I saw Joe. He was brought in by wheelchair. I spoke to him, and he recognized me. He said, 'Max,' but he was in very bad condition."

MARVA LOUIS SPAULDING
Mrs. Joe Louis (1935–1945, 1946–1949)

Joe was on a roller coaster. He couldn't stand still. He always had to be moving. I think the end of the adulation, the noise, the people was responsible for his final breakdown. He was a victim—of stardom, of the IRS, of the system—but nevertheless, he continued to enjoy life.

I saw him in Las Vegas several months before he died. He recognized me. He said, "Hi, Sweetie," and tears rolled down his cheeks. I walked with him in his wheelchair. It was heart-rending to see this magnificent athlete, this magnificent man, this perfect body, in this condition.

As a result of the heart irregularities and severe high blood pressure, Louis suffered a slight stroke. His speech sounded slurred for the last year or so of his life. In 1980, as his condition deteriorated, Doctor DeBakey put a pacemaker into the former champion's chest.

Joe told DeBakey: "I'm ready whenever God wants to take me. I've lived my life and I've done what I need to do."

Joe Louis, American hero, died on April 12, 1981.

CHAPTER FIFTEEN

Final Reflections

"Heroes heed a need. Joe Louis is our hero because he responded when we needed him."
—The Reverend Jesse Louis Jackson

On the morning of April 17, 1981, Good Friday, thousands of the poor and the humble, the rich and the famous, flocked to Caesar's Palace Sports Pavilion in Las Vegas to attend the stirring Gospel service that followed the death of my father. He lay in state in a copper casket in the middle of a boxing ring roped in red, white, and blue and flanked by two honor guards from nearby Nellis Air Force Base. On the previous day thousands more had filed past his casket in the black-cloth-draped hall. Joe Louis died on Palm Sunday, April 12, of cardiac arrest—hours after being hailed by well-wishers who had attended the World Boxing Council heavyweight championship fight between Larry Holmes and Trevor Berbick.

Many people asked at the time why he was displayed in a cavernous hall only yards away from the hedonistic atmosphere of a gambling casino that never even paused to honor him, rather than more respectfully in a church. In the midst of a great deal of influencing by Caesar's Palace, the decision to do so was made by my stepmother; she wanted him where he had been so comfortable and had felt so welcome in his later years. "My father once told me, 'Your whole life is your funeral,' " Martha said when she selected Caesar's as the place where friends and fans alike could pay their last respects. "I insisted on having the service in a ring," she continued, "because Joe's life was in the ring. He would have wanted it this way. It seems appropriate."

Seven years later, as I look back on it, I probably would not have done it differently. It was proper that he last be seen by the thousands of people who loved him in a sports pavilion and ring, a setting not too far removed from the one where they best remembered him. My dad liked the limelight. If there was anything that he missed after he retired, it was being at center stage. Las Vegas, albeit a small arena, kept him close to the likes of Frank Sinatra, Sammy Davis, Jr., and Telly Savalas. I think it also kept him alive. And when Las Vegas recognized the income that boxing could generate, and more fights were held there, my father could see more of the boxing people he enjoyed being around.

Regardless of the setting, I certainly wouldn't have changed the memorial service. It couldn't have been more stirring or respectful if it had been held in a small black Baptist church. My father was honored in song by Sammy Davis, Jr., with "Here's to the Winners," and Dannibelle Hall, who sang a Gospel version of "Bridge over Troubled Water." He was paid tribute in words by Frank Sinatra, a close friend for almost forty years, who called him "a champion of champions, who introduced grace and dignity to the sporting square with ropes around it." Recalling my father's humor, Sinatra spoke of the bantering repartee they frequently enjoyed together. Weighing in at 130 pounds soaking wet and having a "little apple" for a fist, Sinatra was advised by my Dad that the best he could achieve in boxing was a position as cornerman.

On a personal level, I learned of my father's death the previous Sunday. I was still living in Washington, D.C., at the time, although I had just accepted a position as vice president, Corporate Marketing, for Wood Bros. Homes and was scheduled to move back to Denver within two weeks. My roommate—who in my absence received the telephone call from my stepsister Candice—tracked me down at a friend's house to tell me. I immediately called my family in Las Vegas. The lines were busy. As I waited to try the call again, I became introspective, taking the few quiet moments to reflect.

I immediately focused on the last time I saw him. I was in Las Vegas in January 1981, interviewing for the position I ultimately accepted. I called Martha and indicated that I would be in Vegas for the day. She asked me to stop by the house; she would fix dinner for me and Dad. I admired her once again—what she had gone through with my father, how she supported him, and how she had confided in me regarding his mental problems. When I walked into the room Dad had a great smile on his face as he said, "Punchy," my childhood nickname that no longer is a well-kept secret. I told him why I was in Vegas—I was going to leave government service and return to private industry. We talked about my options and my decision to go back to Denver. I was disheartened, watching my father barely able to hold his fork, sitting in a wheelchair. Eventually, it was time to leave. I gave him a big hug—I knew that was probably the last time I would see him.

Other memories came quickly: our wonderful days on the golf course, shared dinners, and, oddly, the day I rode in Chicago's Bud Billiken parade on the Joe Louis Milk Company's float when I was 7 years old. I wore a Chicago White Sox uniform as I stood by Dad waving to his fans. I also remembered going with him when he refereed a wrestling match and wondering who the man was that wanted my father's check when the match was over—an IRS agent. And then I recalled talking with him prior to the 1951 Marciano fight. As a 4-year-old I asked him, "Why are you fighting?"

"I have to," was his sad reply.

"Why?" was my innocent response.

"Because of the money," he answered.

"Is this your last fight?" I asked, not really understanding anything but his pained look.

"Yes, son, this is my last," he said emphatically.

I visited his camp once when he was in training. I begged him to allow me to do roadwork with him. With youthful exuberance, I thought it would be fun. The next morning, I was awakened at 5 a.m. I dressed, went outside, and started running with Dad. The handlers and he laughed because I didn't last long and had to ride in the trainer's pace car. The next thing I remember Dad waking me up, saying, "I wish I could do roadwork that way."

Once when I was quite young I remembered visiting my grandmother Lillie with my father. She lived on a quiet street. I had just learned to cross the street by myself and I practiced incessantly. I looked both ways and, if it was clear, I would dart across. On one crossing, I got careless and was hit by a bicycle. The thought of the red mercurochrome on my bruises and scrapes still makes my body twinge. For years, my father bemoaned having to call my mother about the mishap.

While waiting to redial Martha, I also recalled when I first started to realize the importance of my father to American sport and American history. I was in high school at the University of Chicago Lab School, a predominantly white school. I was struck by the number of classmates' parents who would talk to me about my father and what he meant to America.

Later when I was in my first year at Boston University a friend, John Ford, and I drove to Lewiston, Maine, to watch the 1965 Ali-Liston fight with Dad. Even then he was called "Champ" by his former ringmates and the fans. And three years later, I experienced similar pride when Dad flew to Denver to attend my college graduation. He casually walked into the University of Denver field house, turning all heads. Once again the quiet whispers of acknowledgment began.

I also remembered representing my father in 1970 at a "Salute to the Champ—Joe Louis" in Detroit's Cobo Hall while he was still in the Veterans Hospital in Denver. After the entertainment, my stepmother Martha was introduced to applause. My sister Jackie was announced with equal honors. Then I was. Ten thousand people stood up and applauded for what seemed like two or three minutes. I was moved—no, stunned. My father was so special that 10,000 people, even though he was not present, wanted to acknowledge him through his son. At that moment, I fully understood and realized what it meant to be Joe Louis Barrow, Jr.

As these thoughts and others were going through my mind, I turned on the television. There was CBS Sports' commentator Brent Musburger, breaking off the telecast of the NBA playoffs to tell everyone that my father had died. Had I been watching the playoff game and had my roommate been out, that's probably how I would have learned of his death.

I am no stranger to death; I was first exposed to it at a very young age when a close friend who was born with a birth defect died of a heart attack; we were probably 12 years old. His parents always knew about the disorder, but they never told us. All of a sudden, one day we learned of his death. I later lost aunts and uncles, and then, tragically, at the age of 21 my younger sister Alvita, daughter of my mother and stepfather. Still, these exposures to death, even Alvita's, did not prepare me for the loss of my father. The father-son bond, I sadly discovered, is special.

Although my mother brought me up in religious surroundings, death remained an enigma. Therefore, the eloquence of the Reverend Jesse Jackson in his eulogy for my father was particularly important to me. His words led me toward understanding—and gave me comfort.

THE REVEREND JESSE LOUIS JACKSON
1988 U.S. Democratic Presidential Candidate

This is the Easter season. The season that we celebrate the death and resurrection of Jesus the Christ. The season of pathos and passion has taken on added meaning. Joe Louis died on Palm Sunday. We're celebrating his life on Good Friday. And this is not a funeral; it is a celebration. Funerals are untheological. We must express ourselves in the many ways that God may move through our bodies— if we choose to shout or Amen or run. We are fans of a giant who saved us during a time of trouble. Joe Louis died on Palm Sunday, and we celebrate his life on Good Friday. How marvelous it is to be in the rhythm of thy Creator.

This period has become a very fertile season for the giants. Dr. Martin Luther King, Jr., Duke Ellington, Jesse Owens, Dr. Howard Thurmond and now, Joe Louis. During Passion week. We've also experienced the right to vote for the first time in 100 years, during this same period.

And so as we know death and crucifixion, we also know resurrection. We know that weeping may endure for a night, but joy cometh in the morning. Death, with its might, bids us to be prepared. Death is threatening, perhaps even frightening, but death is democratic. It has the master key to everybody's house. It brings a telegram to your door that you must sign. We live as if life is certain and death is uncertain. In reality, life is uncertain. Death is certain. Death plans family reunions and makes us adjust our schedules. Death makes us humble and accountable. Death deflates our arrogance and reminds us of our finitude, of how limited we are.

Death is another one of God's promises. It challenges our immaturity and makes us face the responsibility to live on. Death bids us to be prepared. You know not the day nor the hour, the time nor the circumstances. It is no respecter of persons. It knocks on the door for courtesy, but not for permission, and disregards all locks and combinations and barriers.

It [death] has scouts running around, advertising its ar-

rival: gray hairs, bald spots, arthritic knees, tired eyes, reduced energy and wrinkles. These are all the appeals to
get your house in order. We dye our hairs and transplant
our bald spots, attribute arthritis to the weather, use glasses
to extend our sight, face-lift our wrinkles—it is self-decep-
tion, but it's not death deception; this moment is real. All of
us must face it. Boldly.

In this natural process of living and dying, we experience
sunrise, the early morning of our existence. We experience
noonday, the peak of our lives, and sunset, the evening of
our lives. God let Joe see sunset. Sixty-six years old, twice
longer than Jesus lived. So many of our geniuses never
survive sunrise. King Tut died as a teenager; he died at
sunrise and so did the four girls bombed at the Sixteenth
Street Baptist Church in Birmingham, Alabama; Jimmie Lee
Jackson in Selma, Alabama, fighting for the right to vote.

So many of our geniuses have their sun eclipse at noon;
Chopin at 39 died of typhoid fever, Mozart died at 36 of
disease of the kidney, Mendelssohn at 38, Schubert at 31,
Bellini at 34, Dr. King and Malcolm at 39, Jesus the Christ
and Donnie Hathaway at 33. But God smiled on Joe. He
experienced the sunset of life. . . .

After the Reverend Jackson began with those words of perspective, the remainder of the service was a joyful celebration for
the "giant who saved us in a time of trouble." The theologian
explained that, although there is never a good time to lose a father,
a friend, or a hero, the blacks might have lost Dad when they
needed him most—during the Depression with "lynching mobs"
threatening their very lives. Fortunately, we didn't lose him then.
And the country didn't lose him at its time of greatest need, in
the post-Depression 1930s and in the midst of World War II. "In
the fullness of time," the Reverend Jesse Jackson elaborated,
"God sent Joe from the black race to represent the human race.
With the combination of diplomacy, determination and timing,

he could not be denied. Joe Louis was a hero by anointment and appointment. The nation didn't choose its doctor, and the nation couldn't refuse its doctor.''

In this unique and trying environment, my father became a champion, Jackson lectured. But ''all champions are not heroes. Heroes are born of necessity. Heroes heed a need. Joe is our hero because he responded when we needed him. . . . With Joe Louis, we had made it finally from the guttermost to the uttermost. From slaveship to championship. Joe made everybody somebody. Usually the champion rides on the shoulders of the nation and its people. But in this case, the nation stood on the shoulders of its hero. The black race was ended because of Joe. The human race was enhanced by Joe.'' And the Reverend Jackson, christened Jesse Louis, noted the ultimate tribute one individual can pay to another—naming one's child after him; boys were named Joe and Louis, and girls were named Josephine and Louise. Jackson's words struck a responsive chord and the entire amphitheater, urged by the reverend, rose clapping to cheer my father in death as they had in life.

Two days later, my father's body was flown by the Air Force to Washington, D.C., where he was buried at Arlington National Cemetery. Dad would have been deeply touched and honored—as were the members of his family—by the selection of his final resting place. My father liked the limelight, but he loved his country. He was proud to have served it during World War II. I remember a conversation with him during the Vietnam War regarding Muhammad Ali's stance as a conscientious objector. Although Dad didn't agree with Ali's view, he respected his right to express his opinion. ''That's the beauty of this country,'' he said. ''You've got to love this nation because I wouldn't be where I am, and you, son, certainly wouldn't be where you are, had it not been for the opportunities that were afforded me in America. You do not have to agree with everything it does, but there's no greater country in the world.'' In his later years, my father had difficulties with his health and was demeaned by the Internal Revenue Service. Regardless, I like to think that although he stumbled, this country never let him fall. My father died with virtually no money, but he was a very wealthy individual in terms of respect and dignity.

June Roxborough Fowler (the niece of my father's manager, John Roxborough) on April 14 set in motion the process of getting authorization for my father's burial in Arlington. Although he had received the European–African–Middle Eastern Campaign Medal with one bronze star and the Legion of Merit during World War II, very high honors for an enlisted man, he did not meet the restrictive eligibility requirements of the cemetery. (As of 1978, you had to have died in active duty, retired from the service, or received the Medal of Honor, Distinguished Service Cross, Silver Star, or Purple Heart to be buried in Arlington National Cemetery.) Quickly, however, President Reagan, acting in his capacity as commander-in-chief, waived the regulations, one of only seventy-three exceptions since the cemetery's criteria were initially changed in 1969. President Reagan said that Arlington Cemetery was "a fitting place for a man whose instinctive patriotism and extraordinary accomplishments have made him one of the most unforgettable Americans of our time." Several years later, he told me at a White House reception how pleased he had been to sign this directive.

Before the burial, my father's body lay in state at the Nineteenth Street Baptist Church. It was at the Reverend Jerry Moore's suggestion that his church, a black church in the heart of Washington, D.C., be his last resting place before burial. The Reverend Moore appealed to my family through the mortician, saying, "Joe Louis ought to be laid out in the bosom of his own community, among his own people." For two days his casket was there for viewing. For two days there were continuous lines. The people came from all strata of society and from almost every state in the Union.

THE REVEREND JERRY MOORE

Pastor, Nineteenth Street Baptist Church, Washington, D.C.

I was upset when they considered Washington Cathedral rather than a Baptist church for your father's viewing before burial. When I found out what was about to be cooked up, I said no. They didn't do anything for him when he was in his prime. They didn't do anything for him when he was in his decline. The only love that he has comes from his own folks. The great respect that he has comes from what he did for us. All he ever did for them was make them money.

The people he mostly inspired were the little people who felt comfortable coming to a black Baptist church, who would never go across town. You could feel a great sense of pride among the people who came because most of them were people that belonged to your father's generation, people like myself who listened to the fights or who had seen fights and read the news articles. They were people who had been primarily subjugated to racial abuse and who had been a part of a hopeful movement of liberation. Joe had become a symbol of breaking out of the chains of segregation and discrimination.

The Reverend Moore expressed the pride and hope many blacks gained from my father's accomplishments. Although clearly important to the black spirit, he also provided inspiration to whites and the country at large. Repeatedly throughout my life, I have been the beneficiary of stories of his influence. Today I know my father transcended race, economics, and social status—he touched everyone.

I remember being invited to a World Boxing Council dinner honoring Sugar Ray Leonard in Washington in 1986. It was preceded by a wreath-laying ceremony at my father's grave in

Arlington Cemetery. Afterward, I accompanied some of the boxers—Joe Frazier, Michael Spinks, Muhammad Ali, Jersey Joe Walcott—to The Palm restaurant for lunch. I was awed to be in their company, yet they wouldn't sit down at the table until I sat down and wouldn't order until I had ordered. They were deferring to me in honor of my father. But I never wanted to follow in my father's footsteps; it was always understood that I was to have an education, to pick a profession, and to do it well. That was the way my father wanted it. He once told a sportswriter that if I ever did want to fight, he'd come out of retirement and hit me with a good right cross.

Even more recently, I felt the influence of my father when I attended a special screening of the film *Cry Freedom*. When I was introduced to the honored guest, Donald Woods, the white South African who befriended Stephen Biko, he immediately began to recall my father's exploits. As a young man, he told me, he eagerly awaited the next issue of *The Ring* so he could read about the great American boxer. Donald Woods told me Joe Louis had a direct and positive impact on the way he viewed blacks. The stories never cease—just as my father's influence on generations never ends.

I said my final good-bye to my father on April 21 at Fort Meyer Memorial Chapel at Arlington National Cemetery. It was hard. In the interfaith service, well organized by the Reverend Walter Fauntroy (the District of Columbia's representative to Congress), readings from the Bible were made by the Episcopal bishop of Washington, the Right Reverend John T. Walker; the Roman Catholic auxiliary bishop, the Most Reverend Eugene A. Marino; and Rabbi Jasua Haberman, from the Washington Hebrew Congregation. In my farewell before the congregation, I said it was my father's "giving that we're celebrating today. It's that inspiration that makes every black American and every American in this country feel proud to know about Joe Louis and to be a part of his life." Former

Secretary of Defense Caspar Weinberger read a message from
President Reagan, who said he felt privileged and grateful to
have had Joe Louis as his friend. And the Reverend Jesse
Jackson read a telegram from Vice President George Bush,
who acknowledged that "there is a little bit of Joe Louis in
every one of us."

More than 800 people filled the Chapel to capacity, and an
equal number outside listened to the service over a public address system. *Newsday*'s Bob Waters suggested it might be
appropriate for my father, as closest to a "king as any American
ever was," to be brought to his final resting place by "a team
of arch-necked horses." The procession was actually one of
limousines; carrying the flag-draped coffin, it ended a few hundred
yards below the Tomb of the Unknown Soldier.

With a three-shot salute and the playing of "Taps," my
father was laid to his final rest on a cool spring day surrounded
by flowering dogwoods, athletes, famed individuals, and thousands of people like you and me. Later I read that a young
black man rang a cowbell as my father's casket was lowered
into the grave. An irritated military guard said, "Time for low
profile, brother." "We been low profile a long time, brother,"
the man replied. "This is the bell of liberty, rung for Joe Louis."
Following a day of tributes from a President, a Vice President,
and other dignitaries, I found this statement from an average
American black citizen a fitting final epitaph.

I will be forever grateful to all those responsible for allowing
my father to be buried in Arlington and for the site selected
by the cemetery for his final resting place. It is a spot thousands
of people pass by each year, and it is surrounded by other
brave soldiers, all heroes in their own right. Whenever I go to
Washington, I go there. I step back. I smile when I hear parents
and grandparents telling stories about Joe Louis to their children or grandchildren as they stop at the gravesite.

The legacy *is* continuing.

AFTERWORD

GERALD R. FORD, Thirty-eighth President of the United States

Joe Louis kicked off a new era and gave to the black community a hero who came along at the right time . . . He not only was a great champion, but he was a great American.

FRANK SINATRA, Entertainer and Friend of Joe Louis

It is nice to know that the man who never rested on canvas now rests on clouds.

BILLY CONN, Former Light-Heavyweight Champion

Joe made an impact on so many people. I was walking down Broadway once when a group of sailors recognized me. One said, "We were sailors aboard the *Ticonderoga* as it was passing through the South China Sea. Over the loudspeaker came an announcement, "All hands on deck. We're going to hear the Louis-Conn fight." Nobody could slow down the *Ticonderoga* but Joe Louis!

HOWARD COSELL, Broadcast Journalist

He was a good man, and it showed through. He was a gentle man, and it showed through. He was the kind of man who cared about people, and it showed through. It's very basic, very simple. It's like the poem written by the great American, Edwin Arlington Robinson:

> *Whenever Richard Cory went downtown,*
> *We people on the pavement looked at him:*
> *He was a gentleman from soul to crown. . . .*

VERNON E. JORDAN, JR., Partner, Akin, Gump, Strauss, Hauer & Feld; Former President, National Urban League Inc.

An era ended the day Joe Louis died. I had the feeling that Joe was relieved. He had lived in a glass house all this time. Now he was free.

JOHN R. THOMPSON, JR., Head Basketball Coach, Georgetown University

I brought my 11-year-old son to see Joe Louis's body lying in state at the Nineteenth Street Baptist Church in Washinton, D.C. I told him: "You've got to remember that I brought you here to see this man. One day you will really appreciate it. Joe Louis carried it for all of us."

LEONARD REED, Joe Louis's Friend and Personal Secretary

Joe's sense of honesty never ceased to amaze me . . . we were in St. Louis on a promotional tour for Joe Louis Punch. The radio commentator asks Joe, "What's your favorite drink?" Joe answers calmly, "Coca-Cola." Can you imagine your father promoting Joe Louis Punch and he says Coca-Cola?

RACHEL ROBINSON (Mrs. Jackie Robinson), Chairperson, Jackie Robinson Development Corp.

I went into deep mourning when I learned Joe Louis died. It was a personal loss. It wasn't just a figure who had died or someone I had admired or even because it was someone I knew. He was connected to me from an early age in terms of establishing who I am and where I stand in this country.

MARVA LOUIS SPAULDING, Mrs. Joe Louis (1935–1945, 1946–1949)

"God, what will I do now?" I thought. It was like losing my father. I could call Joe about any problem. We would discuss it and he'd say, "Well, if I can help you, let me know."

BILLY ROWE, Syndicated Journalist and Joe Louis's Friend

Joe Louis was no ordinary man. In the end, the power he had over me in life continued in his death. I was on my way to Africa for the inauguration of the Nigerian President. Inexplicably, my plane was delayed one day. That evening I learned of Joe's death. Someone didn't want me on that plane to Africa.

ANDREW YOUNG, Mayor of Atlanta, Georgia

I have a very Christian attitude toward death. Death for somebody like Joe Louis is a relief. It moves them onto another dimension of existence without the frailties and without the suffering that they experienced in life. Joe Louis had done his work on earth. It was time for him to go on and claim his Heavenly reward.

FREDDIE GUINYARD, Joe Louis's Friend and Personal Secretary

We were like brothers. He made it possible for me to carry a better grade of food home to my family. Then I didn't pay it any attention, but now, you see what it was.

MARSHALL MILES, Joe Louis's Friend and Manager

In a way, I don't think it made much difference to him that he was heavyweight champion of the world. He was proud because of the prestige and the attention, but I think inside of him he just didn't care. He was just Joe Louis, ordinary guy with extraordinary talent.

ROBERT J. WUSSLER, Senior Executive Vice President, Turner Broadcasting System

What Joe Louis represented was the best of the highest of quality in sports. The fact that he was champion so long left an indelible mark on American society—not black society or white society—but on American society. He was one of the great champions.

BOB DEVANEY, Athletic Director, University of Nebraska at Lincoln

Schmeling had beat Joe Louis in twelve rounds back in 1936. I remember listening to that fight; I really rejoiced in the comeback victory over Schmeling. . . . In the world of sports, Joe Louis was looked on in a very singular way in that he was a person who gave. He was, to me, a very great person all the way around besides in the world of boxing. I was a fan.

J. CLAY SMITH, JR., Dean, School of Law, Howard University

Joe Louis was an American Ambassador for Goodwill. He needed no nomination from the President or advice and consent of the Senate. He held the post of Ambassador by the consent of the American people, supported by people of all nations who knew him.

SHIRLEY POVICH, Sportswriter, *The Washington Post*

Besides his strength, he had a tremendous punch. He probably had the strongest jab that we've ever seen in the heavyweight ranks. His jab was not a flicking thing. He could bust you up with his jab. But even when he'd be punching the hell out of you, you could hardly say it was vicious. It was simply a job to do; it was just a fellow in front of him who had to be knocked down. I would say the man was absolutely devoid of hate or cruelty. I think he regarded all people as people.

MUHAMMAD ALI, Former Heavyweight Champion

Joe, your father *was* the greatest, truly the greatest.

JOE LOUIS'S COMPLETE PROFESSIONAL BOXING RECORD

1934

July 4	Jack Kracken	Chicago	Won on KO in first round
July 11	Willie Davis	Chicago	Won on KO in third round
July 29	Larry Udell	Chicago	Won on KO in second round
Aug. 13	Jack Kranz	Chicago	Won on decision in sixth round
Aug. 27	Buck Everett	Chicago	Won on KO in second round
Sept. 11	Alex Borchuk	Detroit	Won on KO in fourth round
Sept. 24	Adolph Wiater	Chicago	Won on decision in tenth round
Oct. 24	Art Sykes	Chicago	Won on KO in eighth round
Oct. 30	Jack O'Dowd	Detroit	Won on KO in second round
Nov. 14	Stanley Poreda	Chicago	Won on KO in first round
Nov. 30	Charley Massera	Chicago	Won on KO in third round
Dec. 14	Lee Ramage	Chicago	Won on KO in third round

1935

Jan. 4	Patsy Perroni	Detroit	Won on decision in tenth round

1935

Jan. 11	Hans Birkie	Pittsburgh	Won on KO in tenth round
Feb. 21	Lee Ramage	Los Angeles	Won on KO in second round
Mar. 8	Donald (Reds) Barry	San Francisco	Won on KO in third round
Mar. 28	Natie Brown	Detroit	Won on decision in tenth round
Apr. 12	Roy Lazer	Chicago	Won on KO in third round
Apr. 22	Biff Benton	Dayton	Won on KO in second round
Apr. 27	Roscoe Toles	Flint	Won on KO in sixth round
May 3	Willie Davis	Peoria	Won on KO in second round
May 7	Gene Stanton	Kalamazoo	Won on KO in third round
June 25	Primo Carnera	New York	Won on KO in sixth round
Aug. 7	King Levinsky	Chicago	Won on KO in first round
Sept. 24	Max Baer	New York	Won on KO in fourth round
Dec. 13	Paolino Uzcudun	New York	Won on KO in fourth round

1936

Jan. 17	Charlie Retzlaff	Chicago	Won on KO in first round
June 19	Max Schmeling	New York	Knocked out in twelfth round
Aug. 17	Jack Sharkey	New York	Won on KO in third round
Sept. 22	Al Ettore	Philadelphia	Won on KO in fifth round
Oct. 9	Jorge Brescia	New York	Won on KO in third round
Oct. 14	Willie Davis	South Bend	Exh. won on KO in third round
Oct. 14	K. O. Brown	South Bend	Exh. won on KO in third round
Nov. 20	Paul Williams	New Orleans	Exh. won on KO in second round
Nov. 20	Tom Jones	New Orleans	Exh. won on KO in third round
Dec. 14	Eddie Simms	Cleveland	Won on KO in first round

1937

| Jan. 11 | Steve Ketchel | Buffalo | Won on KO in second round |
| Jan. 27 | Bob Pastor | New York | Won on decision in ten rounds |

1937

Feb. 17	Natie Brown	Kansas City	Won on KO in fourth round
June 22	James J. Braddock	Chicago	Won on KO in eighth round; Won heavyweight title; Total gate receipts, $715,470; Louis's purse, $103,684
Aug. 30	Tommy Farr	New York	Won on decision in fifteenth round; Total gate receipts, $325,707; Louis's purse, $102,578

1938

Feb. 22	Nathan Mann	New York	Won on KO in third round; Total gate receipts, $111,716; Louis's purse, $40,522
April 1	Harry Thomas	Chicago	Won on KO in fifth round; Total gate receipts, $48,192; Louis's purse, $16,659
June 22	Max Schmeling	New York	Won on KO in first round; Total gate receipts, $1,015,012 Louis's purse, $349,228

1939

Jan. 25	John Henry Lewis	New York	Won on KO in first round; Total gate receipts, $102,015; Louis's purse, $34,413
Apr. 17	Jack Roper	Los Angeles	Won on KO in first round; Total gate receipts, $87,679 Louis's purse $34,850
June 28	Tony Galento	New York	Won on KO in fourth round; Total gate receipts, $333,308; Louis's purse, $114,332
Sept. 20	Bob Pastor	Detroit	Won on KO in eleventh round; Total gate receipts, $347,870; Louis's purse, $118,400

1940

Feb. 9	Arturo Godoy	New York	Won on decision in fifteen rounds; Total gate receipts, $88,491; Louis's purse, $23,620
Mar. 29	Johnny Paycheck	New York	Won on KO in second round; Total gate receipts, $62,481; Louis's purse, $19,908
June 20	Arturo Godoy	New York	Won on KO in eighth round; Total gate receipts, $164,120; Louis's purse, $55,989
Dec. 18	Al McCoy	Boston	Won on KO in sixth round; Total gate receipts, $51,014; Louis's purse, $17,938

1941

Jan. 31	Red Burman	New York	Won on KO in fifth round; Total gate receipts, $62,899; Louis's purse, $21,023
Feb. 17	Gus Dorazio	Philadelphia	Won on KO in second round; Total gate receipts, $57,199; Louis's purse, $18,731
Mar. 21	Abe Simon	Detroit	Won on KO in thirteenth round; Total gate receipts, $54,736; Louis's purse, $19,400
Apr. 8	Tony Musto	St. Louis	Won on KO in ninth round; Total gate receipts, $52,993; Louis's purse, $17,468
May 23	Buddy Baer	Washington, D.C.	Won on disqualification in seventh round; Total gate receipts, $105,183; Louis's purse, $36,866.
June 18	Billy Conn	New York	Won on KO in thirteenth round; Total gate receipts, $456,743; Louis's purse, $152,905

1941

July 11	Jim Robinson	Minneapolis	Exh. won on KO in first round
Sept. 29	Lou Nova	New York	Won on KO in sixth round; Total gate receipts, $583,711; Louis's purse, $199,500
Nov. 25	George Giambastiani	Los Angeles	Exh. won on KO in fourth round

1942

Jan. 9	Buddy Baer	New York	Won on KO in first round; Total gate receipts, $189,700; Louis's purse, $65,200 (donated to Naval Relief Fund)
Mar. 27	Abe Simon	New York	Won on KO in sixth round; Total gate receipts, $139,136; Louis's purse, $45,882 (donated to Army Relief Fund)
June 5	George Nicholson	Fort Hamilton	Three-round exh.

1944

Nov. 3	Johnny Demson	Detroit	Exh. won on KO in second round
Nov. 6	Charley Crump	Baltimore	Exh. won on decision in third round
Nov. 9	Dee Amos	Hartford	Exh. won on decision in third round
Nov. 13	Jimmy Bell	Washington, D.C.	Exh. won on decision in third round
Nov. 14	Johnny Davis	Buffalo	Exh. won on KO in first round
Nov. 15	Dee Amos	Elizabeth, N.J.	Exh. won on decision in third round
Nov. 17	Dee Amos	Camden, N.J.	Exh. won on decision in third round
Nov. 24	Dan Merritt	Chicago	Exh. won on decision in third round

1945

Nov. 15	Sugar Lip Anderson	San Francisco	Two-round exh.
Nov. 15	Big Boy Brown	San Francisco	Two-round exh.
Nov. 29	Big Boy Brown	Sacramento	Two-round exh.
Nov. 29	Bobby Lee	Sacramento	Two-round exh.
Dec. 10	Bob Frazier	Victoria	Three-round exh.
Dec. 11	Big Boy Brown	Portland	Two-round exh.
Dec. 11	Dave Johnson	Portland	Two-round exh.
Dec. 12	Big Boy Brown	Eugene, Ore.	Three-round exh.
Dec. 13	Big Boy Brown	Vancouver	Three-round exh.

1946

June 19	Billy Conn	New York	Won on KO in eighth round; Total gate receipts, $1,925,564; Louis's purse, $625,916
Sept. 18	Tami Mauriello	New York	Won on KO in first round; Total gate receipts, $335,063; Louis's purse, $103,611
Nov. 11	Cleo Everett	Honolulu	Four-round exh.
Nov. 11	Wayne Powell	Honolulu	Two-round exh.
Nov. 25	Perk Daniels	Mexicali, Mexico	Four-round exh.

1947

Feb. 7	Arturo Godoy	Mexico City	Ten-round exh.
Feb. 10	Art Ramsey	San Salvador	Three-round exh.
Feb. 10	Walter Haefer	San Salvador	Three-round exh.
Feb. 12	Art Ramsey	Panama City	Three-round exh.
Feb. 12	Walter Haefer	Panama City	Three-round exh.
Feb. 19	Arturo Godoy	Santiago, Chile	Six-round exh.
Feb. 27	Art Ramsey	Medellín, Colombia	Two-round exh.

1947

Feb. 27	Walter Haefer	Medellín, Colombia	Two-round exh.
Mar. 10	Walter Haefer	Havana	Two-round exh.
Mar. 10	Art Ramsey	Havana	Two-round exh.
June 6	Rusty Payne	San Diego	Two-round exh.
June 6	Dick Underwood	San Diego	Two-round exh.
June 13	Tiger Jack Fox	Spokane	Four-round exh.
June 23	Harry Wills	Los Angeles	Four-round exh.
Dec. 5	Jersey Joe Walcott	New York	Won on decision in fifteen rounds; Total gate receipts, $216,497; Louis's purse, $75,968

1948

Jan. 29	Bob Foxworth	Chicago	Four-round exh.
June 25	Jersey Joe Walcott	New York	Won on KO in eleven rounds Total gate receipts, $841,739 Louis's purse, $252,522
Sept. 30	Pat Comiskey	Washington, D.C.	Six-round exh.
Oct. 28	Bob Garner	Atlanta	Three-round exh.
Oct. 28	Merritt Wynn	Atlanta	Three-round exh.
Oct. 29	Bob Garner	Norfolk	Four-round exh.
Oct. 31	Bob Garner	New Orleans	Four-round exh.
Nov. 1	Bob Garner	New Orleans	Three-round exh.
Nov. 3	Bob Garner	Nashville	Four-round exh.
Nov. 8	Johnny Shkor	Boston	Four-round exh.
Nov. 9	Bernie Reynolds	New Haven	Four-round exh.
Nov. 17	Jimmy Bivins	Cleveland	Six-round exh.
Nov. 19	Vern Mitchell	Detroit	Six-round exh.
Nov. 23	Kid Riviera	St. Louis	Six-round exh.
Nov. 24	Ray Augustus	Oklahoma City	Exh. won on KO in 2 rounds

1948

Nov. 25	Curt Kennedy	Kansas City	Four-round exh.
Nov. 29	Billy Smith	Cincinnati	Four-round exh.
Dec. 10	Billy Conn	Chicago	Six-round exh.
Dec. 14	Arturo Godoy	Philadelphia	Six-round exh.
Dec. 16	Pat Comiskey	Paterson, N.J.	Six-round exh.
Dec. 20	Willie James	Lewiston, Me.	Four-round exh.

1949

Jan. 10	Sterling Ingram	Omaha	Four-round exh.
Jan. 11	Orlando Ott	Topeka	Four-round exh.
Jan. 12	Hubert Hood	Wichita	Four-round exh.
Jan. 17	Art Swiden	Toledo	Four-round exh.
Jan. 18	Dick Hagen	Moline, Il.	Four-round exh.
Jan. 19	Orlando Ott	Rochester, Minn.	Four-round exh.
Jan. 25	Elmer Ray	Miami	Six-round exh.
Jan. 27	George Fitch	Palm Beach	Four-round exh.
Jan. 28	Nino Valdez	Tampa	Four-round exh.
Jan. 31	Dixie Lee Oliver	Orlando	Exh. won on KO in four rounds
Feb. 1	Elmer Ray	Jacksonville	Four-round exh.
Feb. 3	Bill Graves	Daytona Beach	Exh. won on KO in three rounds
Feb. 4	George Fitch	Savannah	Four-round exh.
Feb. 23	Edgar Edward	Kingston, Jamaica	Three-round exh.
Mar. 1	LOUIS ANNOUNCES HIS RETIREMENT AS HEAVYWEIGHT CHAMPION		
Mar. 1	Ed Crawley	Nassau	Four-round exh.
Mar. 4	Omelio Agramonte	Havana	Four-round exh.
Mar. 5	Omelio Agramonte	Oriente, Cuba	Four-round exh.
Mar. 16	Elmer Ray	Houston	Exh. won on KO in four rounds

1949

Mar. 18	Tex Boddie	Dallas	Four-round exh.
Mar. 22	Hubert Hood	St. Paul	Six-round exh.
Mar. 22	Abel Cestac	Washington, D.C.	Four-round exh.
Oct. 10	Curtiss Sheppard	Baltimore	Four-round exh.
Oct. 24	Bill Weinberg	Providence	Four-round exh.
Oct. 25	Joe Domonic	Hartford	Four-round exh.
Oct. 31	Bill Gilliam	Atlantic City	Four-round exh.
Nov. 14	Johnny Shkor	Boston	Ten-round exh.
Nov. 22	Joe Chesul	Newark	Ten-round exh.
Nov. 28	Johnny Flynn	Kansas City	Ten-round exh.
Dec. 7	Pat Valentino	Chicago	Exh. won on KO in eight rounds
Dec. 14	Roscoe Toles	Detroit	Five-round exh.
Dec. 14	Johnny Flynn	Detroit	Five-round exh.
Dec. 19	Al Hoosman	Oakland	Exh. won on KO in five rounds
Dec. 21	Jay Lambert	Salt Lake City	Five-round exh.
Dec. 21	Rex Layne	Salt Lake City	Five-round exh.

1950

Jan. 6	Willie Bean	Hollywood	Six-round exh.
Jan. 10	Jack Flood	Seattle	Six-round exh.
Jan. 12	Clarence Henry	Wilmington	Four-round exh.
Jan. 13	Al Spaulding	San Diego	Four-round exh.
Jan. 20	Andy Walker	Stockton	Four-round exh.
Jan. 24	Rex Layne	Salt Lake City	Four-round exh.
Feb. 1	Gene Jones	Miami	Eight-round exh.
Feb. 7	Nino Valdez	St. Petersburg	Four-round exh.
Feb. 8	Candy McDaniels	Orlando	Five-round exh.
Feb. 14	Johnny Haynes	Tampa	Four-round exh.
Feb. 21	Sid Peaks	Jacksonville	Six-round exh.

1950

Feb. 23	Dan Bolston	Macon	One-round exh.
Feb. 23	Leo Jackson	Macon	Three-round exh.
Feb. 27	Willie Johnson	Albany, Ga.	Four-round exh.
Feb. 28	Dan Bolston	Columbus, Ga.	Four-round exh.
Mar. 3	Leo Johnson	Waycross, Ga.	Four-round exh.
Mar. 18	Kid Carr	Lubbock, Tex.	Four-round exh.
Mar. 20	Sterling Ingram	Odessa, Tex.	Four-round exh.
Mar. 22	Joe Santell	El Paso, Tex.	Four-round exh.
Mar. 22	John McFalls	El Paso, Tex.	Four-round exh.
Mar. 24	Henry Hall	Austin, Tex.	Four-round exh.
Mar. 26	J. K. Homer	Waco, Tex.	Four-round exh.
Apr. 22	Walter Haefer	Rio de Janeiro	Exh. won on KO in two rounds
Sept. 27	Ezzard Charles	New York	Lost on decision in fifteen rounds; Total gate receipts, $205,370; Louis's purse, $53,908
Nov. 29	Cesar Brion	New York	Won on decision in ten rounds

1951

Jan. 3	Freddie Beshore	Detroit	Won on KO in four rounds
Feb. 7	Omelio Agramonte	Miami	Won on decision in ten rounds
Feb. 23	Andy Walker	San Francisco	Won on KO in tenth round
May 2	Omelio Agramonte	Detroit	Won on decision in ten rounds
June 15	Lee Savold	New York	Won on KO in sixth round
Aug. 1	Cesar Brion	San Francisco	Won on decision in ten rounds
Aug. 15	Jimmy Bivins	Baltimore	Won on decision in ten rounds
Oct. 26	Rocky Marciano	New York	Knocked out in eighth round
Nov. 18	U.S. Serviceman	Tokyo	Won on KO in fourth round
Nov. 18	U.S. Serviceman	Tokyo	Won on KO in fourth round
Nov. 18	U.S. Serviceman	Tokyo	Three-round exh.
Nov. 18	Cpl. B. J. DeCordova	Tokyo	Four-round exh.

1951

Nov. 18	Cpl. B. J. DeCordova	Tokyo	Four-round exh.
Nov. 18	Cpl. B. J. DeCordova	Tokyo	Five-round exh.
Dec. 14	Sgt. Lindy Brooks	Sanda, Japan	Three-round exh.
Dec. 14	Chang Pulu	Taipei, Formosa	Won on KO in first round
Dec. 14	Sgt. S. E. Woodbury	Taipei	Two-round exh.
Dec. 14	D. H. Cantrell	Taipei	Two-round exh.
Dec. 14	Cpl. B. J. DeCordova	Taipei	Three-round exh.
Dec. 16	Cpl. B. J. DeCordova	Taipei	Three-round exh.

LIST OF CONTRIBUTORS

Adele Logan Alexander (Mrs. Clifford L. Alexander, Jr.)
Joe Louis's Fan and Admirer

Clifford L. Alexander, Jr.
Secretary of the Army (1977–1981)
President, Alexander and Associates, Inc.

Muhammad Ali
Former Heavyweight Champion

Alvanious Barrow
Joe Louis's Brother

deLeon Barrow
Joe Louis's Brother

Jacqueline Louis Barrow
Joe Louis's Daughter

Harry Carpenter
Boxing Commentator, British Broadcasting Company

Billy Conn
Former Light-Heavyweight Champion

Howard Cosell
Broadcast Journalist

Jim Cox
Freelance Journalist

Ruth Crump
Historian, Chambers County, Alabama

Emmarell Barrow Davis
Joe Louis's Sister

Michael E. DeBakey, M.D.
Chancellor, Baylor College of Medicine

Bob Devaney
Athletic Director, University of Nebraska at Lincoln

Don Dunphy
Radio Broadcaster

Gerald R. Ford
Thirty-eighth President of the United States

Truman Gibson
Joe Louis's Attorney

Freddie Guinyard
Joe Louis's Friend and Personal Secretary

Reg Gutteridge
Boxing Correspondent,
Independent Television Sport, London

Vunies Barrow High
Joe Louis's Sister

Bob Hope
Entertainer and Boxing Fan

The Reverend Jesse Louis Jackson
1988 U.S. Democratic Presidential Candidate

Maynard Jackson
Managing Partner, Chapman and Cutler
Former Mayor of Atlanta (1974–1982)

Vernon E. Jordan, Jr.
Partner, Akin, Gump, Strauss, Hauer & Feld
Former President, National Urban League, Inc.

Candice Caldwell Joseph
Joe Louis's Foster Daughter

Martha Malone Louis
Mrs. Joe Louis (1959–1981)

Marshall Miles
Joe Louis's Friend and Manager

The Reverend Jerry Moore
Pastor, Nineteenth Street Baptist Church, Washington, D.C.

Rose Morgan
Mrs. Joe Louis (1955–1958)

Albert Patten
Joe Louis's Friend and Admirer

Johnnie Trotter Porée
Joe Louis's Sister-in-Law

Shirley Povich
Sportswriter, *The Washington Post*

Leonard Reed
Joe Louis's Friend and Personal Secretary

Ash Resnick
Executive Vice President, Casino Operations,
The Dunes Hotel and Casino
Former Director, Casino Operations,
Caesar's Palace Hotel and Casino

Rachel Robinson (Mrs. Jackie Robinson)
Chairperson, Jackie Robinson Development Corp.

Billy Rowe
Syndicated Journalist and Joe Louis's Friend

Max Schmeling
Former Heavyweight Champion

Turner Shealey
Joe Louis's Second Cousin

Cliff Shutt
RAF Flight Sergeant during World War II

Frank Sinatra
Entertainer and Friend of Joe Louis

J. Clay Smith, Jr.
Dean, School of Law, Howard University

Marva Louis Spaulding
Mrs. Joe Louis (1935–1945, 1946–1949)

Eulalia Barrow Taylor
Joe Louis's Sister

John R. Thompson, Jr.
Head Basketball Coach, Georgetown University

Jersey Joe Walcott
Former Heavyweight Contender

Sunnie Wilson
Joe Louis's Running Buddy

Robert J. Wussler
Senior Executive Vice President, Turner Broadcasting System

Andrew Young
Mayor of Atlanta, Georgia
Former United States Ambassador to the United Nations

BIBLIOGRAPHY

Campbell, Rex R., and Daniel M. Johnson: *Black Migration in America*, Duke University Press, Durham, N.C., 1981.

Carpenter, Harry: *Masters of Boxing*, William Heinemann, Ltd., London, 1964.

Gutteridge, Reg: *The Big Punchers*, Stanley Paul & Co., Ltd., London, Melbourne, Sydney, Auckland, Johannesburg, 1983.

Harding, Robert S.: *Julian Black Scrapbooks of Joe Louis, 1935–1944*, Archives Center, National Museum of American History, Smithsonian Institution, Washington, D.C.

Hope, Bob, as told to Dwayne Netland: *Bob Hope's Confessions of a Hooker: My Lifelong Love Affair with Golf*, Doubleday & Company, Inc., Garden City, N.Y., 1985.

Johnson, Charles S.: *The Negro in American Civilization*, Henry Holt and Company, New York, 1930.

Louis, Joe, with Edna Rust and Art Rust, Jr.: *Joe Louis: My Life*, Harcourt Brace Jovanovich, New York and London, 1978.

McCallum, John D.: *The Encyclopedia of World Boxing Champions*, Chilton Book Company, Radnor, Pa., 1975.

Mead, Chris: *Champion, Joe Louis, Black Hero in White America*, Charles Scribner's Sons, New York, 1985.

Nagler, Barney: *Brown Bomber*, World Publishing, New York, 1972.

Odd, Gilbert E.: *Encyclopedia of Boxing*, Crescent Books, New York, 1983.

Richards, E.G.: *Reminiscenses of the Early Days in Chambers County*, Court of County Commissioners of Chambers County, Ala., 1942.

Schmeling, Max: *Erinnerungen*, Verlag Ullstein GmbH, Frankfurt, 1977.

Skehan, Everett M.: *Rocky Marciano, Biography of a First Son*, Houghton Mifflin Company, Boston, 1977.